# DATE DUE

# PAUL ROBESON

# PAUL ROBESON
## A WATCHED MAN

## JORDAN GOODMAN

**VERSO**

London • New York

First published by Verso 2013
© Jordan Goodman 2013

1 3 5 7 9 10 8 6 4 2

**Verso**
UK: 6 Meard Street, London W1F 0EG
US: 20 Jay Street, Suite 1010, Brooklyn, NY 11201
www.versobooks.com

Verso is the imprint of New Left Books

ISBN-13: 978-1-78168-131-2

**British Library Cataloguing in Publication Data**
A catalogue record for this book is available from the British Library

**Library of Congress Cataloging-in-Publication Data**
A catalog record for this book is available from the Library of Congress

Typeset in Fournier by Hewer Text UK Ltd, Edinburgh, Scotland
Printed in the US by Maple Vail

For Dallas

# Contents

# Preface

# In the Presence of Greatness

*Toronto, February 11, 1956*

In 1956, my parents, my younger sister, and I were living in Toronto. One day in early February, my mother told me and my sister that later in the week, she would be going out for the evening and our father would be taking care of us. Neither of us really understood what she meant, because this had never happened to us before, certainly not in the two years since we had come to Canada from Europe. Our mother was always there. What could be so important?

She was going to a concert, she told us. She said that the singer (his name, if she told us, meant nothing to me) held very special feelings and memories for her. In her mind she could hear his deep warm bass voice. She had heard him on the radio in Poland before the Nazis shattered her world. She knew what he looked like from photographs, but she had never seen him in person. It was going to be a once-in-a-lifetime experience for her, and for most of those in the audience.

My strongest memory of that evening was the perplexing experience of my mother going out and leaving my sister and me behind. Many years later, after my mother died, that memory, such as it was, came back to me. I knew that I had been seven years old at the time, but much more than that I couldn't say. In the intervening years I had also learned that the singer had been Paul Robeson. I became curious. When was that concert? It didn't take me long to find out: February 11,

1956. But why had my mother been so determined to go? That required more research.

In 1956, I discovered, Paul Robeson, one of the most famous African Americans of the twentieth century, had been allowed out of the United States for the first time since 1950. He was to perform in Toronto at Massey Hall to a sold-out audience of 2,800. The scheduled program was eclectic: Robeson would sing Negro spirituals, folk songs (Canadian, Chinese, Eastern European, and Yiddish—at which my mother, who could speak very little English, probably cried her eyes out), and his signature tune, "Ol' Man River"; he would be reading excerpts from *Othello*, poems by Shelley and Schiller—especially the "Ode to Joy"—and poems by his own contemporaries and close friends, the Chilean poet Pablo Neruda and the African-American poet Langston Hughes.

The evening went exactly according to the plan laid out in the program. What was not announced was Robeson's encore. The last time he had performed in Toronto, nine years earlier in May 1947, city officials told him that his appearance was on the condition that he would sing, but not speak. This time, no one stopped him. Robeson rounded out the tumultuous evening with a rousing speech about peace, freedom, and brotherhood. "My purpose in life," he proclaimed powerfully and deeply from the stage, "was to fight for my people, that they shall walk this earth as free as any man."

*Oakland, September 20, 1942*
When Paul Robeson arrived at the Moore Dry Dock, a recently integrated shipyard labor force was waiting there to greet him. In the previous year, President Roosevelt had issued an executive order banning all forms of discrimination in the country's defense industry, and the men Robeson met were working together round the clock to make Liberty and Victory ships for the war effort.

As the country's most famous African American, Robeson, who stood six foot three and weighed more than 220 pounds, was at the pinnacle of his career and his popularity. He was a household name. His voice, which one critic had described as "one of the most beautiful in the world . . . in the [sic] soft mellow resonance . . . in its organ-like ease and power . . . it exercises a spell that is inescapable," was known from coast to coast.

Robeson had dropped into the shipyard during the lunch break for a morale–boosting concert. Although the organizers may have hoped for a patriotic performance, what they got instead was pure Robeson, art and politics uncompromisingly combined.

The workers were scattered around the yard looking for places to sit and eat their lunch. A reporter from the *Oakland Tribune* who was on hand described the scene:

> They put down their sandwiches and thermos bottles as Robeson sang 'Water Boy' for the sheer entertainment value. They stopped chewing and listened silently as he introduced his 'Ballad for Americans.' 'This will never be a real America until my colored brothers are working by your side. We too are real Americans . . . We all have to be here together. That's what democracy really means' . . . Then as the sun climbed over a steel shop, Robeson cupped his ear with his right hand . . . took off his hat and broke into the Star Spangled Banner. Off came the shiny helmets, the goggles and the greasy hats, and three thousand men and women shouldered in beside the Big Negro to sing the national anthem. The whistle sent [them] back to their jobs. A thousand war workers hummed 'Old [sic] Man River' and 'Water Boy' as they arced their welding torches and went back to putting steel together for victory.

In contrast with the fantasy heroes of the present age, it is important to remember there have been celebrities who actually did something real, famous people who risked their careers and reputations and sometimes even their lives for their principles.

Paul Robeson was such a hero. From the 1930s to the 1960s,

Robeson was the voice of the people. He once described what this meant to him in these words: "When as a singer I walk onto the platform, to sing back to the people the songs they themselves have created, I can feel a great unity, not only as a person, but as an artist who is one with his audience."

Robeson was a magnet, a rallying point for people who shared his concerns. Enormous crowds listened to him spellbound, deeply moved. He drew millions from all over the world to his struggle, in a way that showed them their own struggles mirrored in his. He sang their songs to them in their own languages, Russian, Yiddish, Welsh. He was an international human being. In the United States, he fought strenuously for the human rights of African Americans; in the colonial world he supported movements for national liberation; and in the international arena he worked tirelessly for world peace.

His message of peace, equality and justice was understood as clearly on the streets of Manchester, Moscow, Johannesburg, and Bombay as it was in Harlem and Washington, D.C.

There has never been another popular entertainer with so much political impact. Robeson was also unique in the extent to which his politics and his art were inseparable. He was at the center of the most urgent political issues of the period—racism, colonialism, and the looming threat of nuclear war. He didn't just sing and speak his ideals; he put them into direct action. He cofounded the Council on African Affairs, a radical African-American organization to aid national liberation struggles in Africa; he was a driving force behind the world peace movement, which during the 1940s and 1950s was vital in keeping international pressure on both the United States and the Soviet Union to avoid war; and he played a critical role in the Civil Rights Congress and the National Negro Congress, organizations that paved the way for the 1963 March on Washington and the 1964 Civil Rights Act.

Robeson's concern was not for his fellow African Americans only; he identified with oppressed people everywhere, and they identified with him. He was instrumental in linking the African-American struggle with similar movements for equality throughout the world, and was welcomed as a political voice for freedom in Africa, Asia, and the West Indies. He counted among his close friends Jomo Kenyatta, Kwame Nkrumah, Pandit Nehru—future leaders of the postcolonial world—and C.L.R. James and Albert Einstein, all of whom shared his vision of peace, equality and justice.

His popularity and the fact that he inspired so many people to believe in the possibility of freedom also alarmed governments across the Western world. When Robeson visited Spain during the Spanish Civil War to encourage the Republican Army and the International Brigades, security services in the United States, Britain and Canada started to pay attention. They feared Spanish Republicanism as tantamount to Communism, and they kept files on Robeson for the next forty years.

During the Cold War the United States government became so worried by his impact abroad that it tried to silence him by seizing his passport, making it impossible for him to travel outside the country.

This confinement only deepened and broadened the support of his devoted audience. Beyond the United States, peace groups in Europe, South America, and Africa all piled pressure on the US State Department to reverse their decision and reinstate Robeson's right to travel. The "Let Paul Robeson Sing" campaign, which started in Manchester in 1955 and spread across Britain over the following years, was a deliberate attempt to embarrass the US government.

It was typical of the man that he would not submit to unjustified exercise of authority. When he was prevented from crossing into Canada for a concert, he managed instead to sing across the border, standing on the back of a truck. Later, unable to cross the Atlantic without a passport, he gave a concert for an audience of Welsh miners by telephone. And when he was called before the House Un-American Activities Committee, on June 12, 1956, he defied his inquisitors, accusing them of being un-American themselves.

At stake that June morning were fundamental issues about the rights of individuals in a free society: the right to travel, the right of political affiliation and the right of dissent. These are so basic that we take them for granted, but it's important to remember that they have to be fought for, again and again.

The issues raised that day in a Washington committee room remain unresolved and have, if anything, become even more crucial. We are now living in a world where government surveillance is ubiquitous; where civil liberties, won against fierce opposition, are being eroded as information about individuals is constantly gathered and shared among private and public agencies; where the freedom to assemble and protest is being treated by the authorities as terrorism; and where individual movement is increasingly seen as suspicious behavior.

Throughout his career, Robeson's growing political involvement polarized his audience. This is a book about Robeson, but it is also about the people who watched and listened to him—about the fans who revered him and flocked to his concerts, and about those who watched him silently from the wings, waiting for a slip for which he could legitimately be punished. But above all, this book is about the politics, the burning issues of the 1950s, how we see the Cold War and its aftermath—topics that are as controversial now as ever they were. The ideological struggles of these years were embodied in Robeson himself and in people's attitudes to him. Through him, we can gain a unique view of this moment in history.

This book, focused on Robeson's political battles and based on entirely new sources, should reinstate him as a defiant and defining figure of the twentieth century for a generation who are in real danger of never knowing anything about him.

# Introduction

# Being Paul Robeson, Becoming Radical

Paul Robeson was born in Princeton, New Jersey, in 1898, the youngest of five children born to William and Maria Louisa Robeson. William, a runaway slave from North Carolina, graduated from the all-black Lincoln University and Divinity School in Pennsylvania, and had established himself in 1879 as Reverend William Robeson at Princeton's Witherspoon Street Presbyterian Church.

As Lloyd Brown, Robeson's close friend and biographer explained, Princeton, whose population was one-fifth black, was "the South up north." The university's all-white student body was drawn largely from below the Mason-Dixon Line, and "Princeton—college and town—was like the Big House of a Southern plantation, with the black townspeople as its servants." Despite being in the north, it was also a Jim Crow town: There were strict rules about how black people should behave, about where they could go, about what they could do. In later life, while Robeson was staying at Albert Einstein's home in Princeton, his close friend and host was surprised to learn that he had been born in the college town. "I didn't know anyone was ever *born* here," remarked the seventy-three-year-old scientist. "I thought Princeton was only a place where people *died*."

When Paul Robeson was five years old, a terrible tragedy struck the family. While William and the children, including Paul, were away, Maria Louisa Robeson lost her life in a horrible domestic fire. Reeve, Ben, and Paul, three of the four boys, stayed on in the family home with their father; Marian, the girl, went to live with a family friend and fellow minister.

Paul attended the local segregated elementary school, but in 1907, his father decided to quit Princeton and the Presbyterian Church and moved thirty miles to the north, to the town of West-field, where he took the post of pastor at the local African Methodist Episcopal (A.M.E) Zion Church, an independent black denomination founded at the end of the eighteenth century. There were too few blacks in town to fill a segregated school, and Paul, for the first time, attended school with white children.

The Reverend William Robeson and Paul, now the only child at home, did not remain long in Westfield. In 1910, when Paul was twelve, he and his father moved to the town of Somerville, closer to Princeton. Somerville had a larger black population than Westfield and boasted a substantial congregation at the local St. Thomas A.M.E. Zion Church, where Reverend Robeson became pastor.

Somerville suited both father and son. Paul did very well at the town's integrated high school, where he was one of only a hand-ful of black students, excelling in his academic studies, in the glee club, the debating club, the drama club and, significantly, on the playing field. In his senior year, for all of these achievements, Paul, now a six-foot-two-inch imposing man, won a state schol-arship to attend Rutgers College (later Rutgers University).

The college, then an all-male institution, had fewer than 500 students. He was the only African-American student. Until then, Paul had not really encountered the racism that infected his coun-try, but in his first year at Rutgers he came face-to-face with all its ugliness. It was an experience he never forgot. One day, he went down to the playing field to try out for the college football team. He'd been a star player in high school and thought he had a decent chance of getting on the team. As Robeson recalled it years later, "The white boys didn't want a Negro on their team . . . at the scrimmage one boy slugged me in the face and smashed my nose . . . and then when I was down, flat on my back, another boy got me with his knee . . . he managed to dislocate my right shoulder." The coach intervened; Paul was just too good to exclude. He made the team and forged an impressive college football career while rising to the top rank of his class in academic studies. No such ugly incident occurred again.

In 1919 Robeson graduated, having proved himself a gifted scholar and player. But his father was not there to share in his son's success. William Robeson had died the year before.

Now on his own, Robeson moved to New York, where he enrolled in Columbia Law School. Until his graduation in 1923, he continued to pursue all of his interests: He played three seasons of professional football, sang numerous recitals at schools, churches and community halls, coached football, played semipro basketball, clerked in a Wall Street law office, and made his debut on Broadway, first as a dramatic actor, in the play *Taboo*, and then as a singer, in Noble Sissle and Eubie Blake's *Shuffle Along*—the first Broadway musical written by an African American. He even appeared in London in a play starring opposite Mrs. Patrick Campbell, one of the country's most famous actresses, and then toured England with her. He met Larry Brown, who would be his accompanist for forty years, through John Payne, an African-American musician who opened his home to passing African-American artists. He also managed to get married, to Eslanda (Essie) Goode. All of this in just three years.

When he returned to New York, Robeson, like many other African Americans at the time, was drawn to Harlem, the most populous black urban center in the world. This was his first exposure to a whirlwind diversity of black people from every walk of life and from other parts of the world. Harlem was in the throes of a remarkable and vibrant cultural and political flowering—where jazz, theater, cinema, literature, painting, and photography confronted the politics of the color line. The Harlem Renaissance, or "New Negro" movement, continued to resonate through New York and beyond, across the Atlantic, for the next decade.

Although he graduated from law school, Robeson never took the bar examinations and never practiced law. It was a highly segregated profession—as were all professions in the United States at the time. Instead, the stage and the movie set claimed him, both as an actor—he starred in two Eugene O'Neill plays, *All God's Chillun Got Wings* and *The Emperor Jones*, which he also took to London, and in a silent film, *Body and Soul*, by the radical African-American filmmaker Oscar Micheaux—and as a singer.

On April 19, 1925, Robeson gave a concert at the Greenwich Village Theatre featuring Negro spirituals. Previously most recitals in major American or European cities consisted of pieces from the classical repertoire. That night Robeson began with "Go Down Moses" and went on to "Nobody Knows the Trouble I've Seen" and "Swing Low, Sweet Chariot," among others. The combination of Robeson's deep, sonorous tone and dramatic power and Larry Brown's original arrangements and deft accompaniment elevated these spirituals to a new plane. The audience screamed their delight and asked for more.

Critics applauded, too, comparing Robeson's voice to that of the Russian Fyodor Chaliapin, the most famous bass of the time. Two more concerts were scheduled, and both sold out. W.E.B. Du Bois, already known as an intellectual giant in the "New Negro" movement, personally congratulated Robeson and Brown on their second concert, calling it very beautiful. This was probably the first time that Du Bois wrote to Robeson, and it marked the beginning of a bond of intense friendship and loyalty that would continue until Du Bois' death in 1963.

While starring in Greenwich Village in November 1924 in *All God's Chillun Got Wings*, Robeson penned a note of appreciation to Roland Hayes, the renowned classically trained lyric tenor and the first African American to sing spirituals in a recital. Hayes had just arrived in New York after a short European tour. Robeson referred to him as a pioneer and described hearing him at a Carnegie Hall recital in the previous year: "As I listened to him . . . I knew he possessed that 'something,' incapable of definition which we most inadequately call 'soul.' I watched the people of both groups sit reverent and enchanted as he sang. Here there was no problem. We were not black not white . . . I have seen a star. I will follow."

The poet and critic Carl Sandburg was much more impressed by Paul Robeson than by Roland Hayes. After hearing Robeson sing, Sandberg concluded that he was the best interpreter of the Negro spiritual, and a more genuine article than Hayes. He wrote, "Hayes imitates white culture and uses methods from the white man's conservatories of music, so that when he sings a Negro spiritual the audience remarks, 'What technic; what a remarkable musical education he must have had!' When Paul Robeson sings spirituals, the remark is: 'That is the real thing—he has kept the best of himself and not allowed the schools to take it away from him!'"

Robeson had profoundly and wholly injected himself into the history of the Negro spiritual and made it his own. He and Brown would fill recital halls for decades to come, and Roland Hayes's name would be largely eclipsed.

For the next two years, the pace of Robeson's public appearances intensified. His face and voice became widely known and recognized on both sides of the Atlantic. His name was hardly out of the papers. In 1927, he and Brown made their first recordings for Victor in the United States and for HMV in Britain. Robeson also appeared in London at the Ambassador Theatre in *The Emperor Jones* and broadcast a recital on the BBC. In London he met Emma Goldman and in Paris he met Ernest Hemingway, James Joyce, and Rebecca West. Back in the United States, he and Brown undertook a grueling winter tour in the Northeast and the Great Lakes States, returned to the Broadway stage in Jim Tully and Frank Dazey's play *Black Boy* and then did another tough tour, of the heartland of the American Midwest where, in Kansas and Missouri, the two African Americans found a less liberal welcome than they were used to in New York.

Jerome Kern, one of the most successful Broadway composers, saw Robeson in a tryout for *Black Boy* at a theater north of New York City and later recalled that it was hearing Robeson's "organ-like tones" that inspired him to write "Ol' Man River" for Robeson to sing. Kern and his new lyricist, Oscar Hammerstein II, wrote the musical *Show Boat* as a vehicle for Robeson, intending him to play both the stevedore Joe, who sings "Ol' Man River," and Joe's son, who was to incorporate a recital of Negro spirituals into the action. However, Robeson, despite being interested at first, eventually turned down the offer. Instead Jules Bledsoe was cast as Joe, and the role of Joe's son was cut.

On October 15, 1927, while *Show Boat* was in rehearsal, Robeson and Brown joined the *S.S. Majestic* in New York for its transatlantic voyage to Europe, on their way to a recital tour of European cities, beginning in Paris at the prestigious and opulent Salle Gaveau.

African Americans were not a rare sight in Paris in the 1920s. The jazz scene, especially in Montmartre, was in full swing, and there were other places where African Americans gathered. Josephine Baker had already debuted at the Folies-Bergère and was running her own club, Chez Josephine. Roland Hayes had given his first recital in the city, and scores of writers, musicians, and artists, as well as many ordinary African Americans, were making the City of Light their home. Besides African Americans, Paris also drew a wide range of francophone Africans and West Indians, who were attracted by the city's cultural and intellectual atmosphere.

So when Robeson and Brown appeared in the Eighth Arrondissement at the Salle Gaveau, the city's main recital hall, on October 29, the Parisian audience was ready. They may have been unused to a full program of spirituals, but the artists' reputations had preceded them. This was an important landmark in Robeson and Brown's career, the first time they had taken their successful American formula abroad.

Black and white Americans as well as the French filed into the 1,700-seat hall for the nine o'clock concert, billed mostly as spirituals but with a few folk songs, such as "Water Boy," thrown in. Reporters associated with mainstream and African-American newspapers were present and noted the array of celebrities attracted to the performance. James Joyce and Sylvia Beach, the owner of the famous Left Bank bookshop Shakespeare & Company, were there, as were Roland Hayes and Alberta Hunter, the African-American blues singer and songwriter. Parisian notables abounded. The seats were sold out, and according to one newspaper report, some 500 people who turned up in hope of one left disappointed. Those who were lucky enough to get in were treated to a unique experience. The encores lasted for half an hour. The critics agreed that Robeson and Brown were fantastic. Repeat performances were planned.

Early in 1928, back in the United States, and now a father, Robeson accepted the role he had turned down the previous year. The producer Florenz Ziegfeld convinced him at last to play Joe in *Show Boat*. Not on Broadway, but in London—a city Robeson had grown to love—at the Drury Lane Theatre, with Alfred Butt, the influential manager, who had just taken over running the theater and who had produced *The Emperor Jones*, starring Robeson, a few years earlier. What hadn't seemed right for Robeson in 1927 seemed perfect now. It was not a taxing role— he had only to sing "Ol' Man River." He knew and respected Butt, the money was good, and he would have ample opportunities to give concerts. Robeson sailed for England in early April 1928, to prepare for the show's opening on May 3.

*Show Boat* was one of the most spectacular productions ever staged in London. The cast numbered more than 160 people; the number of costumes topped 1,000; the money poured in. People queued for twenty-four hours to get a ticket. It was well worth it, audience and reviewers agreed, and the biggest hit of the show was Paul Robeson singing "Ol' Man River," After the opening night, Jerome Kern is supposed to have telephoned Florenz Ziegfeld at his country home outside New York City to tell him that he should expect a long run. He was right. The Drury Lane Theatre *Show Boat* played until March 2, 1929—350 performances in total.

Paul Robeson and "Ol' Man River" were now firmly locked together in the public imagination. Where one went, the other followed. Recording the song certainly helped promote Robeson as its chief interpreter. Although almost forty separate recordings of "Ol' Man River," vocal and instrumental, were released between 1928 and 1939 by the likes of Bing Crosby, Al Jolson, and Jules Bledsoe, the original Joe on Broadway, Robeson himself, recorded five of those releases. As gramophone records spread through the world, so did Robeson's voice. But that was only one of the forces that created his international impact. An even more powerful one appeared in 1936, with the black and white film of *Show Boat*. Now those who were not fortunate enough to have seen Robeson on stage or in a recital could see the man on celluloid.

From the time that *Show Boat* opened in London in May 1928 until the end of September 1939, London was Robeson's base. In the early part of that period, Robeson moved between the United States and Europe as he broadened his artistic endeavors. Highlights of the time included his first public recital in London, held in Drury Lane Theatre, with Larry Brown at the piano, on July 3, 1928; his debut at the Royal Albert Hall, on April 28, 1929; two concerts at Carnegie Hall, on November 5 and 10, 1929; tours of British seaside towns, Central European capital cities, and the continental United States; performances in Toronto and Montreal; a run at London's Savoy Theatre playing Shakespeare's *Othello* (May 19 to July 5, 1930); a return to Broadway to play Joe in the 1932 revival of *Show Boat*; and the making of two films, the experimental silent *Borderline* (1930), shot in Switzerland, and *The Emperor Jones* (1933), shot in the United States.

But when 1935 came around, Robeson found himself concentrating on his British career. By 1939, he had made five British films, starred in four plays on the London stage and toured British industrial cities and the Welsh coalfields.

As a performer, Robeson had conquered the world: in theater, in musicals, in film, in recitals. He was the most famous African American in the world.

How things would have turned out had he accepted the role of Joe in 1927 is hard to guess, but his decision to make London rather than New York his home in the 1930s had a profound impact not only on his art but also, more importantly, on his political evolution.

In the 1920s and 1930s, London, like Paris, was the center of a rich and vibrant anticolonial, radical intellectual community, drawing its membership mainly from the Caribbean and Africa but also from the Indian subcontinent. Many organizations sprang up to foster and feed this growing call for self-determination, and they spanned the political spectrum, including such diverse organizations as the West African Students Union, the League of Coloured Peoples, the League Against Imperialism, the Negro Welfare Association and, notably, the International African Service Bureau, founded in 1935 in the wake of Italy's invasion of Ethiopia.

The organizations sponsored meetings and conferences and published magazines, pamphlets, and books. They attracted some of the leading black intellectuals of the period, people such as C.L.R. James, George Padmore, I.T.A. Wallace-Johnson, Una Marson, Amy Ashwood Garvey, Jomo Kenyatta, and Nnamdi Azikiwe, (the latter two would eventually play leading roles in their own national liberation movements). Robeson circulated through these organizations and got to know all of these thinkers

As Robeson developed politically, his art, too, changed. He studied a host of foreign languages so that he could sing folk songs in their original tongues, to speak directly to the people.

He had already discovered Africa, its history, culture and its political struggles, for himself, and now learned several African languages, in order to incorporate African folk songs into his concert repertoire. He also began gravitating toward edgier roles in edgier plays, typically the sort shunned by the commercial theater establishment. In *Stevedore*, in 1935, he played a dockworker who tried to organize fellow blacks into an integrated union. The following year, he took the lead role in *Toussaint Louverture* [sic], a play by C.L.R. James about the leader of the successful Haitian revolution that began with the slave rebellion of 1791. In 1938, he starred again in a play about union organization, racism, and violence. *Plant in the Sun*, with Robeson in the lead role, opened at London's Unity Theatre, a creation of the Left Theatre Movement, which was dedicated to bringing theater to the working class. Its advisory council included as members such prominent intellectuals and artists as Sean O'Casey, Harold Laski, and Victor Gollancz.

Andre Van Gyseghem, who directed Robeson in *Stevedore*, recalled that the play's political character was not what had attracted Robeson to it: "Paul was hardly a political radical then . . . his focus was still almost exclusively on his art and improving himself professionally . . . he liked talking about politics, but he really did not see any link between what he did—his life—and politics."

But by 1937, Robeson's political persona had started to emerge. Early that year, he and Max Yergan, an African American who had lived and worked in South Africa for more than fifteen years, founded the International Committee on African Affairs in New York. Although African-American newspapers occasionally carried African stories in their pages, there was no voice in the United States dedicated to publicizing African issues and the necessity for colonial liberation. The International Committee on African Affairs was designed to fill that gap.

On June 24 of the same year, Robeson cut short a holiday in the Soviet Union to attend a mass rally at the Royal Albert Hall in aid of Basque refugee children. Following the German, Italian and Spanish aerial bombardment of the northern town of Guernica on April 26, 1937, the Basque government in Bilbao had launched a worldwide appeal to take in 20,000 children whom they were evacuating, and in May, 4,000 of these children had arrived in Southampton. The London rally drew a crowd of 6,000, who generously contributed a substantial amount of money to the refugee fund. Robeson sang, of course, but there was something new and different about his performance: He also spoke.

It was a very emotional evening, and its highlight, according to newspaper reports, was Robeson's speech. In that speech, possibly for the first time on a public stage, Robeson made the link between art and politics. "Every artist, every scientist, every writer must decide now where he stands," he said. "The artist must take sides. He must elect to fight for freedom or for slavery. I have made my choice. I had no alternative." In powerful language he went on to link fascism in Spain with the oppression that his own people faced throughout the world: "Despoiled of their lands, their culture destroyed, they are in every country save one denied equal protection of the law, and deprived of their rightful place in the respect of their fellows."

Five months later, Robeson was once again the star attraction at the Royal Albert Hall, at a 9,000-strong rally to raise funds for the victims of the Spanish Civil War. Surrounded by the stalwarts of the British Labour Party, which included Clement Atlee, leader of the Opposition, and members of Parliament Herbert Morrison, Ellen Wilkinson, and Stafford Cripps, Robeson now took up the political mantle more decisively than ever before. He began to sing his signature tune, "Ol' Man River," but instead of the passive words "I'm tired o' livin' and feared o' dyin'," he belted out defiantly, "I must keep on struggling until I'm dyin'."

The following day, the *New York Times* reported that Robeson had made this change. The paper made no comment on it at the time.

Now that he had discovered his political voice, Robeson felt impelled to go to Spain. It took a little time to arrange the necessary papers, but on January 21, 1938, Robeson, Essie, and Charlotte Haldane, wife of the biologist J.B.S. Haldane, made their way to Paris and from there to the Spanish border and on to Barcelona. After a short stay in Barcelona, the center of Catalonian resistance, the party headed to the Mediterranean town of Benicasim, which had become the hospital base closest to the front line. There Robeson sang and met African-American members of the Abraham Lincoln Brigade, one of the mobilized companies in the International Brigades—and integrated. One of its volunteers, Oliver Law, was the first African American in the history of the United States to lead white soldiers into battle.

Wherever Robeson went he was instantly recognized and cheered. Tommy Adlam, a British volunteer who was there, said, "The whole place lit up . . . [Robeson] was just like a magnet drawing you . . . as if somebody was reaching out to grasp you and draw you in."

After stopping in Madrid and Valencia, where Robeson sang many more times, the party of three returned to France and Paris, arriving on February 1.

The invasion of Ethiopia, the rise of brutal fascism in Spain, the radical black presence in London and Paris—all of these were the building blocks of a political Paul Robeson. But another profound revelation awaited him. Unlike many of his political contemporaries, who were generally metropolitan creatures, Robeson traveled extensively; his voice took him to parts of Britain that most London-based black people knew only by name. By touring Britain's industrial cities, where in music halls and cinemas he drew huge audiences, Robeson was able to see for himself the condition of Britain's industrial working class.

On December 7, 1938, he appeared in Mountain Ash, South Wales, as the honorary guest of the National Memorial Meeting to commemorate the thirty-five Welshmen who had given their lives in the Spanish Civil War. There he came face to face with the universality of oppression and the cry for freedom, a universality that he was only now coming to understand. Arthur Horner, president of the South Wales Miners' Federation, who introduced Robeson, expressed it for the miners. "In South Wales we have always lived for freedom," Horner explained, "and are determined to fight for it, challenged as it is in a hundred ways at the present time. What we must demonstrate is that we are ready to work tomorrow and the day after against the forces which work to destroy our rights." And Robeson replied, before an audience of more than 7,000 people—Brigaders, black men, women, and children from Cardiff, a group of Basque children and others, of many ethnicities and from all walks of life, "I am here because I know that these fellows fought not only for Spain but for me and the whole world. I feel it is my duty to be here."

Tommy Adlam, who had met Robeson in Spain and was in Mountain Ash that night, was proud when Robeson remembered him: "It was 'Our Paul.' You know, it wasn't Paul Robeson, like that, it was 'Our Paul.' He's ours. He doesn't belong to any class but he's ours . . . It was a marvelous occasion. It's a thing you never forget, really." A year later, Robeson began filming *The Proud Valley*, in which he played a black miner in the Welsh coal pits who tries to improve the miners' lot and ultimately sacrifices his life for theirs. Produced by Michael Balcon and shot on location in the South Wales coalfield, the movie, released in 1940, would turn out to be Robeson's last British film and his penultimate appearance on the big screen.

In the North of England and in Wales Robeson began to understand something that few others did: The color line was not unique, but instead one of many barriers, including class, that divided people historically, politically, and culturally.

In his speech at the rally for the Basque children refugees, at the Royal Albert Hall, Robeson had said that African people and people of African descent had been oppressed and despoiled everywhere except for one place on earth. He was referring to the Soviet Union.

Robeson had been to the Soviet Union on several occasions. He made his first visit, together with Essie, in late 1934 and early 1935, and while there he met Sergei Eisenstein and talked of various film projects. Paul and Essie were very impressed by the life in Moscow and particularly by the way minorities were treated. They met William Patterson, whom they knew from Harlem and who would play a large part in Robeson's life in the two decades to come, and other members of Moscow's sizable African-American community, who told the visitors of how well they had been received, how Russian society was devoid of racial prejudice.

A second trip, made in late December 1936 and the first half of January 1937, included a four-city concert tour with Larry Brown. Around this time Robeson placed his son, Paul Jr., in a Moscow school, declaring to the press that this way the boy would be spared the racial discrimination he himself had faced attending college in the United States.

The Soviet Union made a lifelong impression on Robeson. He always spoke warmly of it and of the Russian people. He would pay dearly for this sentiment.

It wasn't long before the FBI was referring to Robeson as a Communist. The Council on African Affairs soon attracted its own surveillance and a file that quickly expanded. Meanwhile, in Ottawa, the Special Branch of the Royal Canadian Mounted Police (RCMP), began clipping newspaper articles about Robeson. One of the first entries in their dossier was a report that his ten-year-old son had won an award at his Moscow school.

In London, Robeson's file with British MI5 was filling up. There were reports on his activities with the League Against Imperialism and with the Left Theatre Movement, and one stating that he had become a Communist after visiting the Soviet Union. They also noted that at a meeting of the League of Coloured Peoples some members expressed the hope that Robeson would "not identify himself so closely with the Communist Party." A Special Branch Report of November 22, 1937, that is, from the period between the rally in aid of Basque refugee children and the rally for victims of the Spanish Civil War, asserted, "Paul Robeson is a secret member of the Communist Party" and added that he had joined in Moscow. Surveillance of Robeson was stepped up and his file grew thicker. On September 30, 1939, Special Branch provided news that Paul Robeson, "the well-known variety artist and Communist Party sympathizer," had boarded the liner *Washington* for New York.

In common with many Americans, Robeson and his family, now reunited in London, were fleeing the outbreak of World War II in Europe for the relative safety of the United States.

For the next ten years, Robeson remained in North America. During this time, he consolidated his nationwide reputation as an artist and a committed political activist. His voice, which for many Americans was familiar from recordings alone, was heard live for the first time on every radio across the United States when he sang "Ballad for Americans" in November 1939 and January 1940. Both the record and the sheet music sold tens of thousands of copies. But Robeson stopped making films after 1942; he played in *Show Boat* for the last time in 1940; he withdrew from the American theatrical stage following his final performance in *Othello* in 1945.

Instead, Robeson concentrated his art on recitals, which he took on several tours across the country and into Canada, Panama, Hawaii, and the British West Indies. Politically, however, he broadened his interests and commitments, becoming involved in the labor and peace movements and in anti-lynching campaigns, and widened his geographical sympathies to include China and Latin America. The African-American community honored him with the prestigious Spingarn Medal, awarded each year by the National Association for the Advancement of Colored People (NAACP) since 1914 to the "man or woman of African descent" who had realized the highest achievement in his or her field. In the country as a whole, he made his political mark when he campaigned vigorously for the Progressive Party and for Henry Wallace's bid for the presidency in the country's 1948 general election.

# PART I

# EUROPE 1949

# I

# Postwar Britain

It was 1949, and Paul Robeson had not set foot in in Britain for ten years. In the meantime everything had changed. During his previous stay, the country had been in good economic and social shape, even though war was already looming. The Great Depression had passed. The empire continued to feed the mother country with the rich bounty of the tropics and to supply its industries with raw materials. Sterling was the most widely traded currency in the world.

In 1949, the devastation of the Second World War was still visible everywhere. Many British cities had been bombed by the German Luftwaffe, and though rebuilding was a postwar priority, large chunks of the urban landscape were still rubble.

This material damage could be, and was being, repaired, but many other changes in the country would be permanent. Britain's place in the world order was altered. The United States had emerged as the single most powerful nation, and the dollar now reigned supreme. The British Empire was unraveling: India had gained independence in 1947, and Palestine, renamed Israel, in 1948. The guerrilla war in Malaya continued, and growing unrest and dissatisfaction with British rule in East and West Africa was widespread. The enshrining of apartheid in law in South Africa had created international repercussions as well as increasing internal divisions.

~

Robeson's return to Britain had only recently been arranged. Indeed, just two months earlier, Robeson had been resting at his home in Connecticut, fully expecting to begin a grueling four-month concert tour of the United States. But then came the shocking news from his agents that all of his engagements until April 1949 had been canceled at a stroke. Robeson was not the only entertainer to be treated in this manner at this time. The political climate in the United States had become extremely difficult; the entertainment industry was being subjected to a vicious anticommunist attack. The number of people blacklisted, not only in the film industry but also throughout the media—radio, television, the stage, the press—ran into the hundreds. Agents booking engagements soon shied away from drawing up a contract if there was a whisper that the star in question was in any way "red."

Just when all seemed lost, Harold Fielding, Britain's leading theater producer, contacted Robert Rockmore, Robeson's close friend and attorney, and proposed a British tour. Robeson jumped at the chance. The State Department renewed his passport, but according to Paul Robeson Jr. in his biography of his father, Robeson had to sign a waiver stating that he would restrict his public appearances to the concert dates and would refrain from showing up at political events. As the tour progressed it became clear that Robeson had no intention of submitting to this restriction.

His passage on the *Queen Mary* was secured. Tickets for his first appearance, at the Royal Albert Hall on March 18, went on sale January 29. They quickly sold out.

On February 17, 1949, Paul Robeson disembarked in Southampton. His had almost certainly been the most famous face on that seven-day voyage across the Atlantic from New York; anyone who passed him on the decks or saw him in one of the ship's restaurants would have recognized him instantly. During that trip, the ship's crew were luckier than the passengers: They'd had the special treat of a Paul Robeson recital given just for them.

From Southampton Robeson took the train to London. When, a few hours later, he arrived at Waterloo Station, a reporter from the *Daily Worker*, Britain's foremost working-class newspaper and an organ of the British Communist Party, was waiting for him. On the front page of the next day's issue, readers learned that Robeson was in Britain for an extended and "sensational" tour that would take in Britain's major cities—Birmingham, Manchester, Glasgow and Sheffield, to mention just a few. And he was in Britain to talk about peace. "I represent here," he told the reporter, "that fraction of American opinion that feels we can build a world in peace, and that the next war would certainly mean the end of whatever we mean by civilization." The FBI received a copy of that interview very shortly thereafter, and it went straight into Robeson's file.

At Waterloo Station Robeson was thronged by a large group of people, most of whom were just waiting for trains but instantly recognized this larger-than-life world celebrity. One of these struck it lucky, asking for his signature. A photograph shows a train guard from Southern Railway staring upward in awe at Robeson, who, looming over him in a gentle fashion and smiling, is signing the autograph book. Behind Robeson were the two men, one of them just visible in the photograph, who had come to meet him; as soon as they could, they whisked him away to his hotel in St. James.

We know about the presence of Peter Blackman and Desmond Buckle, the two men waiting for Robeson, only because of another photograph that captured the moment that day in Waterloo Station. We don't know whether Robeson expected to see both men, but it is highly likely that he was expecting Buckle. William Patterson, a prominent American lawyer, human rights activist, leader of the Civil Rights Congress, and very long-standing friend and adviser of Robeson's, had met Buckle in London in November 1948 when both attended a meeting of the preparatory committee for the International Conference on

Human Rights. The two men found they had a lot in common, and when it became clear that Robeson would be traveling to Britain, Patterson arranged for Buckle to organize his activities there.

Robeson had first met Blackman and Buckle in the 1930s, when he lived in London, and meeting them there at Waterloo Station provided him with a direct link to those early days of his political education. They were members of the Communist Party of Great Britain, having joined in the late 1930s, when they were active and critically important participants in London's anticolonial political scene.

Blackman had an uneven relationship with the Party. MI5, which tracked him very carefully from the 1930s through 1950s, were convinced that he had broken with the Party during the war but had recently reacquainted himself with some of its leading members. Buckle, on the other hand, was an undeviating life-long member.

Peter Blackman was born in Barbados in 1909 and entered Britain in 1930 to study theology. He was ordained in the Anglican Church and spent some time in Gambia as a missionary, then left the church and upon returning to Britain devoted himself to political activity and writing—in the 1940s he was a regular contributor to the *Nation* and the *New Statesman*, the latter a decidedly left-wing political magazine under its longtime editor Kingsley Martin. Blackman belonged to several leftist anticolonial organizations in London, including the League Against Imperialism and the League of Coloured Peoples, but his main achievement in this area was his chairmanship of the Negro Welfare Association, a prominent black organization founded in London in 1931 to fight racism and the color bar in Britain. It was in the Negro Welfare Association—which included, at various times, leading luminaries such as Nancy Cunard, Reginald Bridgeman, and Jomo Kenyatta—that Blackman became closely associated with Desmond Buckle, though the two men had probably met before.

Blackman was from a relatively humble background; Desmond Buckle was privileged. Born in 1910, in Accra, Ghana, Buckle came to England in 1920 to attend boarding school in Cornwall and remained in the country permanently. He studied medicine in London, and then abandoned it to throw himself into the same metropolitan political world as Blackman. A prolific journalist and a committed trade unionist, Buckle became increasingly interested in pan-Africanism and, in the postwar era, the struggle for African national liberation and the world peace movement. For many years he was secretary of the British Communist Party's Africa Committee—which worked closely with anticolonial groups in Africa and Africans in Britain—and a member of its International Affairs Committee.

Blackman and Buckle were key figures in Britain's postwar racial politics and its transnational political world, in which Robeson would have been as much at home as he was in the 1930s. Throughout the next few months, both men kept close to their charge.

We know that Blackman and Buckle were at Waterloo Station on the afternoon of February 17, 1949; it's less clear whether an MI5 officer was in the crowd. The security service certainly knew that Robeson was on his way to Britain and that he would arrive that day in Southampton. The information had come from two sources. The first was an intercepted telephone call from Jack Brent, secretary of the International Brigade Association, to Maud Rogerson, based at the London headquarters of the Communist Party of Great Britain in King Street, Covent Garden, and in charge of the Party's International Department and a member of its Africa Committee, about Robeson's travel plans. Intercepting telephone calls to the Party's King Street offices was a daily MI5 activity.

Several days later, the intercepted information was confirmed when Richard Thistlethwaite, MI5's representative at the British embassy in Washington, D.C., wrote to Sir Percy Sillitoe, director-general of MI5, to tell him that Robeson was scheduled to

board the *Queen Mary* in New York on February 11 and that aside
from touring Britain—MI5 noted especially that Robeson was
going to perform in front of the surviving members of the British
Battalion of the International Brigade Association in London—
he also planned to go to Paris and Bucharest. Thistlethwaite
admitted that he did not know precisely what Robeson's purpose
was in visiting Europe, but added, " . . . in the past he is known to
have engaged in political activities during his tours and he is, of
course, known to have been active in Communist circles for many
years. In view of his intended appearance before the International
Brigade which fought in Spain, it seems more than likely that this
tour will follow the usual pattern." The FBI, Thistlethwaite
noted, had already been informed of Robeson's movements and
he would keep the American agency in the picture as MI5 watched
him during his stay in Britain. Indeed, the FBI was also doing its
bit to keep track of Robeson's movements. In a telegram dated
February 8, the agency informed the US embassy in London that
Robeson was about to sail.

As Thistlethwaite's letter suggests, Robeson had been of interest to MI5 from as early as 1933, and reports of his activities,
particularly of his association with a group of politically active
African and Caribbean intellectuals in London and, later, of his
work for the Republican cause in the Spanish Civil War, filled his
growing file.

In the immediate postwar period, MI5's interest in Robeson
reflected the tensions surrounding the burgeoning national liberation movements throughout the British Empire, particularly in
Africa and the Caribbean. Although he wanted to, Robeson never
visited Africa, but several months before arriving in England, he
had toured the West Indies, giving concerts in Jamaica and Trinidad. There had been some question whether "in view of [his]
reported professed communist sympathies" it would be in Britain's interest to bar Robeson from the West Indies, but this course
was not pursued, because the authorities were confident that he
was only going to sing.

The governor of Trinidad, Sir John Valentine Wister Shaw, attended the first of Robeson's two concerts in Port of Spain. Reporting back to London as well as to his opposite numbers in Jamaica and British Guiana, the governor seemed impressed, though he took exception to having to pay for his seat (presumably out of his own pocket) at the top price of $10. Robeson's voice had triumphed over terrible acoustics and the continuous noise of the milling crowd outside "anxious to hear the great artist without paying . . . Only a singer of his physique and capacity could have sustained such an ordeal," Shaw noted. "The coloured population went mad about Robeson—not unnaturally, for he is undoubtedly a great artist and commanding personality . . . I intended, if he had signed my visitors' book, to ask him to lunch, but he omitted that trifling formality."

Robeson had not made any political pronouncements, Shaw reported, apart from altering a few lines of "Ol' Man River" (something he had been doing since the late thirties): "If I had not had my ears pricked for communistic sentiments, I should not have noticed this." In addition to the line changes, Shaw also noticed that Robeson was complimentary about the political situation in Trinidad. To Shaw this meant Robeson was arguing that "there was something to be said for British rule" and that "in this respect Trinidad compared favorably with the United States."

As the *National Guardian*, a New York–based left-wing newspaper, reported in its coverage of the Caribbean tour, Robeson said that indeed, he was impressed by Trinidad and the position of its black population. "I feel now," he commented, "as if I had drawn the first breath of fresh air in many years." But it was not for the reason that Shaw believed; it was not British rule but black rule that impressed Robeson. "I felt for the first time," he continued, "I could see what it will be like when Negroes are free in their own land."

This was the first time that Robeson had been among a sizable community of people of African descent outside of the United States. In concluding his *National Guardian* interview, Robeson repeated the connection between the Caribbean experience and his own: "The march to freedom by the Negroes of the West Indies is a matter of profound importance to Americans. The sound of their marching can be heard by the Negroes of our country, and their own marching time will be quickened by it."

These concerns from the colonies, then, were added to Robeson's MI5 file. At this time, MI5 cooperated closely with the American security services, the FBI and the CIA, on many sensitive issues, and Robeson was now one of them. Sillitoe was asked by the CIA to report back to them once Robeson's British tour was completed; Thistlethwaite in Washington would be reporting to the FBI. Because of his stature as one of the most popular singers alive, Robeson was seen as an international threat.

A reporter from the *Manchester Guardian*, who attended a function given on Robeson's first evening in London, was deeply impressed, even humbled, by the man. "It is common enough for reporters to show a somewhat desultory interest in celebrities," his note began, "but tonight's great man held a ring of people so closely around him that a waitress had almost to elbow her way to offer drinks . . . Paul Robeson . . . towered above us, spoke quietly in his rich voice, and by his manner alone, forbade any but serious questions." Robeson told the assembled audience that he was planning to sing a program of "serious songs" in a number of European languages, including Russian and Yiddish, in about twenty British towns. Once his itinerary had been dealt with, Robeson proceeded to talk about theater and "after forty minutes he still held his crowd as he discussed the position of coloured people in the United States and the British Empire."

The *Manchester Guardian* did not go into any details about the content of Robeson's remarks that evening, but a little over a week later, Robeson gave the British public a better idea of what was on his mind, in an in-depth interview with *Reynolds News*. This left-leaning London-based paper was an organ of the

Co-Operative Party, an affiliate of the Labour Party that believed that cooperative effort, rather than individuals working on their own for their own ends, was the only way to achieve a just and fair society. On February 27, 1949, the newspaper published the first installment of a two-part article based on this interview, titled "I, Too, Am American."

There was a photograph of Robeson, his hands resting on a tabletop and his face turned halfway toward the reader, alongside a poem by Langston Hughes: "They'll see how beautiful I am, and be ashamed—I, too, am American." The article began by telling readers that "the great singer, great Socialist, (and) great human being" had become politically aware in Britain. "Sometimes when I go back to my home State in New Jersey, friends of my student days say to me, 'Paul, what has happened to you, you used to be such a mild sort of chap and now you are so militant and political.'" Robeson had told the paper. "I realized then that I learned my militancy and my politics from your Labour Movement here in Britain . . . I realized that the fight of my Negro people in America and the fight of the oppressed workers everywhere was the same struggle."

Robeson's packed concert tour began with a recital at Birmingham's Town Hall on February 25, then wound its way through the British Isles, taking in all of the major cities, including Belfast and Glasgow, until mid-April. Larry Brown, Robeson's longtime accompanist, traveled with him throughout the tour. Their program was conventional and, in comparison with how it would change in the years to come, safe. Robeson sang a couple of songs from the seventeenth century, one English and the other French; a Hassidic Chant; and a selection from European classical masters such as Mozart, Beethoven, Mendelssohn, and Mussorgsky. It was only toward the end of the program that Robeson sang from his heart, when he launched into a number of well-known spirituals, such as "Swing Low, Sweet Chariot," arranged for him by Brown.

It seemed that to draw the crowds who knew and loved his voice he had to present such a program—and draw the crowds he did. Both his major London recitals at the Royal Albert Hall sold out well in advance—almost 20,000 tickets. But he had not abandoned his political agenda, and in some cases—as at his March 6 concert in Croydon—his audience was as admiring of his political views as of his art. After that concert, a deputation of locals and African students who were in the town presented Robeson with a letter signed by nearly 500 individuals. It said very much what a lot of people in Britain and elsewhere thought about Robeson. "Your singing," the letter read, "has delighted millions, but it is not only for your artistry that this appreciation is written. It is also for the magnificent work that you have done in the fight against race hatred, and the sincerity of your efforts to secure peace."

The sentiments expressed also came from two local interest groups, the Croydon chapter of the British-Soviet Society and the Croydon Peace Campaign Committee. Robeson thanked the delegation but reserved a special message for the African students. Drawing from his deep understanding of how the postwar world operated, he reminded them of "the need for unity between the African peoples, both in the United States and in Africa, to combat the big boys of Wall Street who are grabbing the copper and the raw materials of Africa for the benefit of a few." The African peoples' dream of a share in the wealth of the world and that of the people of Croydon for peace were inextricably linked, he said. Fairness and equality, peace and prosperity were not disparate issues but essential components together of the process of bringing progress to all.

Desmond Buckle, who with Peter Blackman was responsible for the political side of Robeson's tour, ensured that the singer's concert-free days were taken up by rallies, speeches, or meetings, under the auspices, usually, of the British Communist Party. As MI5 learned, Robeson didn't want Buckle to advertise the Party's association with the public engagements he was arranging, for fear that such publicity would jeopardize his "contractual commitments."

Most of Robeson's speaking engagements, therefore, were arranged only after his arrival in the country, usually by interested groups contacting Desmond Buckle. As MI5 discovered, Buckle, who took complete charge of Robeson's arrangements outside of his scheduled tour, had no phone in his own home and took calls at the central London offices of the Communist Party. However, he did not go in to the office every day, and the anxiety this caused his callers is palpable in the records of intercepted calls. The competition for Robeson's time was intense, and the disappointment of not getting him booked for an occasion was deeply felt. Many of the requests for a Robeson appearance could not be fulfilled.

His movements over the first long weekend of April demonstrate how packed his program was. On Thursday evening, Robeson gave his second and final Royal Albert Hall concert. The next evening, Friday, he was the featured guest performer at a private recital for an invited audience at the Polish Embassy. Aside from an impressive line-up of dignitaries, including ambassadors from the Soviet Union and its Eastern European satellites (the MI5 report was at pains to add that no member of the Yugoslavian embassy attended), the invitees included four prominent left-wing MPs (two of them, Leslie Solley and Konni Zilliacus, would soon be expelled from the Labour Party for their objection to Britain signing up to the North Atlantic Treaty); Gordon Schaffer, the assistant editor of *Reynolds News*, whom Robeson would meet again; a Nigerian who MI5 noted was in close touch with the Nigerian National Liberation Council; and Desmond Buckle.

Robeson spent part of the following day, April 9—his fifty-first birthday—on the train to Manchester. Arriving at platform one at London Road Station that evening, he was met by a reception committee of prominent Manchester trade unionists, who accompanied him to a dinner in his honor sponsored by Manchester's

New International Society, a left-wing organization founded in 1946 in Moss Side, an area near the university and cosmopolitan in character. Lester Hutchinson, the Moss Side MP, left wing like Solley and Zilliacus and soon to be expelled from the Labour Party for the same reason, toasted Robeson's birthday.

On April 12, Robeson was on his way to Blackpool, for an evening performance at the town's New Opera House; he would go back to Manchester the following evening for an appearance in Belle Vue. Next day, Robeson was back in his London hotel.

There is no doubt that, in one sense at least, endearing himself to his enormous and devoted British fan base by choosing their nation as the venue for this postwar concert tour made Robeson happy. In another sense, however, it left him with a feeling of anxiety: He had left unfinished business behind in the United States. On March 7, 1949, one of the most significant political trials in American history had opened in New York City, and he had not been there.

On July 20, 1948, six FBI agents armed with arrest warrants had raided the national offices of the Communist Party of the United States near Union Square in Manhattan and arrested five top party leaders. Over the next few weeks, others were found and arrested, so that by early August twelve leaders in all had been arraigned. Why? The twelve were indicted on the charge of violating the Smith Act, otherwise known as the Alien Registration Act, which became law in 1940. Intended, as President Roosevelt insisted, to protect the United States, primarily it required noncitizens to register with the government and refused entry to anyone who was associated with the Communist Party abroad. But in one of its subsections, the Smith Act also gave powers to arrest "whoever, with intent to cause the overthrow or destruction of any such government, prints, publishes, edits, issues, circulates, sells, distributes, or publicly displays any written or printed matter advocating, advising, or teaching the duty, necessity, desirability, or propriety of

overthrowing or destroying any government in the United
States by force or violence, or attempts to do so." The Communist Party of the United States was the target of this clause, and
the twelve party leaders had been arrested as an example to all.

The presiding judge, Harold Medina, opened the trial at the
Foley Square Courthouse in Manhattan on January 17, 1949, but
almost immediately the proceedings got bogged down in the
issue of jury selection, which seemed unlikely to be resolved in
the short term. Robeson had appeared at the courthouse before
the trial was scheduled to begin and met each of the defendants.
He certainly already knew one of them very well—Ben Davis,
who represented Harlem for the Communist Party in the New
York City Council—but he may have known others in the lineup.
One he was unlikely to have met before was John Williamson,
who was British by birth but had been living in the United States
since he was ten years old. He had made his name within the
Party initially through the Young Workers League, but by the
late 1930s he was on the Party's Central Committee. Now
Robeson shook Williamson's hand and vowed to fight with them.
Williamson never forgot that moment. Later, after years of
suffering for his beliefs at the hands of the American authorities
and finally being deported back to Britain, he would find himself
in the unique and satisfying situation of being able to repay
Robeson for his support.

Robeson decided he had time to make his British tour while the
lawyers argued about jury selection. According to an FBI report,
when he left New York for Southampton, Robeson planned to
remain in Britain only until the end of March, at which point he
intended to return to New York and testify at the trial. He would
then return to Europe and continue his tour.

In what was a very fluid situation, the plan fell through. On
March 9, in Glasgow, where he was the guest of honor at a meeting of the Scottish-USSR Society, Robeson announced publicly
and apparently for the first time that he would be cutting his tour
short. Speaking to his Glasgow audience, Robeson declared,

"Marxism is on trial. It is a way of life, a philosophy." He was planning to return to the United States at the end of May, he said. The trial of the Communist leaders at Foley Square Courthouse was just about to enter its second day. He reiterated his intention on several occasions in March and, according to MI5, in early April, at a private meeting of the Paddington branch of the Communist Party where about seventy people were present, Robeson expanded on why he might have to change his plans at a moment's notice: He would be needed "if the trial of the leaders of the United States CP goes badly, and it becomes necessary to arouse public sympathy."

The part of Robeson's British tour organized by Harold Fielding, which Desmond Buckle referred to as "something of a triumphal procession," was nearing its end. His final two concerts, billed as "Two Recitals for the People" and held on April 17 and 18—Easter Sunday and Monday—at Harringay Stadium in north London, were hugely successful. Over the two evenings 20,000 people heard Robeson sing. Though arranged by Fielding, the concerts had departed as far as it was possible to get from Fielding's formula. Their billing gave this away, and the essential spirit of the occasion was emphatically underlined by its pricing—considerably cheaper than that of the previous eighteen concerts. The most expensive seats cost seven shillings and sixpence, instead of the usual twenty-five shillings. "Last night," reported the *Daily Worker* after the first concert, "Paul Robeson belonged to the people of London . . . a wildly cheering, roaring throng, they took him to their hearts. Harringay arena was packed to the roof to hear the great Negro singer . . . at prices which he insisted should be at rock bottom. It was above all a friendly crowd—made up of people who loved him for his great progressive record as well as for that magnificent voice."

Robeson was as good as his word. He had said from the early days of being in Britain that after this tour, no one who wanted to listen to him would be priced out. "From now on," he said to

Rose Grant, a *Daily Worker* reporter, "I shall sing only for the people. No more concerts for me in England at a pound a seat. The guy who can afford only a shilling has just as much right as anyone else to the entertainment I can give." Radical pricing was fully in line with Robeson's view of his art and of the artist. "No artist can afford to stand aside in this struggle," he declared in a message to a London meeting in late March, "for art which fails to reflect the mood of the people is barren art. The choice confronting every artist at this hour is either to side with the people or to knuckle under to the forces of imperialist obstructionism. There is and there can be no middle course. In making my choice I am aware of no crippling doubt or indecision, for I know that I belong to the people."

The day following the second triumphant Harringay recital, Robeson packed his bags. His destination was Paris. He was heading to the world's largest-ever peace gathering, and into a maelstrom of controversy from which he would never escape.

# 2

# Peace Talks in the Salle Pleyel

On the morning of April 20, 1949, the austere Modernist front of the Salle Pleyel, Paris's main concert hall, was festooned with bright and colorful flags from around the world. The usually quiet rue du Faubourg Saint-Honoré in the Eighth Arrondissement was thronged with more than 2,000 delegates and observers from sixty countries. They were there for the biggest peace conference ever held, the World Congress of Partisans of Peace.

Paul Robeson was not on the program, but he was on his way. He had decided to go to Paris only a few days previously. According to *Action*, the Paris organ of one of France's main peace groups, Combattants de la Liberté et de la Paix, Robeson was coming to the city entirely on his own account, not as a delegate or an observer.

The official delegates and observers passed into the building through pillars garlanded with posters showing Pablo Picasso's dove, especially drawn for this congress, to take their designated seats. Streamers covered the surrounding walls, declaring, in English, Spanish, French, Italian, and Russian—the five official languages of the congress—that the defense of peace was everyone's duty and that uniting for the defense of peace was the most sacred of duties. The auditorium was packed.

This unique international meeting had only been made possible by the coming together of two other forces in the previous year.

The first, the World Congress of Intellectuals for Peace, had convened in the Polish city of Wrocław, August 25–28, 1948. Its theme was a rallying cry for writers, scientists, and artists from throughout the world, who proclaimed, for the first time since the ending of World War II, a united stand against armed conflict. Four hundred and fifty delegates from forty countries had been invited; many of these representatives were household names in their own countries, and more than a few had international stature. Notable among them were the writers Jorge Amado from Brazil and Aimé Césaire from Martinique; scientists Julian Huxley and J.B.S. Haldane from Britain, and Frédéric Joliot-Curie from France; and the artists Pablo Picasso from France and Leopoldo Mendez from Mexico. The congress called for peace instead of war and for the free exchange of ideas—artistic, literary, and, above all else, scientific.

At the close of the proceedings, delegates voted unanimously to take the spirit and letter of the meeting further in their own countries by undertaking to form national committees for peace, organize national congresses, and strengthen international intellectual networks. The Wrocław resolutions envisioned a permanent international committee headquartered in Paris, the International Liaison Committee of Intellectuals for Peace, which would decide upon future international peace meetings. The names of those who would make up this committee were suggested in Wrocław, and over the coming months its composition was fixed.

The second meeting that greatly influenced the Paris Peace Congress (as the World Congress of Partisans of Peace was commonly known) was held in Budapest, December 1–6, 1948, under the banner of the Women's International Democratic Federation, founded in Paris in late 1945 by Eugénie Cotton, a French scientist and educator. The federation, which had become an umbrella organization for many women's groups worldwide between its founding and the Budapest meeting, was viewed suspiciously by Western governments as a Soviet front.

Its aims, however, appealed to many women. The federation stood against the resurgence of fascism and the recurrence of war,

but always within the context of women and children. Its mani-
festo, "For the Defense of Peace," adopted at the end of the
conference, spoke entirely about the urgency of peace and the
singular importance of women standing up to those who would
instigate a new war. It called for mass demonstrations and rallies
throughout the world "exposing the criminal plans of the aggres-
sors" and for peace to be made a central demand on International
Women's Day.

The Paris Peace Congress and the peace movement in general
were part of the new Cold War politics, in which the Soviet
Union and the United States vied with each other to become the
dominant global power.

The postwar amicable settlement of 1945, when the United
States, Great Britain, and the Soviet Union sat side by side deciding on the shape of the world to come, was but a faint memory. In
1947, a new and tense world order was created as the foundations
of what came to be known as the Cold War were laid down.

The first building block laid on this foundation was the Truman
Doctrine, which President Harry Truman first expressed in a
speech to a joint session of Congress on March 12, 1947. He
wanted Congress to approve a $400 million military and economic
aid package to Greece and Turkey: to the former to help a regime
that was threatened by a communist insurgency and to the latter
to provide assistance in Turkey's dispute with the Soviet Union
over rights to the Dardanelles—Stalin had stationed troops near
the Turkish border. In arguing his case, Truman explained that
the world was divided into two ideologies. "One . . . is based,"
he stated, "on the will of the majority . . . free institutions, representative government, free elections, guarantees of individual
liberty, freedom of speech and religion and freedom from political oppression . . . the second . . . is based on the will of a
minority forcibly imposed upon the majority . . . it relies upon
terror and oppression, a controlled press and radio, fixed elections and the suppression of personal freedoms." And then he

came to the part of the speech that formed the thrust of the doctrine: "I believe it must be the policy of the United States to support free peoples who are resisting attempted subjugation by armed minorities or by outside pressures. I believe we must assist free peoples to work out their own destinies in their own way."

The second building block of the Cold War was the Marshall Plan, launched by George C. Marshall, the US Army's wartime chief of staff and now Truman's secretary of state, in a speech he gave at Harvard University on June 5, 1947. Known formally as the European Recovery Program, Marshall's proposals for distributing American funds to aid in the reconstruction of Europe were initially intended to include all of Europe, both Western and Eastern. But over the summer months, the Soviet position toward the plan changed from interest to caution to rejection and finally to the launch of a propaganda campaign against it. On September 18, Soviet Deputy Foreign Minister Andrei Vyshinsky made Moscow's position clear to all in an address to the United Nations. The Marshall Plan, he argued, was no different from the Truman Doctrine. Both, he insisted, paved the way for the United States to interfere in the internal affairs of European countries and "to complete the formation of a bloc of several European countries hostile to the interests of Eastern Europe and most particularly to the interests of the Soviet Union."

The final building block was put in place when Stalin, in response to the Truman Doctrine and the Marshall Plan, created Cominform, the Communist Information Bureau. The founding conference of the new organization—a successor to Comintern, the Communist International, which Stalin had dissolved in 1943 when it was nearly a quarter of a century old—was held in the southern Polish ski resort of Szklarska Poręba on September 22–27, less than a week after Vyshinsky's UN speech.

All the leading lights of the Soviet system and their satellites were there. The most important was Andrei Zhdanov, a former Leningrad party boss and now Stalin's ideology chief, favorite, and most likely successor, who laid out the thinking behind a new

Soviet foreign policy. In his speech on September 22, he began by declaring that a shift in the international dimensions of ideology had taken place, and proposed what came to be known as the two camps doctrine. He explained that it was apparent that the political world had now become polarized, a direct nod to Truman's own articulation: "the imperialist and antidemocratic camp, on the one hand, and the anti-imperialist and democratic camp, on the other." The United States, whose main purpose according to Zhdanov was to strengthen imperialism and to support reactionary and antidemocratic, profascist regimes and movements everywhere, was in the first camp. Facing the United States in the second camp was the Soviet Union, "to which motives of aggression and exploitation are utterly alien, and which is interested in creating the most favorable conditions for the building of a communist society. One of these conditions is external peace."

The gauntlets were thrown down. Communist parties in Western countries were told to abandon their immediate postwar stance of participating in movements of national unity and instead to do everything they could to undermine their respective governments. In Eastern Europe, the Soviets imposed control on all aspects of political, social, and cultural life. Talk of war was to be banished; the Communist Party's watchword was now "the struggle for peace." The Cold War had begun and the Soviets had claimed the moral high ground.

The West was slow to understand fully that the enemy had grasped the initiative on world peace. The name of Cominform's biweekly newspaper, first issued in November 1947, *For a Lasting Peace, For a People's Democracy*, said it all. The Truman Doctrine and the Marshall Plan, according to Moscow, foretold of American interference and domination; Cominform spoke about peace.

When the West realized what had happened, its first response was to pour scorn on the Soviets' moral claim on world peace. It was a ploy, without substance, no more than a cynical piece of propaganda, the Americans, British, and French proclaimed.

Western governments were contemptuous of those who attended the peace meetings, particularly in Wrocław and Paris, branding them as naive, duped and manipulated by Moscow. Privately, however, they worried that they had lost the peace initiative to the Soviets. Jefferson Caffrey, the American ambassador to France, warned his State Department colleagues back in Washington, D.C., during the run-up to the Paris meeting, that "the emotional appeal of [the] peace campaign will have far-reaching and highly unsettling effects on French opinion not only on [the] internal political level but with regard to the Atlantic pact, proposed military aid program, US foreign policy in general and [the] role in foreign affairs of [the] present French Government." Behind the scenes, Western governments seemed to have been resigned to the fact that they had been caught on the defensive, "barred," as one British Foreign Office paper made clear, "from attempting to use the slogans of peace ourselves." Instead, they decided on a variety of ad hoc methods in the short term to counter the Soviet initiatives: refusing to grant visas to peace conference delegates (a ploy used by the French, American, and British governments at various times); planting pro-Western delegates at peace meetings (what the British Foreign Office referred to as "stout-hearted democrats . . . somebody to bat for us"); using whatever propaganda devices were at their disposal, including the press, national radio, and the Voice of America, to discredit the peace meetings ("Our publicity should emphasize the unrepresentative nature of the Congress and the undemocratic procedure which will be used in it. It should be presented as an instrument of the Kremlin's expansionist foreign policy, a gathering of Russia's fifth columns to undermine the defense of Western Europe"); and, finally, staging counter-conferences. Taking its cue from its own governments, the Western mainstream press now began speaking of a Soviet "peace" offensive, the word *peace*, in order to signify its deceitful nature, always appearing in quotation marks.

~

On January 6, 1949, several months after the declarations passed at the Wrocław meeting, the Soviet Politburo signaled its approval of an international peace congress. The response from peace groups was quick. Several days after the Politburo's statement, the French Wrocław delegation began to plan for a congress in France, and a month later, in early February, the International Liaison Committee of Intellectuals for Peace announced that national peace congresses would be taking place in a number of other cities, in the United States, Romania, Mexico, and Italy. On February 25, the International Liaison Committee and the Women's International Democratic Federation issued a formal call worldwide, signed by seventy-five leading peace activists, many of whom had been at Wrocław, for partisans of peace to gather in Paris for an international congress. By the end of March, Picasso had designed his dove as the symbol of the peace congress and most of the seventy-two countries that would be represented in Paris had answered the call. On April 1, the French cabinet authorized the French capital as the venue for this international gathering.

As the inaugural meeting of the Paris Peace Congress was called to order, eyes turned toward the front of the hall, where the members of the congress's organizing body had poured into the stage area. Behind them were flags, "each surrounded with a dove," representing the countries of the world. There was a bustle of delegates and observers preparing themselves in anticipation of a packed program. Simultaneous translations would be provided through 2,000 headphones. At precisely 10:40 a.m., Françoise Leclercq, secretary of the Union of French Women, one of the congress's sponsoring bodies, welcomed the participants and officially opened the five-day proceedings. Moments later, she handed the microphone over to Frédéric Joliot-Curie, president of the congress's organizing body, and the first speech was under way.

~

Joliot-Curie was France's most famous living scientist. Born Frédéric Joliot, in 1926 he had married Marie Curie's daughter Irène and the couple took Joliot-Curie as their married name. In 1935 they were jointly awarded the Nobel Prize for Chemistry for their work on artificial radioactivity—only the second married couple to be awarded a Nobel Prize (the first was Marie and Pierre Curie). At the close of World War II, Charles de Gaulle had appointed Joliot-Curie as France's first high commissioner for atomic energy, despite his having been an active member of the French Communist Party since 1942.

Joliot-Curie's speech this morning was eagerly awaited. In the words of the congress's official proceedings: "Silence was total; emotions were indescribable. Three thousand people intensely experienced this solemn moment: delegates, observers, cameramen, photographers, reporters, stenographers." No one familiar with his position on war and peace and especially atomic weaponry would have been surprised by the scientist's speech. As the man at the very heart of France's nuclear research program, Joliot-Curie was a fervent advocate of the peaceful application of atomic energy. He predicted huge advances in medicine, chemistry, physics, and industrial applications, as long as research activities were not diverted to military applications. Atomic scientists who were developing bombs were, in his opinion, committing a crime. That their research was kept secret from their colleagues, he pointed out, ran counter to the open spirit that had guided scientific work for centuries.

No one at the congress knew as much about nuclear energy as Joliot-Curie, but he did not confine himself to this issue, pursuing instead a broader argument, one that would be repeated by many speakers in the days to come: that rearmament was the greatest danger the world now faced. Both the Marshall Plan and the recently signed North Atlantic Treaty (the basis of NATO), Joliot-Curie contended, were enabling states to increase their military budgets and materials at the expense of urgent social programs, such as health and housing. All of this was contrary to the principles of the United Nations. Should the warmongers get their way, the future would be bleak.

This world peace congress, Joliot-Curie concluded, was the best means by which individuals could make their voice for peace heard throughout the world. He reached out to the delegates and observers with a final rousing statement. "We call upon all good people to prevent this scourge—war. Together, conscious of our force, we will wage battle with the certainty of victory." The congress jumped to its feet and wildly applauded its world-renowned president. Then the meeting was adjourned and the audience was asked to return to its seats for the afternoon session at 2:30 p.m.

There were few in that audience confident enough to take peace for granted. Only four years earlier, the world had been suffering through the end game of the most horrible war of all time. Only four years earlier, the United States had dropped atomic bombs on Hiroshima and Nagasaki—a technological terror never witnessed before. The United States was the only country with an atomic bomb and had already used it in a military conflict. These were dangerous times, and Joliot-Curie's plea for world peace was impassioned.

At the afternoon session, Professor John Desmond Bernal, one of the dozen vice presidents of the organizing committee, took the chair. Bernal was a leading British scientist, noted for his biomolecular research at London's Birkbeck College. He and Joliot-Curie knew each other well; they had met in the 1930s. They shared political beliefs and were instrumental in the creation in 1946 of the pro-Soviet World Federation of Scientific Workers, with Joliot-Curie as president and Bernal as one of the two vice presidents. The federation preached scientific internationalism.

Bernal handed the podium over to Pietro Nenni, national secretary of the Italian Socialist Party. Frequently interrupted by applause, Nenni spoke for an hour on the need for peace, offering a sustained criticism of the United States for abandoning the principles and spirit of the United Nations to pursue the Truman Doctrine and Marshall Plan and urging vigorous protest against the belligerent behavior of Western governments in signing the North Atlantic Treaty. Nenni's speech ended on a note of defiance: "Should the promoters of the Atlantic Pact [ignore] our call for peace and solidarity . . . and assume the responsibility of a new war . . . we would respond by a revolt of all the peoples against the warmongers."

The audience rose to applaud. The next speaker in line was Yves Farge, leader of the Combattants de la Liberté et de la Paix, formed in Paris before the Wrocław congress and recently part of the international peace movement. But instead of motioning him forward, Bernal took the microphone and announced that Paul Robeson had just arrived at the front door of the Salle Pleyel. When, several minutes later, Robeson entered the auditorium, the audience stood up and greeted him with rousing cheers and applause. Bernal invited him to take a seat on the platform.

When the demonstration for Robeson had died down, Farge took the microphone. At least some of the audience must have wished for a short speech, but Farge pressed ahead with a carefully crafted address that lasted as long as Nenni's.

Bernal then announced that Robeson, who had not been scheduled to appear, had taken this day out of his busy tour to join his fellow peace travelers. The chairman thanked Konni Zilliacus, the British Labour MP for Gateshead, who was to have spoken after Farge, for stepping aside to allow Robeson to perform. Bernal asked for a half-hour break to give Robeson time to prepare. A piano was provided and an accompanist, Helen Thierry, was found. Robeson had brought his sheet music from London, and he and Madame Thierry conferred on the songs he would sing.

At 6 p.m. sharp, everything was ready and Robeson stepped forward. "As his powerful figure appeared on the platform, caught in the rays of the spotlights, all delegates and guests rose to cheer this indefatigable fighter for the equality of coloured and white people." Even *Le Figaro*, the conservative Paris paper, could hardly withhold its delight at Robeson's appearance: "No famous political person," its April 21 article read, "neither a writer nor an intellectual invited to the Congress has had such a long applause as the black singer. When he arrived, one could see the audience, including the Russian Metropolitan, the Bulgarian Pope, and the Hungarian Protestant Bishops, rising to cheer him."

And then Robeson began to speak. "I am very happy to greet all of you who are assembled here to fight for peace in order to show the world that the people can direct their own destinies and come together for the well-being of humanity."

James Crowther, the widely read scientific journalist, secretary-general of the World Federation of Scientific Workers, and member of the British delegation in Paris, called Robeson's "short fighting speech" electrifying. He added that Zilliacus was not missed.

When Robeson finished talking and the ovation had subsided, he began the recital. He performed "The Four Insurgent Generals," a popular revolutionary song of the Spanish Civil War, partly in English and partly in Spanish; "Joe Hill," his friend Earl Robinson's 1936 setting of a poem honoring the memory of a labor activist unjustly executed by a firing squad in Utah in 1915; and "Ol' Man River." Some sources add that he also sang in Russian from the opera *Quiet Flows the Don* by Ivan Dzerzhinsky, and a few other songs, but no further details are known. The applause was rapturous and, at the very end of the program, many in the auditorium began banging their feet on the floor in appreciation.

The first day's program ended on that resounding note. Afterward, Robeson relaxed and socialized with a number of people he knew. He even introduced Peter Blackman, who had accompanied him from London and who had been invited to speak, to members of the American delegation. Later that evening

Robeson left Paris and arrived in Stockholm for a concert sched-uled for the next day, April 21. He must have thought the evening had gone well. The audience certainly appreciated his speech and his singing. Photographs of him taken at the time show a very happy man.

But unknown to Robeson, his political life was beginning to spin out of control.

Alphaeus Hunton, secretary of the Council on African Affairs, telephoned Robeson with the devastating news: The American mainstream press wanted his blood; the African-American press had turned on him. He no longer represented their views. His remarks in Paris were being reprinted across the nation, and Robeson was being called a traitor to his country.

# 3

# Garbled Words

"Nuts to Mr. Robeson."

"Paul Can't Speak for Us."

"Robeson Blasted for Paris Speech."

These are headlines from leading African-American newspapers at the end of April 1949. The message was unambiguous.

Sitting with other members of the press in the Salle Pleyel on the evening of April 20, was Joseph Dynan, a Midwesterner who had been with the Associated Press since 1941, when he joined the global news service in Tokyo four months before the Pearl Harbor attack. In 1944, after working in various parts of the world, he reported from Italy with the Allies and then landed with the invading French forces in southern France, eventually getting to Paris, where he lived for many years.

Dynan filed his report as soon as Robeson had finished singing. As was customary, it went by wire to all the US newspapers that bought copy from the Associated Press. The coverage it got was immense, from coast to coast.

Typical of what readers saw in their morning paper on April 21 was what appeared in the *Florence Morning News*. This newspaper, founded in 1887, was the only one in Florence, South Carolina, a thriving town with a population of some 20,000, half white, half African American. What appeared on its front page on April 21, 1949, was typical of what readers across the United States saw in their papers that Thursday morning. There was a smattering of local and state items, but the bulk of the page was filled with international news, all copied from the Associated Press wire. The banner story described the crossing of the Yangtze River by the Communist forces engaged in the civil war in China; another story reported on rumors that the Soviets were lifting the Berlin blockade; a third told of segregation in the American armed forces. About halfway down was a piece by Joseph Dynan—one of the three front-page articles with a byline. The headline was powerful and unsettling: "Negroes Loyal to Russia, Says Robeson."

Datelined "Paris, April 20," the article began: "Paul Robeson, American Negro singer told the communist-inspired world peace congress today that American Negroes would never fight the Soviet Union." The article went on to mention briefly the predominantly anti-American attacks—on the Atlantic Pact, the Marshall Plan, US atomic policy—that were the themes of the speeches that first day in Paris. Then Dynan returned to Robeson: "I bring you a message from the Negro people of America," he quoted Robeson as saying, "that they do not want a war which would send them back into a new kind of slavery."

Dynan next referred to Robeson's criticisms of Truman's foreign policy as it applied to Africa, and brought his article full circle with the following statement, with the quotation marks exactly as they appeared in the Florence paper that morning: "'It is unthinkable,' said Robeson, that American Negroes 'would go to war on behalf of those who have oppressed us for generations' against a country 'which in one generation has raised our people to the full dignity of mankind.'"

This quotation appeared in every American newspaper that day from the *Florence Morning News* to the *New York Herald Tribune* and the *New York Times*.

~

But did Robeson actually say those words?

Neither contemporary newspapers, aside from those subscribing to the Associated Press wire, nor government reports could agree on what was said that evening at the Paris Peace Congress.

The Paris newspapers all carried different versions of the events. *L'Humanité*, the official newspaper of the French Communist Party, not surprisingly, covered the congress throughout. Reporting on the opening day, the newspaper headlined with Joliot-Curie's words: "To those who want war, we say calmly but resolutely, you will have to deal with the Partisans of Peace." Just underneath those words was a drawing of Robeson and his greetings to the newspaper's readers. On the next page was the text of his speech.

Robeson's speech as reported by *L'Humanité* began with a message brought by Robeson from the Coordinating Committee of Coloured and Colonial Peoples in London demanding a decent life and a program of freedom without new forms of slavery. "We have decided to fight for peace," Robeson continued. "We do not want to go to war for anyone against anyone . . . we support peace and friendship with the Soviet Union and with popular republics." Then, according to the paper, he began to sing.

*Les Lettres Françaises*, the weekly literary magazine supported by the French Communist Party, produced a more nuanced account, portraying Robeson as a larger-than-life representative not only of an oppressed people in his own country but also of oppressed people everywhere. His was the voice of solidarity and understanding. "It is only when I went to the Soviet Union that I felt human," were the only words that the magazine quoted directly. *Le Figaro* simply reported the quote, "We are fighting for the people with the Soviet Union and the eastern democracies." It was only *Liberation*, the republican daily, that quoted Robeson as saying that an imperialistic war was "unthinkable for me and for all the black people that I represent. Never will black Americans wage war against the Soviet Union." The newspaper added that he then said, "We denounce the politics of the

American government which allies itself to the Hitlers and the Goebbelses."

British papers, too, had differing reports of Robeson's appearance. The *Times*, one of the only mainstream papers to cover the Paris congress on a daily—though meager—basis, said only that Robeson enlivened proceedings by singing. Alistair Cooke, writing in the *Manchester Guardian*, took it as read that Robeson said, "No American Negro would ever fight the Soviet Union." The *Daily Worker*, which had sent its foreign editor, the celebrated journalist Derek Kartun, to Paris to cover the daily proceedings, reported Robeson as saying something similar to, but not exactly the same as, the Associated Press's version: "It was unthinkable, he said, for himself and for the Negro people at home, that they should go to war in the interests of those who have oppressed them for generations, against a country which had shown there was no such thing as a backward people."

Confusion was rife. The *National Guardian*, also published in New York and very friendly to Robeson (who had occasionally written for the paper), initially reported Robeson's remarks in much the same way as the *New York Times*. But then, on May 2, in a response to the furor, the *National Guardian* attempted to set the record straight once and for all, by stating "from the official record" that Robeson had simply said: "We do not desire to go to war for anyone against anyone," then added that he had noted that the fight of the American black people was also a fight for the freedom of white people—a remark that certainly did not appear in the official proceedings—nor, it would seem, anywhere else.

The *New York Times*'s assertion that Robeson's speech was improvised is probably correct: If Robeson had anything written down, it was probably no more than a few notes. The only verbatim account of Robeson's speech is contained in the proceedings of the congress, which were published later in the year (on the day following Robeson's speech, the *World Peace Congress Bulletin*, published through the period leading up to as well as during the congress, carried a shortened but otherwise accurate version of the speech). That account not only contains Robeson's actual words but also, and perhaps even more importantly, when closely read offers a clue as to why and how Robeson was misquoted. And that process tells us quite a lot about the politics of identity that were at the heart of this controversy.

In this shortened verbatim account, Robeson is reported as having said a great deal, which obviously pleased the audience. He said, for instance—as also reported by some of the newspaper accounts—that black and colonized people wanted a life more human and that the recent Western business investments in Africa, wholeheartedly supported by Western governments, would lead to new forms of slavery. He also said that he had felt human for the first time on a visit to the Soviet Union; that the wealth of the United States was built on the backs of poor white European immigrants and enslaved Africans, who now wanted a fair share of that wealth; and that "we" wanted to fight for peace and did not want to go to war for anyone against anyone else. At no point in this account did Robeson say the words attributed to him by the Associated Press.

The key to what happened that evening lies in the word "we." Robeson clearly stated at the very beginning of his speech that he was speaking on behalf of black and colonized people everywhere. At no point did he talk exclusively about himself, nor did he ever distinguish between American blacks and other black people. When he said, therefore, that "we do not want to make war against the Soviet Union," he was not talking about American blacks only, but about all black and colonized people. This was exactly how Robeson thought about the struggle for civil, social and economic justice. He never singled out the African-American experience from that of colonized peoples in general. That was his genius and his great contribution to understanding oppression. But, on this occasion, it also spelled his doom.

There was nothing particularly startling about what Robeson had to say as such. For many, the Soviet Union still, in 1949, held the promise of an end to colonialism and oppression. Many of those who spoke at the Congress argued strenuously that their countrymen would never go to war against the Soviet Union. Robeson's special contribution was to make a point about the need for peace, not along national lines, like the other speakers, but along international and class lines.

In a secret report sent by the American embassy in Paris to the State Department in Washington on June 7,1949, the account of Robeson's speech was simply taken from the article in *L'Humanité*, which as far as it went was faithful to the verbatim proceedings of the congress. The embassy clearly saw nothing extraordinary about Robeson's speech.

Why, then, did Joseph Dynan report Robeson's speech inaccurately? It may be that he misheard it. The speech was frequently interrupted by applause from an audience 2,000 strong. Or it may be that what he saw influenced what he heard. Dynan, a white American, may have *heard* Robeson say that he was bringing a message from the Coordinating Committee of Coloured and Colonial Peoples, that they did not "want to go to war for anyone against anyone," but he *saw* a black American, representing his people, say they would not fight against the Soviet Union. He may have misunderstood Robeson or he may have slanted his report for dramatic effect. The effect certainly was dramatic for Robeson.

The damage was done. When he was given a chance to explain himself during the Scandinavian tour that followed his Paris appearance, Robeson tried to clarify the situation, but his answer was awkward, though accurate. On May 3, in Copenhagen, a reporter asked him to outline "the tasks of your people in the present situation." Robeson rambled on about the challenges of undoing centuries of colonialism in Africa, the West Indies, and Asia, and then he said something that agreed with what he had said in Paris, explaining specifically who he had included in his definition of "we." "When you talk about Negroes," he told the reporter, "you mostly think about the fourteen million in the United States, but you are apt to forget the forty million colored people in the

West Indies and Latin America and the hundred and fifty million in Africa." When asked whether in Paris he had said that the Negroes would never fight the Soviet Union, Robeson reminded the reporter, "I was referring to all the forces I mentioned here." He emphasized that his speech in Paris "was on the struggle for peace, not about anybody going to war against anybody."

Anyone encountering this interview—which was reprinted in a news release from the Council on African Affairs on May 11, 1949—would have had to read it very carefully in order to understand it as a correction to the other press reports. Unfortunately, news releases from the Council on African Affairs were not widely distributed and certainly never made it into the mainstream American press. Thus the fatal distortion of Robeson's words stood as a public document.

The fallout in the United States from what became known as the Paris speech was fast and furious, particularly in the African-American press and among the African-American leadership.

During the Second World War and for a few years after, African-American journalists had generally been sympathetic to the Soviet Union, where, they believed, racial discrimination did not exist. This did not go unnoticed at the time. J. Edgar Hoover, in particular, was concerned enough about the Communist tendency of the African-American press to launch an investigation during the war years of the people who worked for it.

By 1948, however, as the Cold War polarized ideological positions, the leading African-American newspapers, which had previously taken a sympathetic stance, now became staunchly anticommunist. At the same time, these papers were clamoring for a change in the law, demanding integration in the armed services, as set out in President Truman's executive order of July 26, 1948, which called for an end to racial segregation in the military. The papers kept up the pressure on Truman to put into practice what he had promised, while the military dragged its heels or even blocked progress completely.

A crucial turning point came in late April 1949, that is, at precisely the same time as delegates were gathering for the Paris Peace Congress, when Louis Johnson, the newly appointed secretary of defense, realizing that changes were not taking place, issued a deadline of May 1 for the armed services to present their plans for racial integration. The African-American press received this news cautiously but was generally optimistic. When, at about the same time, the secretary of the army, who had impeded progress, unexpectedly resigned from his post, hopes for a quick transition to an integrated service were raised even higher.

It is in this context that Robeson's reported remarks need to be viewed. Many white Americans remained unconvinced of the loyalty of African Americans to the United States in the event of military conflict, despite their unswerving dedication as soldiers in both world wars. For the most part, African-American leaders and their newspapers pressed the point that loyalty was not and would never be an issue. Robeson's reported remarks apparently directly contradicted that.

On the morning of April 21, when the Associated Press reports appeared in newspapers across the country, Marilyn Smith, who worked in the State Department's International Press and Publications Division, phoned Walter White, secretary of the NAACP. At some point in the conversation, White was asked for a statement about Robeson's remarks, which he agreed to prepare. Smith assured him that his statement would have the widest possible coverage, wherever in the world the State Department had access to information media. She could certainly promise that the statement would go out over the Voice of America radio network and be filed in Europe, the Middle East, and the Far East.

White's friendship with Robeson went back more than twenty years. Recently their relationship had cooled considerably, but still White had felt that although he did not agree with Robeson, he respected him for speaking his mind. Now he no longer felt that way. In his statement, he turned on his old friend. He began by referring to his respect for Robeson, but only for his artistry. "When Mr. Robeson declares in Paris," White continued, "that American Negroes will not fight against Soviet Russia and sets himself up as the authorized spokesman for 14,000,000 persons, he and I part company." He went on to state that no African American or African-American organization had mandated Robeson to speak for others. He firmly insisted that loyalty was not an issue. "The overwhelming majority of American Negroes think of themselves as Americans and will respond to the call of their country in time of war."

At this point White, having distanced himself from Robeson, took the mantle on himself and the NAACP and addressed the issue of loyalty directly, emphasizing that it was not absolute but conditional. He warned that the African American, who was "daily subjected to contemptuous and condescending treatment, perpetually forced to live under the threat of physical violence, herded into ghettos and almost constantly barred from jobs, places of public accommodation and opportunity to live in dignity and peace," would not accept "without question a summons to arms irrespective of the treatment given him by his own country." White America needed to "wake up to the determination of Negroes to break the shackles which race prejudice fastens upon them."

And then Walter White did something brilliant. He basically told white America that Robeson's reported remarks were part of the political territory of African America. White America had to tread very delicately around this controversy, he advised. "[It] would be wise to abstain from denunciation of the Paul Robesons for extremist statements until it removes the causes of the lack of faith in the American system of government. Until the United States cleanses itself of its own racial sins, it will not have the right to criticize without hypocrisy such statements as those of Mr. Robeson at Paris."

How much of this statement reached the audience the State Department targeted is not known. Walter White's final paragraph would have made some people very uncomfortable, for it put the United States, not Paul Robeson, under scrutiny.

In addition to White, the State Department sought the views of Mary McLeod Bethune. Bethune, who was older than Robeson and like him fathered by a slave, had become one of the most formidable civil rights leaders in the United States and certainly the most respected and influential woman in the movement. She was president of the National Council of Negro Women, which she had founded in 1935. She and Robeson were friends. At a massive gathering in New York in April 1944, to celebrate his forty-sixth birthday, Bethune, who couldn't attend, sent Robeson a message of congratulations, calling him "the tallest tree in our forest," a description that stuck to him for decades. Soon, however, the winds of the Cold War were blowing between them. Already by 1947, Bethune was staying away from events at which Robeson was featured, even though the two leaders shared the same aspirations.

Bethune's State Department submission showed how far she had separated from Robeson in such a short time. When she had read the report from the Paris Peace Congress, Bethune told Smith, it "chilled my blood." She went on to defend the loyalty of African Americans, questioning Robeson's right to appoint himself as their spokesman. "Negroes have always stood by America in any emergency and Negroes will always stand by America in any emergency." Robeson, she added, "does not speak for the Negroes of America. He speaks for himself and for those who think as he does." No national African-American organization, Bethune insisted, had ever suggested "by deed or implication or resolution that Negroes would ever fail to support the American flag."

Over the next few days, the African-American press gave space to those African-American leaders who disagreed, sometimes violently, with Robeson. The *New York Amsterdam News*, typical of many African-American newspapers, headlined its April 30 story "Leaders Disagree With Robeson." Congressman Adam Clayton Powell, who represented Harlem, spoke for many of those named in the article when he declared that Robeson's views were entirely Robeson's own. He did not speak for African Americans, whose loyalty to the United States was not in question.

Channing Tobias, a long-time civil rights activist and director of the Phelps-Stokes Fund, an organization devoted to improving the educational opportunities of African Americans, was more critical of Robeson than was Powell. What irked Tobias most was that Robeson chose to "declare his disloyalty to his native land" in Europe. "There's a sort of unwritten law that if you want to criticize the United States you do it at home," Tobias said. This sentiment was widely shared.

On April 30, less than two weeks after making her declaration to the State Department, Bethune weighed in behind these community leaders when she made her views on Robeson public in a blistering column in the *Chicago Defender*:

> When Mr. Robeson presumes to speak for me . . . in expressing disloyalty to our country, then I think he has missed his cue and has entered the stage during the wrong scene. I am chagrined at his presumption and its implication.

What did Robeson make of all this? We have one clue. On May 1, just after Alphaeus Hunton of the Council of African Affairs had put him in the picture, Robeson wrote to his longtime friend Freda Diamond, in whom he had confided on many occasions. He was hurt—"This has been such a long, long ache that I'm numb"—was how he put it. He repeated that what he had said had been distorted; that he had said "Negroes would fight for peace." And then, the defiant Robeson took charge. "I am ready enough," he told Diamond. What he meant by that would become clear in a few months' time.

~

The argument that Robeson had shown himself to be disloyal to his country and to his own people found its most caustic expression in an editorial that appeared in the May issue of *Crisis*, the magazine of the NAACP. Penned by Roy Wilkins, a prominent civil rights activist who had been editor of *Crisis* for 15 years, the piece was crass and showed clearly how far some people were willing to go to parade their anticommunist, pro-American credentials.

Its main purpose was to portray Robeson as a Communist sympathizer; a man more at home with white people than with his own; a man who spent as little time in his own country as possible and made as much money as he could, hobnobbing "in very select British and Continental society," even going to Russia; a man who maintained an exclusive country property in Connecticut, with an unlisted telephone number; a man who made himself available to "all-white left-wing groups," when ordinary African Americans "could not get even a reply to a letter."

The editorial did not deny that Robeson had oodles of talent and charm but maintained it had all been misused. Wilkins ended: "At Paris and elsewhere Mr. Robeson fancied himself a general (or at very least a colonel) in the Communist-led army of the proletariat, but if he takes occasion to glance behind him he will find but a thin sprinkling of American Negroes following the banners and parroting the monotonous slogans." This theme would be played again to devastating effect a few months later.

The debate over Robeson's speech in Paris continued until well into the next year. The question of who spoke for whom would continue to be a battleground, as the community leaders who criticized Robeson claimed that they, not he, knew best what the African-American people thought and wanted. It was abundantly clear that the split between those who espoused radical solutions to big problems and those who wished to work within the system for more limited gains had grown rapidly and was now extremely—irreversibly—wide.

Robeson was being pushed out into the American political wilderness, where, as far as his critics were concerned, he belonged. But he was not as easily silenced nor so easily abandoned as his critics hoped he would be.

# 4

# Legal Lynching, Jersey Style

Late in January 1949 Robeson had attended a legislative conference of the Civil Rights Congress in Washington, D.C., along with more than 600 delegates. There he met Bessie Mitchell, sister of one of the defendants of the notorious case of the Trenton Six. Only a few days later, in early February, just before he sailed for Southampton on the *Queen Mary*, Robeson joined a mass rally in Trenton, New Jersey as chairman of the newly formed Committee to Free the Trenton Six.

What was it about this case that had made such an impression on Robeson that he immediately became so involved in it even though he was about to leave the country? As he reminded his audience at the rally, he had grown up near Trenton. "I know what's been done to these boys could have been done to my own boy," he said, and, continuing in a defiant tone, "But your presence here will show the Trenton authorities that my people have allies who will fight for them. We've come here to tell the enemies of democracy in Trenton and everywhere else that we're not staying 'in our place' anymore."

The ordeal of the Trenton Six began on January 27, 1948 Around 11 a.m. that day, William Horner, the proprietor of a second-hand furniture and bric-a-brac store, and his wife, Elizabeth, were attacked in their shop by a group of men who then fled the scene. Both Horners sustained head injuries, and when a patrolman found him, William was unconscious. With the help of other officers who had come on the scene, he was bundled into an ambulance and rushed to the nearest hospital. He never regained consciousness and died several hours later. Elizabeth had a lucky escape. She was bleeding and in pain but conscious and told the patrolman as he rushed past her to William's side that they had been attacked by three "young, light-skinned Negroes."

Over the next two weeks armed police officers patrolled black Trenton, questioning, roughing up and eventually arresting suspects. They had more than twenty men in detention but charged none of them. Then, on February 7, the police actually arrested a first suspect, twenty-three-year-old Collis English. Over the next few days, other men were taken until the police got to the sixth, John MacKenzie, a relative of English's, arrested February 10. All six men were arrested without warrants and held and questioned without legal representation. While in custody, five of them signed statements confessing to murder and attempted murder.

The trial began on June 7. The defendants couldn't afford lawyers, so the court appointed their counsel. The county prosecutor had already had success in his eighteen months in the job finding African-American men guilty of robbery, though he had pursued with less enthusiasm a Southern white man accused of shooting off a black man's head in a Princeton public park. Over fifty-five days, the all-white jury heard evidence, examination, and cross-examination, and on August 6 all of the accused were found guilty and sentenced to death. So appalled was the defense team by the outcome of the trial that they immediately launched an application for appeal. A stay of execution followed automatically.

Before the convictions were announced, only the local newspaper, the *Trenton Evening Times*, had covered the story from the arrest through the trial. Now news of the Trenton Six began to appear elsewhere, starting with a short item deep inside in the *New York Times*.

For a long time after that, no more was heard of it, but behind the scenes remarkable events were taking place that would eventually put the case of the Trenton Six on the international stage. Bessie Mitchell, the thirty-six-year-old sister of Collis English, refused to let things lie. Without help from anywhere, Mitchell contacted anyone who would listen to her tale of injustice. She began, incredibly, with the FBI; she then tried the NAACP and then the American Civil Liberties Union. Almost a month passed and she had succeeded nowhere.

And then, at what must have seemed to her the end of the road, Mitchell stumbled across the Civil Rights Congress, an organization of which she knew nothing. Using the information on a leaflet, she contacted the director of the New Jersey chapter, and for the first time in her search for help she found hope and encouragement.

On September 1, 1948, the silence surrounding the case started to break when the New York *Daily Worker* carried an article that for the first time gave a voice to the defendants, introducing Bessie Mitchell and her cause to readers throughout the country.

Further press publicity came when the New York–based weekly *National Guardian*, which appeared on newsstands for the first time in October of that year, devoted a major article to the case in its second issue, on October 25. Titled "Is There a 'Scottsboro Case' in Trenton, N.J.?" and written by William Reuben, it was the first national coverage to describe the crime, the evidence and the trial in any detail. Indeed, Reuben pointed out toward the end of his piece that the press outside Trenton had been silent on the case. He asserted that the only evidence the prosecution had was the signed confessions, which the police admitted had been forced out of the defendants. In court each of the six defendants repudiated his statement. No witness, Reuben added, had reported that more than three youths had been involved, yet six young men were being charged. He concluded by saying that certainly two were completely innocent and there was sufficient uncertainty about the remaining four defendants to call for a retrial.

The article was a turning point for Mitchell. When the paper's editors realized that they were scooping this story, they sent Reuben down to Trenton to investigate. Reuben interviewed and reported extensively on Mitchell and found many other informed people who were willing to talk. The Trenton Six was called another Scottsboro case, in a deliberate move to evoke public sympathy. In 1931, nine black youths in Scottsboro, Alabama, had been arrested, convicted and all but one sentenced to death for the alleged rape of a white woman. The Scottsboro trial was notorious; it became a benchmark case that continued for most of the rest of the thirties.

Robeson's old and close friend William Patterson had spearheaded the Scottsboro case. Now, the lawyer turned his attention to the Trenton Six. Patterson had been executive secretary of the Civil Rights Congress (CRC) since 1948. Founded in 1946 through the amalgamation of a number of organizations, including the National Negro Congress and the International Labor Defense (also headed by Patterson), the CRC took a broad view of civil rights, one beyond race, calling itself "a defender of constitutional liberties, human rights, and of peace." It had already been involved in a number of high-profile cases, many of them involving African Americans who were being unjustly treated in the country's courtrooms.

One afternoon in December 1948, Patterson went to Trenton and met the families of the accused men. He convinced them that the CRC was their best chance of seeing justice done. He then embarked, as he had learned to do on previous occasions, on a double-edged program, one political and the other legal. To sway public opinion to the defendants' side, Patterson rolled out a nationwide campaign to take the cause of the Trenton Six to the streets, union halls and churches. Petitions, letters, rallies, and even a play and a filmstrip helped publicize the case.

On the legal side, Patterson personally hired lawyers to represent the defendants in what he hoped would be a successful appeal leading to a new trial. To lead the team Patterson selected an extremely experienced radical lawyer, O. John Rogge, whom he retained on January 20, 1949. Rogge had had a distinguished career, breaking onto the public stage before the outbreak of World War II, when he initiated a series of probes into the corrupt machine politics associated with Huey Long, the notorious governor of Louisiana. He became the assistant to the attorney general in the Roosevelt administration, but left Washington politics once Truman, to whom he was opposed politically, became president. His adherence to the progressive left continued throughout the early postwar years, when he also became involved in the international peace movement. He held a place on the organizing committee of the Paris Peace Congress and was a senior member of the American delegation.

The story now crosses from Trenton to Britain. In late December 1948, *Reynolds News* published an article titled "They Must Die for Being Black," written by William Reuben. One of those who read the story was Len Johnson, who became very interested in the case.

Len Johnson was a black boxer, born in 1902 in Manchester, where he lived for most of his life. Although he had won more than ninety contests, he never held a British title, as the British Boxing Board of Control allowed only British-born white contenders this distinction. Though boxing was his first love, the color bar made it difficult for him to make much of a career out of it, so after struggling through the late 1920s and 1930s until the outbreak of the Second World War, he finally gave up the ring.

As soon as the war was over, Johnson joined the Communist Party. Early in 1946 he and two fellow Mancunian members of the Party—Wilf Charles, the secretary of the Moss Side branch, and Syd Booth, a long-serving party member who had fought in the International Brigades during the Spanish Civil War—founded the New International Society. They hoped that their organization's broad aims of promoting respect for human rights irrespective of color, gender, or religion would appeal to Moss Side's mixed population. To help establish the New International Society, Johnson, Charles, and Booth engaged a building with a bar and a billiard table that provided a much-needed social center for the area.

The society did not attract as many members as the founders had hoped. In 1949, after three years, the membership was only about 200, a figure that had hardly budged since the society's first flourish. Most of the members were white, and aside from Johnson himself, so were the officers.

But the New International Society made up for what it lacked in numbers and diversity with the success of its campaigns. Most of the society's work took place outside of Moss Side and focused primarily on highlighting discriminatory practices in the British workplace and pinpointing instances of the color bar in operation. They had been involved in some well-publicized cases: when the shipping firm Manchester Liners attempted to sack all its black seamen but later backed down; when the Manchester Labour Exchange opened a queue for blacks only, then abandoned it under pressure; when the Ministry of Labour banned black men from volunteering to train in Lancashire coalfields, a ban that was ultimately withdrawn after the New International Society drew attention to it in the press.

International issues also attracted the society's interest, especially the many miscarriages of justice in the American South. The Trenton Six, a case of "legal lynching, Jersey style" was right up its alley. The New International Society wasted no time getting involved. On January 2, 1949, the society hosted a protest meeting; its theme placed the ordeal of the Trenton Six within the context of the continuing lynching of black men in the Southern states. What happened across the Atlantic was "our business," as the society's leaflet put it: "The lot of the American negro is the running sore of world civilization, for a nation that persecutes minorities is a threat to democracy."

~

In mid-February 1949, Johnson spotted an announcement in the *Daily Worker* that Paul Robeson was to give two concerts, one in March and the other in April, at the Royal Albert Hall in London.

Johnson had met Robeson in 1932 in Manchester, and the singer had encouraged Johnson in his long-running battle with the British boxing color bar. "Paul Robeson is a great man," Johnson wrote in the *Topical Times*, a weekly sports magazine, soon after the encounter. "[He] put new life in me with a few words. He drew me a picture of his fight for recognition. He pointed out that my job was fighting, and that if I could fight in the ring I ought to able to fight outside it. I took his words to heart and made every effort to show the British public that the color bar is just so much nonsense."

Now Johnson jumped at the chance of seeing Robeson again, and in his capacity as secretary of the New International Society he wrote to Robeson inviting him to Manchester to "a big propaganda meeting . . . a turning point in all our work," to speak on the case of the Trenton Six. He promised that Robeson would be in an impressive lineup of committed speakers, all of whom had close personal connections with anticolonial issues. One was Lester Hutchinson, the local Labour MP and veteran of the notorious Meerut Conspiracy trial of the early thirties. On that occasion, thirty-three men, three of them, including Hutchinson, British, had been tried in the garrison town of Meerut, northern India, for conspiring to organize strikes and civil unrest with the aim of bringing down the colonial government.

Another promised speaker was H. B. Lim (Lim Hong Bee), a Malaysian political activist who had been in Britain since the mid-1930s and was leader of the pro-Communist Democratic Malayan Students Organisation and, since 1947, editor and publisher of the strongly anti-British monthly magazine *Malayan Monitor*. Finally, Johnson said, Yusuf Dadoo, the highly prominent and outspoken Muslim, Communist and anti-apartheid chair of the South African Indian Congress who had recently agreed to a cooperative pact with the African National Congress to effect a united stand against the aggressively racist South African government, would also participate. These three speakers were all outstanding; but, Johnson intimated in his letter, it would be Robeson's appearance that would really draw an audience.

On the evening of May 10, 1949, Robeson took his place on the platform at King's Hall in Belle Vue for the Trenton Six public meeting. The hoped-for lineup of anti-colonial speakers did not, however, materialize; Robeson was the only famous person there. Neither Hutchinson, Lim, nor Dadoo appeared. Taking their place on the platform were Horace Newbold, secretary of the Lancashire and Cheshire Federation of Trades Councils; Len Johnson himself; and Gordon Schaffer, assistant editor of *Reynolds News*, who had sponsored William Reuben's breaking the story of the Trenton Six in Britain.

The timing of this meeting could not have been better. The story of the Trenton Six had developed significantly since mid-February, when Johnson first asked Robeson to take part in the meeting. Thanks to William Patterson's management of publicity and the legal case, the story of these six black men was stirring the imagination of Americans beyond the narrow confines of Trenton. Patterson had appeared on television, a rare event for a black radical activist. John Rogge, leading the defense team, had given a press conference, the details of which appeared in the *New York Times*, and launched a series of articles in the *National Guardian* in which he explained why the men had not received a fair trial.

As a result, the Civil Rights Congress geared into action, printing more than 150,000 copies of its pamphlet "Lynching Northern Style" and distributing them nationwide. In late March, Dashiell Hammett, the well-known crime novel writer and author of *The Maltese Falcon*, started a petition to free the Trenton Six, a campaign that received the backing of Arthur Miller, whose play *Death of a Salesman* had just premiered on Broadway. In early April, Bessie Mitchell wrote to Eleanor Roosevelt asking for her help, and several days later the New Jersey State House in Trenton was surrounded by pickets. The governor of New Jersey, Alfred Driscoll, who a few months back had admitted to representatives of the Civil Rights Congress that he had never heard of the Trenton Six, was now receiving letters from ordinary citizens demanding a retrial.

How many came to listen to the speakers in Belle Vue is not known with any certainty; one source says 4,000; another says 10,000. The New International Society considered Robeson's Trenton Six appearance one of the more important in its history and believed it even had an impact on the level of public support for the cause in the United States.

Not everyone in Manchester was as pleased as Johnson and the New International Society with Robeson's appearance at this meeting. In particular, another organization in Manchester, which claimed authority to be the sole voice of the city's black community, seriously objected to Robeson's participation.

The Pan-African Federation had been formed in Manchester in 1944 to present a united pan-African front in Britain. It was the brainchild of George Padmore and Ras Makonnen, who knew each other from London when they, together with C.L.R. James, founded the International African Service Bureau. The new federation included a number of well-known British black organizations, as well as three African ones, one of which, the Kikuyu Central Association, was represented by Jomo Kenyatta. The federation appointed Dr. Peter Milliard, a British Guiana–born physician who had settled in Manchester in the 1930s, as its president, and Ras Makonnen, another British Guianan now living in Manchester, as its general secretary.

Ras Makonnen had come to Britain in 1937, aged about thirty-seven, after a peripatetic life that had also taken him to the United States and Scandinavia. In London, Makonnen knew C.L.R. James and Jomo Kenyatta, became fast friends with George Padmore, and first met Paul Robeson. Makonnen moved to Manchester in 1939, studied briefly at the University of Manchester and began to get involved in black politics in the city. The presence of African and West Indian students studying at the university and African-American soldiers who remained behind rather than returning to the United States inspired Makonnen to open two restaurants and a bar especially to cater for this community.

Makonnen used his earnings from the restaurants and bar to help the black cause in Manchester, eventually branching out to a bookshop and a publishing venture that brought pamphlets written by leading black radicals such as Kenyatta, Padmore, and Eric Williams, the future prime minister of Trinidad and Tobago, to public awareness.

At the time of the Pan-African Federation's creation, the idea of staging "a postwar conference to consider the needs and demands of Negroes" was being discussed among a small number of black activists and centered on W.E.B. Du Bois in New York. Du Bois, now seventy-seven and one of the most esteemed African-American writers, thinkers and activists alive, could rightly claim to be the grand old man of pan-Africanism. With the support of the NAACP behind him he had organized the first Pan-African Congress, held in Paris in 1919 and timed to coincide with the early meetings of the Versailles Conference. Du Bois' pan-African vision embraced the existence of a racial, cultural, and historical bond between all peoples of Africa and of Africa's diaspora throughout the world. He believed in the dignity of every human regardless of race and was committed to getting economic and political self-rule for the world's colonized people, especially in Africa. Following close on the heels of the 1919 congress, three more were held, the first two in London in the 1920s and the last one in New York, in 1927, all of them organized by Du Bois and supported by the NAACP.

It made perfect sense, both historically and politically, that the Fifth Pan-African Congress should be held in either Paris or London. But it didn't turn out that way. The meeting was eventually staged in Manchester in October 1945 and organized by the city's new Pan-African Federation. For the first time since 1919, the congress was no longer under Du Bois' and American control. The common bond of this congress's main participants—ninety individuals from fifty organizations, including such outstanding African delegates as Kenya's Jomo Kenyatta and Ghana's Kwame Nkrumah—was British colonial rule. It was the first time that African representatives and organizations had actively participated in a Pan-African Congress. The issue of labor was put at the very center of pan-Africanism and independence was the focus. In this, the congress aligned itself with the aspirations of the World Federation of Trade Unions, created in Paris earlier in October, to which many of the delegates in Manchester had given their support in person. Proposing a broad program of human rights and economic and social justice, the Fifth Pan-African Congress demanded an end to colonial rule and racial discrimination.

The Pan-African Federation had scored a triumph and naturally saw itself now as the authoritative voice of British black people. Because of his close association with Du Bois, whom he had known since Harlem days, Robeson would have known all about the Pan-African Federation and its central role in the Manchester Pan-African Congress. He wouldn't have known that a bitter animosity existed between the Pan-African Federation and the New International Society, but he was soon to find out.

On May 8, 1949, the train carrying Robeson from Gateshead arrived in Liverpool. There, a large crowd who had been invited to welcome him to the city met him and marched with him to an open-air engagement in a car park, a former bomb site. According to the *Daily Worker*, 10,000 people came out to listen "to the rich tones of 'Old [sic] Man River' and 'Joe Hill' coming through powerful loudspeakers and drowning the sound of the trams and the bustle of the city streets." Also appearing on the outdoor platform was Olaf Stapledon, the philosopher and science fiction writer, who had been a delegate at the World Congress of Intellectuals for Peace in Wrocław the previous year, and Len Johnson.

The New International Society, which by now had a branch in Liverpool, had taken charge of all the Liverpool arrangements, which included, apart from the open-air meeting, a special reception and an evening concert in the city's neoclassical St. George's Hall, which had sold out well in advance.

From Liverpool, Robeson made his way to Manchester for the great rally in the cause of the Trenton Six that Johnson had proposed back in February. The scene was set for the evening of May 10 in King's Hall in Belle Vue. But before that, there would be two events that the New International Society had organized on its own premises in Moss Side, one of which Peter Blackman was to join.

There was no reason to think that anything untoward might happen, but then, between the two events, a counter-rally began. Orchestrated by Ras Makonnen, the demonstration, attended by fifty to eighty people, reflected the bitter competition between his and Johnson's organization to represent black people in Manchester.

Makonnen had contacted Robeson earlier in the year, at about the same time as Johnson, as soon as he had learned from the press that Robeson was in England. As general secretary of the Pan-African Federation (its letterhead now boasted the additional title Pan-African Congress, with W.E.B. Du Bois's name prominently displayed), Makonnen took the opportunity of writing Robeson to outline the aims and accomplishments of the federation. He congratulated Robeson on what he had done for "our people" (meaning Africans and West Indians) but suggested that the singer might not know much about the organization that represented them.

Makonnen then went on to describe the federation's work in uncovering and righting instances of injustices to black people, mostly in northwest England, styling it as the voice of those people. His letter ended by extending an open invitation to

Robeson to visit and meet "our people either formally or informally" in Manchester and Liverpool.

Two weeks later, Peter Blackman wrote to Makonnen on Robeson's behalf thanking him for the invitation and telling him that he would be coming to the northwest but that other "adequate arrangements" had already been made.

Makonnen was incensed. It took him two weeks to reply. Blackman's "peculiar tone" he said, had "demanded time and thought, before a fitting answer could be made." Then he got to the point. Someone in either Manchester or Liverpool, had already been in touch with Robeson and made arrangements. But who would do this? "Where is there an individual African or group of Africans in the environs of Manchester and Liverpool," Makonnen asked, "and known to the Pan-African Federation, who could make such arrangements in the name of his fellows and without their knowledge?"

Makonnen did not mention which group he thought might have appropriated Robeson but he did not mince his words when he referred to this as a "usurpation," a determination "to have the last word in these matters." Then he raised the temperature, asserting that the Pan-African Federation had the "right to make arrangements for our own communities and [did] not need the intervention of others."

Makonnen shared all of this correspondence with Hilton Prescod, chairman of the Emergency Defense Committee for Coloured People in Liverpool, who duly wrote to Blackman. It is clear from the tone of Prescod's letter that things had gotten out of hand; both organizations were evidently insulted by Robeson's attitude—"we can only interpret it as a deliberate slight."

And why? Because they had both hoped to "give an African welcome to Mr. Robeson as a distinguished son of our race," and someone, who clearly was not and could not by definition be African, had usurped their position. When Robeson was last in Britain in the 1930s, Prescod pointed out, the singer had expressed his sympathy with the "under-dogs" of Wales and industrial

England. Now, Prescod continued, "we may with some justification . . . assume that he has the same sentiments toward the African communities in the United Kingdom . . . indeed, an even greater sympathy and identification."

To make matters worse, on the very day this letter was written, March 24, Robeson was in Liverpool preparing to give a concert at the city's prestigious Philharmonic Hall. That fact, however, was not what really caused the next upset. Rather, it was that Prescod had learned that Robeson had already been entertained at a reception given by the British Council. Prescod concluded from this that the "adequate arrangements" which Blackman had mentioned referred to a white organization that "would not dream of issuing invitations to any member of our community." And with that conclusion clearly in mind, Prescod ended his letter. "We wish to put on record," he stated succinctly, "our condemnation of the policy being followed by Mr. Robeson, or his advisors, in confining his associates to an exclusive circle while ignoring the very 'under-dogs' he says he wishes to meet."

In his reply to Prescod, Blackman revealed that it was the New International Society under Len Johnson's guidance that was taking care of Robeson's political engagements in Manchester and Liverpool. Prescod made it clear in his reply to this that he had little time for the New International Society and that, certainly, despite the fact that Johnson was of African descent, his group did not represent African people in the northern cities. On the contrary, he reiterated, "the Africans in these two cities" had decided to organize their own affairs and to "exercise [them] to the full through the Pan-African Federation." Robeson's appearance in Manchester was therefore not at the invitation of the African people but at those of the New International Society and the Manchester and Salford District Trades Council. Under no circumstances, Prescod emphasized, "should any attempt be made to indicate otherwise."

~

Robeson's concerts were now decidedly political, and tussles would periodically erupt over how Robeson fit into and furthered other people's and organizations' agendas. The disagreement between the Pan-African Federation, a loose organization of African- and British-based black organizations that had turned its back on Communism as a guiding principle, and the New International Society, a predominantly white organization with an internationalist, antiracist agenda, supported by the British Communist Party, was just one example of the competition for Robeson's public persona.

The strength of feeling Robeson produced in those who saw, heard, or knew him was powerful. Even after he returned to the United States following this tour, feelings in Britain were still running high. On July 3, 1949, Dr. Peter Milliard, president of the Pan-African Federation, wrote to Larry Brown about it. Evidently Milliard knew Brown well, though how and why he had met Robeson's longtime accompanist is not clear.

Milliard's letter began fairly innocuously, thanking Brown for a package of hard-to-get food Brown had sent him in the post, then turned into a stinging attack on Robeson and particularly on his Belle Vue performance.

Milliard did not pull his punches. The depth of his feeling was palpable. First, he accused Robeson of joining the Communist Party in Britain, a party that Milliard saw as made up of and acting on behalf of "Anglo-Saxon whites." In his mind, Robeson, by associating himself with the New International Society, was aligning himself with the wrong side.

As for Robeson's speech in Belle Vue, Milliard called it "a howling success as a Communist show," but as a political meeting "exposing the iniquitous charges against our Trenton lads," it had been a failure. Robeson utterly missed the opportunity of explaining the Trenton case, Milliard argued, as an example of "what happens in America." "Paul succeeded," Milliard continued, "in making himself a buffoon. He sang 'Water Boy' like a 3rd rate comedian." On top of all this, and what Milliard found most objectionable, was that, as it seemed to him, Robeson preferred the company of whites: He had, in short, "lost his soul."

Manchester would come back into Robeson's life. When he visited the city many years later, he found it completely altered. The African and African-American populations had been superseded by a large influx of West Indians. Milliard was dead, and Makonnen was in Ghana. Hardly anyone remembered the day that Manchester had hosted the Fifth Pan-African Congress. Only Johnson was left.

# PART II

# NEW YORK AND WASHINGTON, D.C., 1949

# 5

# Strike Two

June 16, 1949. As Robeson crossed the Atlantic on a Pan American Clipper en route to New York he might have been reflecting on his successful British and Scandinavian tours. Or he could have been wondering what kind of reception awaited him at home. The fallout from his Paris speech was still in the air. The American press, both white and black, had printed many hurtful accusations and allegations about him. One attack must have been particularly disturbing—a piece by Max Yergan, formerly his close friend and political ally.

"The American Negro and Mr. Robeson" appeared in the *New York Herald Tribune* on April 23, 1949. It was a long essay—well over 2,000 words—written the previous day as a letter to the editor. What was particularly significant about this article was that it had been written by a leading African American and published in a mainstream newspaper. It was one thing for white Americans to denounce Robeson in the white press, as they had done, and for black Americans to denounce him in the black press, as they had done and would continue to do. But it was quite another matter for a black American to do it in the pages of a white newspaper. It was meant as a clear signal that Robeson was speaking on his own behalf and not as a spokesman for African Americans.

Yergan used the article not only to denounce Robeson but also to establish himself as an anticommunist African-American patriot. He told his readers that his grandfather had fought for the

Yankees in the Civil War; that he had served his country during the First World War; that his three sons had served in World War II. Even now, two of his sons were in the Army medical service: "I encouraged them to volunteer and I am proud of their action," Yergan said.

But Yergan's main aim was to link Robeson to the Communist Party and to the damage they were doing and intending to do to the country and particularly to the place of African Americans in it. He argued that it was the Communists, including, by implication Robeson, who were driving a wedge between black and white Americans, trying to persuade African Americans "to think of themselves as a 'nation' . . . to popularize the term 'Negro people,'" and "to divide, disrupt and create confusion and disorder." But, he went on, African Americans knew what the problems were and how to solve them and didn't need Communists to speak and act for them. All "thoughtful" Americans, Yergan argued, knew that African Americans were subjected to limitations on their "constitutional guaranties and citizenship rights" and that these needed to be removed—not, as the Communists would, by "driving Negroes off into some separate compartment" but by joining with the white majority in the great democratic institutions that were already making progress in this area.

Africa, too, Yergan insisted, would progress through the expansion of democracy, an ideology "of a far more ancient vintage than Marxism." He knew Africa well, he told his readers, but he knew it, he insisted (and this gave him special qualifications), as an African American living in a democratic society. He reminded those who might not know much about the Council on African Affairs (most of white America did not) that he had cut his ties with the organization precisely when and because it had become a tool of the Kremlin. Hijacked by Robeson and his Communist friends, the organization, which had been established to publicize conditions in Africa to Americans, became instead a channel for criticizing America's foreign policy and praising that

of the Soviet Union. "It is what it is," Yergan wrote, "an instrument of the Communist Party, Communist intrigue and . . . not
in the interest of the people of Africa, but in the interest of the
Kremlin masters of Communists everywhere." Robeson, Yergan
concluded, "did not speak for us in Paris."

Who was Max Yergan, and why did his attack matter so much?

Paul Robeson met Max Yergan in London in the early 1930s.
Yergan, a native of North Carolina, was six years older than
Robeson. After completing his university education, he had
begun working for the black YMCA, and his first assignments in
the missionary work of the organization had been in India and
East Africa. In 1922 he arrived in South Africa and spent the next
fifteen years with the YMCA there, although he frequently visited
the United States and Britain.

It was during this period that Yergan became more radical,
moving away politically from the liberal stance of the YMCA,
which was, as Yergan and others saw it, silent and complicit in
the injustices committed in South Africa. Over time, Yergan was
increasingly influenced by left-wing members of the African
National Congress and acquaintances in the South African
Communist Party. In March 1936 he decided that his personal
views and those of the YMCA's had diverged too much, and
resigned from the organization whose loyal servant he had been
for almost one third of his life.

Robeson fully supported his friend's decision to radicalize,
praising his courageous and outspoken position. "Yergan's
admirable stand," Robeson wrote, "provides a fine lead for
other Negro intellectuals who are occupying false positions
from which they may wish to escape, but who are wavering."
Robeson himself was inspired by Yergan, who was probably
the only African American he knew with so much firsthand
experience of Africa.

Yergan returned to the United States in 1936 and quickly
became involved in the politics of the National Negro Congress,

a body that grew out of the need, as its founders saw it, to coordinate and support the progressive work of black groups in the United States. At its founding meeting in Chicago in February 1936, Yergan made an important speech in which he emphasized his African experiences and, most significantly, drew a direct link between African and African-American struggles for economic and social justice.

The speech alluded explicitly to the recent Italian invasion and conquest of Ethiopia—here Yergan made the connection between fascism and imperialism—in the context of a Marxist analysis of imperialism and capitalism. This point pleased many members of the Communist Party who were in the audience. Yergan's speech also caught the attention of Ralph Bunche, one of the architects of the congress and one of the country's leading African-American intellectuals, and Paul Robeson, whose interest in Africa had been growing throughout the decade and who had recently converted to the radical cause himself.

Robeson and Yergan seemed destined to join forces. Indeed, at some point in the year they began talking about forming a new organization dedicated to disseminating information about, and lobbying for, Africa. The conversations they had ultimately led to the organization of the International Committee on African Affairs, , in January 1937 in New York, with Yergan as director.

Yergan began the task of assembling the membership. While it appeared that anyone could be asked to join, in fact the shape of the committee was governed, from the outset, by three stipulations: It should be interracial; it should be radical and black-led; and it should be international in composition, with members from North America, Europe, and Africa. Drawing on both his own and Robeson's wide appeal, Yergan had no problem attracting some of the leading intellectuals of the day to the organization. Some of the names were very well known—Ralph Bunche, Mary Van Kleek (director of industrial research at the Russell Sage Foundation), and René Maran, the writer from Martinique whose novella *Batouala* was the first work by a black person to be awarded the Prix Goncourt—and others less famous, but the caliber of the membership was always of the highest order.

In April 1937, Yergan was in London, and toward the end of that month he was invited to a meeting that included Ralph Bunche and Paul Robeson. The main purpose was to introduce Yergan to the leading British-based African and Caribbean radicals, including Jomo Kenyatta, George Padmore, and Ras Makonnen.

Yergan believed that Robeson was key to the success of the organization. His admiration for Robeson as a force for global political good, as he confided it in a letter to Ralph Bunche, was deeply touching: "I know of no person more constructively effective in the international life of people of African descent than Paul Robeson . . . he is a power in many ways, and as we talked and planned together, I became increasingly aware of the significance of his membership in the International Committee on African Affairs." A few weeks later, Robeson sent Yergan a check for $1,500 (approximately $50,000 in today's purchasing power) as "seed money."

Despite Robeson's cash injection, money always was a problem in the early years and because of that many of the committee's objectives could not be met. In 1941, the organization's name was changed to the Council on African Affairs, with Robeson appointed chairman and Yergan as executive director. Over time the composition of the membership became decidedly less international and more African-American. Thanks to Yergan's skill in fund-raising and the inclusion of wealthy whites as members—especially Frederick Field, the Vanderbilt heir, and John Hammond, the famous record producer and musician—lack of money was no longer a pressing problem.

During World War II, the Council on African Affairs became one of the most important American voices in its field. Through the activities of Yergan and Robeson, who often crisscrossed the United States, raising funds through concerts and rallies, the council became known both nationally and internationally as a potent force for African political liberation. Its monthly publication, *New Africa*, edited by Alphaeus Hunton, who had joined in 1943, kept subscribers informed of contemporary political developments in the continent, information that was not available through any other channel.

Then, in July 1947, as anticommunist hysteria grew, Yergan was named by the House Un-American Activities Committee as a "Negro Communist from New York." Yergan reacted by switching sides. His first move was to fire Doxey Wilkerson, the Communist editor of a radical Harlem-based weekly newspaper, the *People's Voice*; Yergan sat on its board. In November, the publication issued a statement making it clear that its political stance was now nonpartisan. Next, Yergan resigned from the National Negro Congress—he had been associated with the organization for a decade and in 1943 had become its president. Having abandoned his left-wing colors, Yergan turned around and joined the Cold Warriors in their fight against world communism. By February 1948, he had begun a bitter and public battle against Robeson for control of the Council on African Affairs—a battle that took up most of that year and involved moves and countermoves reminiscent of a French farce. In September, the sparring resulted in Robeson's victory and Yergan's permanent discharge from office and expulsion from membership.

Robeson heard nothing more from Yergan personally, but the latter was busy building up his anticommunist credentials both in the United States and abroad. In Washington, for example, late in 1948 and then again in January 1949, Yergan testified before the grand jury in the Alger Hiss case. Then in March he fired off a memorandum to the South African embassy in Washington warning them of the dangers of communism and the importance of forging a Christian anticommunist policy in the country.

The FBI, which had kept a close eye on Yergan's political activities since 1942, paid particular attention to this about-face.

On February 7, 1948, J. Edgar Hoover wrote to the New York office to say that he had noted that Yergan had come out as a dissenting voice in the Council on African Affairs and that "he desires that the Council disavow any Communist or Fascist ties." He also made a point of noting that Yergan's new anticommunism was not just a matter of words but, as Yergan showed by firing Wilkerson at the *People's Voice*, of action too. For that reason, Hoover said, he wanted the New York office to seek out "reliable and established sources" to affirm that Yergan had broken with the Communist Party and to then consider "contacting Yergan in an effort to develop him as a source of information or confidential informant."

A little over a month later, the New York office of the FBI wrote to Hoover and confirmed that Yergan had cut his ties with the Communists. The informants all agreed: "Yergan is an opportunist who would cooperate with anyone if it meant furthering and improving himself." They added that they considered him untrustworthy.

That did not seem to bother the FBI, for by September 1948, the bureau had already been in contact with Yergan and he was already passing confidential information and documents to them. In October, the special agent in charge at the New York office advised Hoover that they were now satisfied that Yergan's name could be safely removed from their Security Index Card. By the end of the year, the FBI felt themselves in possession of a most useful informant, one who could advise them on their battle against Communists and the communist infiltration, as they saw it, of several key African-American political organizations, including the Civil Rights Congress, the National Negro Congress, and the Council on African Affairs, as well as on the tactics of the Communist Party itself.

When Robeson's plane touched down at New York's La Guardia airport on June 16, 1949, more than sixty of his friends were there, anxiously awaiting their hero's return. First to welcome him was

William Patterson, but others, notably Alphaeus Hunton, secretary of the Council on African Affairs, Charles Howard, a prominent attorney and newspaper publisher, and Bessie Mitchell, who had done so much for the Trenton Six, soon came up and "hugged and kissed" him. Twenty uniformed policemen escorted Robeson from the plane, though why they were there remains a mystery: the *New York Times* simply explained it away by asserting that this was normal practice "for the arrival of prominent persons."

Robeson was more concerned about the police presence than was the reporter from the *Times*. "This is an interesting welcome," he was quoted as saying. "There is a squad of police to meet me . . ." The *Times* reporter added that Mr. Robeson "displayed annoyance" over their presence.

As Robeson made his way through customs, his bags were searched carefully; a photographer was on hand in case there were any "documents of interest." Milling around were a number of FBI agents. Robeson's effects—"one suitcase, a music scrapbook and two packages of sheet music"—yielded nothing of interest to the officials and agents present. One of the FBI men informed the Washington office that a motorcade of a dozen cars, bearing signs advertising a welcome-home rally at Harlem's Rockland Palace, on June 19, left the airport together, intending to drive through Harlem. According to the same agent, "The motor cavalcade bearing Robeson received no ovation of recognition from Harlemites." Local newspapers told a different story.

Reporters at the airport had been full of questions, especially about what Robeson had said in Paris. Robeson promised to answer them later at a press conference; all he was prepared to say now was that the Associated Press and other agencies had distorted his words and that he would be giving a full reply at the meeting at Rockland Palace.

~

Rockland Palace, located on 155th Street near Eighth Avenue and the Harlem River, had a seating capacity of 5,000 and was a popular venue for rallies, dances and sporting events. Robeson had played basketball there when he was a student. On Sunday, June 19, it played host to Paul Robeson's homecoming.

One strike had gone against Robeson in Paris. The time had come for him to face his critics, Max Yergan included.

The rally, held under the auspices of the Council on African Affairs, began at 3 p.m. Sources differ as to how many attended—anywhere from 3,500 to 5,000—but they all agree the audience was half black, half white. The program, as it was advertised at the end of May, was designed to strike directly at the hostile reception to Robeson's Paris speech and to defend the returning hero. The program flier called it a celebration for Paul Robeson, "demonstrating the high esteem which we have for him and our gratitude for his courageous insistence that the Negro people—all people—want peace." The theme for the afternoon was "Harlem Speaks for Peace and Freedom"—two issues inexorably linked in Robeson's mind and in the minds of many of the radicals who supported him. The flier noted that speeches would focus "on the struggles of the American, West Indian and African Negroes for political rights and economic security, and their relationship to the vital question of world war or world peace."

The program was opened by Charles Howard, a prominent attorney and longtime leader of the NAACP in Des Moines, Iowa. Howard had had the distinct honor of giving the keynote speech at the national convention of the Progressive Party, the first time that an African American had done this for any American political party. Taking his place at the podium, Howard wasted no time in assailing Robeson's critics, who, "using the basest character assassination" hoped to destroy Robeson "as a people's leader." But, he told his audience, it was not that easy to "turn the people against Paul Robeson, any more than they can turn the people against themselves." The fact that some of the basest attacks came from the African-American press was shameful, Howard noted. But even they could not destroy the man, for to do that they would have to erase his record, to discredit his past: In effect, they would have to "crawl into every newspaper office in the country and destroy all back copies" with headlines such as "Robeson Leads Thousands to Washington to Protest Lynchings"; burn countless trophies, medals, and citations; and finally "perform mass surgery upon the brains and the hearts of millions of Americans to make them forget the things they themselves have heard Paul say and seen him do."

There were more speeches, by Alphaeus Hunton; W.E.B. Du Bois, now vice chairman of the Council on African Affairs; Mary Van Kleek; Benjamin Davis, the Communist Party member for Harlem in the New York City Council; and Vito Marcantonio, the American Labor Party congressman for New York's 18th District. At 4:50 p.m., Robeson entered the hall. He was greeted by a five-minute ovation. Then Pete Seeger and the Weavers burst into the song "Welcome the Traveler Home."

After initial thanks and a few songs, Robeson launched into the main event—his speech, his big speech. The audience, whatever they were expecting, were not disappointed.

Building up his theme by running through key moments in his upbringing, Robeson soon came to his first, and by now familiar, point: that the wealth of America "had been beaten out of millions of the American Negro people, enslaved, freed, newly enslaved until this very day." And then, he broke the emotional atmosphere by announcing in no uncertain terms his absolute right to be called an American.

"I defy," he proclaimed from the podium, looking out over a sea of white and black faces, taking aim at the white ruling classes and their African African-American apologists, "any part of an insolent, dominating America, however powerful; I defy any errand boys, Uncle Toms of the Negro people, to challenge my Americanism, because by word and deed I challenge this vicious system to the death." He continued: "I fight for the right of the Negro people and other oppressed labor-driven Americans to have decent homes, decent jobs, and the dignity that belongs to every human being."

But it was the African Americans in the audience who were his primary concern this day. Human dignity, he said, was denied him in his own land, and he blamed Wall Street and its African-American stooges for this "travesty." "Let them snatch their bit of cheese and go scampering rat-like into their holes, where, by heaven, the Negro people will keep them, left to their dirty consciences, if any they have." The African-American people would not be duped. He laid out his radical program. "I'm looking for freedom," he told his audience, "*full freedom*, not an inferior brand."

Robeson then described, in glowing terms, his recent reception in Europe and criticized the United States and its client states for the Marshall Plan and the Atlantic Pact. Next on his agenda was the controversy over the Paris speech, which he had promised to address that afternoon. It was time to state absolutely clearly what he had said on the evening of April 20. No more garbled words:

"At the Paris Peace Conference I said it was unthinkable that the Negro people of America or elsewhere in the world could be drawn into war with the Soviet Union. I repeat it with hundred-fold emphasis: *They will not*." And then, mindful of how his words in the Salle Pleyel had been mistaken, he spelled out, so that there could be no misunderstanding, whom he meant by the phrase "Negro people of America or elsewhere in the world": not only the fourteen million in America, but also the forty million in the Caribbean and Latin America and the 150 million in Africa. They were, Robeson said, an inseparable mass, and they wanted peace.

This desire had nothing whatsoever to do with loyalty, as his critics in the press had maintained. African Americans, he repeated, must not be lured "into any kind of war with our closest friends and allies." Their fight was "*right here in America*," for their constitutional rights, for their right not to be lynched. This was their battlefield. In a direct reference to the appalling way in which African-American soldiers returning from the devastating war in Europe and the Pacific were treated in the United States, Robeson exclaimed, "We do not want to die in vain any more on foreign battlefields for Wall Street and the greedy supporters of domestic fascism. If we must die, let it be in Mississippi or Georgia! Let it be wherever we are lynched and deprived of our rights as human beings."

For the Soviet Union, on the other hand, he had nothing but praise. By contrast with big businessmen on Wall Street, its people wanted "peace and an abundant life–freedom is already theirs . . . Yes," he proclaimed, "I love this Soviet people more than any other nation, because of their suffering and sacrifices for us, the Negro people, the progressive people, the people of the future of the world."

With a rousing cry for unity, Robeson brought the day's proceedings to an upbeat end: "We will help to insure peace in our time—the freedom and liberation of the Negro and other struggling peoples, and the building of a world where we can all walk in full equality and full human dignity." With those words concluding one of the longest speeches he had ever made, Robeson left the podium to thundering applause.

The next day, the *New York Times* carried a piece on the speeches given in Rockland Palace headlined "Loves Soviet Best, Robeson Declares." It was typical of the press reaction. The nation-wide-syndicated Hearst papers carried an editorial headed by the phrase "An Undesirable Citizen." The *Afro-American* headlined its coverage of the homecoming rally "I Love Above All, Russia."

American citizens did not take Robeson's words lying down. They wrote to President Truman and told him what to do with Robeson. "He should be given a one-way ticket to the Soviet Union since he had expressed how much he would like to live in Russia," said one correspondent from Joplin, Missouri. That was not an isolated reaction. J. Edgar Hoover at the FBI got calls suggesting he send Robeson to Russia permanently. Robeson got his own share of hate mail.

More garbled words. Paris had been put to rest, but Robeson had stirred a new hornet's nest. The charge of disloyalty was back in the picture.

Strike two.

# 6

# Like a Duck

An entire new chapter in Robeson's political struggles now opened. The scene moves to the sweltering heat of Washington, D.C., on Wednesday, July 13, 1949. It is 10:30 a.m., and in the New House Office Building, part of the complex of congressional buildings surrounding the Capitol, the House Un-American Activities Committee is about to open its first of several public hearings "regarding communist infiltration of minority groups."

The House Un-American Activities Committee, better known by its acronym HUAC, came into existence in 1938. It was chaired initially by Martin Dies Jr., a Democratic congressman from Texas, and from 1938 until 1944, the committee's brief was to investigate alleged instances of subversive communist and fascist activities by American organizations, citizens and federal employees. After 1945, HUAC, now constituted as a standing, or permanent, committee of the House of Representatives, was charged to investigate alleged attempts, through subversion or propaganda, to undermine the American government. Throughout its thirty-year history it was the most feared, aggressive, and formidable official instrument of American anticommunism. Though the name of Joseph McCarthy is usually associated with its repressive activities, it is well to remember that Senator McCarthy's field of activity was alleged communist infiltration of the US government and first surfaced in 1950, when McCarthy publicly accused the State Department of harboring communists. From 1953 until the end of December 1954, McCarthy was chairman of the Senate Committee on Government Operations, and it was this committee that investigated government departments, and agencies—particularly two propaganda agencies, the Voice of America and the United States Information Agency—and the US Army. HUAC, by contrast, investigated the alleged un-American activities of ordinary American citizens and nongovernmental organizations, and it had the power to invite and to subpoena witnesses as it saw fit.

By the time of the July 13 hearing, HUAC had already thrown its net widely over the United States and was very busy indeed. Though the idea of an un-American activity could be applied without regard to political color, it became very clear from the moment that HUAC became a permanent committee that it would be turning a blind eye to right-wing organizations, such as the Ku Klux Klan, and concentrating exclusively on communist and alleged communist organizations and individuals. It didn't take long for HUAC to initiate several hearings on the Communist Party of the United States—that was one of its first actions after becoming a permanent committee. Next, in 1947, HUAC concentrated on communist infiltration, as the committee called it, of various high-profile American institutions such as the motion-picture industry and labor unions, and on the issue of espionage in the United States government. In 1949, hearings were held on Soviet espionage in the aircraft and jet propulsion engine industries and on communist infiltration of the radiation laboratory of the University of California, Berkeley. Meanwhile, a very close relationship had developed between HUAC and the FBI. All manner of material flowed from Hoover's offices to those of the House committee.

In 1949, the first year of the Eighty-first Congress, several changes were made to the rules governing who could or could not sit on HUAC; these were intended by the Truman administration to prevent certain individuals who were considered troublesome from exercising power through the committee. Nobody who was a chairman of another committee could have a seat on HUAC; of the rest, only congressmen who were lawyers were qualified. Because the Democrats controlled the House of Representatives (as well as the Senate), Democrats were in the majority on all House committees. Of HUAC's nine members five were Democrats, including the chairman John Wood, and four were Republicans, including a thirty-six-year-old lawyer from California named Richard Nixon, who had been elected to Congress two years before.

John Wood was a Southern Democrat from Georgia, elected to his second term in the House in 1945. During the time he served as a member of the committee, he was involved in investigations into the motion-picture industry, the American Communist Party and the Joint Anti-Fascist Refugee Committee, an organization established to provide medical care to Spanish Civil War refugees living in France. As far as Wood was concerned, the Joint Anti-Fascist Refugee Committee was anti-American because it was anti-Franco. HUAC charged that the group was engaged in political activity for communists. Wood was ideologically in the same mold as Martin Dies, and under his leadership HUAC could be trusted to root out Communists wherever they had insinuated themselves in the United States.

"Minority groups" as a collective target were as ripe as any other for communist infiltration, and for HUAC investigation. On the morning of July 13, 1949, only five members of the panel were present. Francis Case was the only Republican there, though another, Harold Velde, an Illinois Republican, came in later, bringing the total to six. Seated with the congressmen were the committee's six staff members, including Frank Tavenner, the committee's counsel, Benjamin Mandel, its director of research, and Alvin Stokes, an investigator who would be asked to make a statement.

The hearing began, surprisingly enough, not with Stokes's statement but with John Wood's reading of a letter he had just received from General Dwight D. Eisenhower. Eisenhower, who had recently been elected president of Columbia University, was writing in reply to a letter from Wood asking for his comments on "the loyalty record . . . during World War II by members of minority races," and specifically "the record of American Negro soldiers." Eisenhower had no doubts on the subject: "It no more occurred to me," he wrote, "to question their mass patriotism and loyalty than it would have occurred to me to entertain such doubts about the entire force." Almost 50,000 African American troops, Eisenhower recalled, had been deployed in Europe and North Africa, and there was not a whisper of any "unwillingness to serve." This was "irrefutable proof of the loyalty of our Negro troops." In concluding his testimony on African-American military loyalty, Eisenhower went one step further and ended on an unassailably positive note. Since the ending of the war, he wrote, he had neither seen nor experienced anything that led him to believe that "our Negro population is not fully as worthy of its American citizenship as it proved itself to be on the battlefields of Europe and Africa."

After this reading, Alvin Stokes was called before the panel. Stokes, a forty-year-old African American, had been working as an investigator for HUAC since early 1947, when J. Parnell Thomas, the previous chairman, hired him because of his excellent undercover work when he was employed by a county sheriff's department in New Jersey. In the intervening time he had become, according to his own testimony, a specialist on "Communist attempts to infiltrate, control, and dominate Negro organizations and to recruit, capture, and control outstanding Negroes and others for service in the Communist movement."

After interviewing hundreds of prominent African Americans, Stokes had concluded that the Communist Party had hardly made an inroad into this community, enlisting only about 1 percent of the entire black population of the United States. For this low incidence, Stokes praised the work of organizations such as the NAACP and the churches, and women, whom Stokes honored because they had rejected communism and put a brake on their menfolk falling prey to the Communist Party.

Nevertheless, Stokes insisted, the Party had been stirring things up, encouraging disunity in the country, "setting race against race, religion against religion, and class against class." It had also continued its clandestine program to create a "Negro Soviet Republic" in what was called the Black Belt of the Southern states.

Whether Stokes raised the issue of the Black Belt republic in order to put the fear of God into the panel and especially its Southern representatives, John Wood and Burr Harrison, Wood's Democratic colleague from Virginia, is unclear, but whatever his motives there is little doubt that it would have unnerved these two and possibly others on the panel. Stokes was alluding to a pronouncement made at the 1928 Sixth World Congress of the Communist International that African Americans concentrated in the Black Belt counties—areas where African Americans were in the numerical majority—of the southern United States constituted an oppressed nation. As such, according to the guiding principles of Comintern, this population had the right to self-determination, to control its own resources and to secede from the rest of the country.

This was a signal to the American Communist Party to begin political work in a region that until then they had virtually ignored, on the grounds that it had no radical tradition, being overwhelmingly conservative and paternalistic. Birmingham, Alabama, was chosen as the site of the headquarters of its new district, which covered six Southern states, and in 1929, the Party got down to the job at hand. In 1938, a map showing the location of the proposed Black Belt Republic was published in a Communist Party pamphlet; this was reprinted for all to see in the 1949 hearing's official publication.

Stokes insisted that though this republic had never materialized, plans for it still formed part of Communist Party policy. As an example of how actions furthering the policy had been camouflaged, Stokes referred to the recent homecoming rally for Paul Robeson—the first time Robeson's name had come up in the hearing. Stokes said that he attended the June 19 rally at Rockland Palace and that the theme of the speeches was the deplorable "lack of rebellious spirit on the part of the Negro people." It was Stokes's opinion that the purpose of the meeting was to incite rebellious action against the American government, even though he admitted without being asked that no single speech overtly took this line.

Anyone sitting in the audience—the hearings were public—might have been excused for wondering what was going on. No one so far, the chairman included, had stated the purpose of the hearing. How many minority groups HUAC would be discussing this morning and afterward was anyone's guess. African Americans, obviously, but who else? As the days wore on, it would become patently clear that, aside from a small nod to Jewish groups, all of the witnesses were being drawn from and asked to speak about the African-American community. Now, as Stokes unveiled his analysis of the political will of African Americans, it became even more obvious that nothing general in the African-American political community was under review, but rather, specifically, Paul Robeson. What he had said in Paris, along with its implications about the loyalty of his people, was the Committee's jumping-off point.

Why Wood chose not to follow standard practice of announcing the purpose of the hearing at the outset is not known. The NAACP had certainly heard in the days before the session opened that HUAC was holding hearings for "certain leading Negroes who would like to go on record to dispute statements made by Paul Robeson that American Negroes would not fight the Soviet Union if a war should break out between America and Russia." The loyalty of the African American, the NAACP stated, was not in question, and they couldn't see why a hearing should be held to affirm something that the government already knew.

Wood replied to the NAACP that his committee had no doubt about the African American's loyalty. What bothered him was that Robeson had "made disloyal and unpatriotic statements . . . organized and planned for world-wide reception." He confirmed that he was acceding to requests from "members of [Robeson's] race . . . for the expression of contrary views" in a public forum. Who these "members" were remained hidden from the public.

Stokes reported that Robeson had repeated his Paris assertions at Rockland Palace. He took issue with those who simply attacked Robeson by arguing that he only spoke for himself. The situation was much more dangerous than that. According to Stokes, Robeson was spouting the Kremlin line, designed to foment disunity, to reactivate old hatreds and stir up new ones. And in this, Robeson had been successful. Stokes pointed to a recent survey that showed that in seven American cities, more than half of the whites believed that African Americans were overwhelmingly Communist and that in the event of war would be disloyal to their country. "Mr. Robeson," Stokes insisted, "was the first to smear the historical loyalty of the Negro people since . . . the Revolutionary War." Robeson, acting on his Kremlin instructions, was driving a wedge into American society in order to destabilize it, convincing white Americans that African Americans were disloyal.

When Stokes had completed his statement, he was questioned (gently) by the panel. Francis Case, a Republican congressman from South Dakota, asked a few innocuous questions about matters of fact, and then, without the slightest signal that he was about to change tack, he asked Stokes, "Do you know whether or not Mr. Robeson is a member of the Communist Party?" To which Stokes answered, "I do not," though he added the qualification that, in any case, Robeson was openly loyal to the Communist movement. Then Case asked similar questions about other speakers at Rockland Palace whom Stokes had earlier identified as having made (indirectly) inflammatory statements. Stokes had no information for him.

Next in line, but not questioned for very long, was Rabbi Benjamin Schultz, national executive secretary of the American

Jewish League Against Communism, who, echoing Stokes, proclaimed that Robeson's "attempted provocation of American Negroes against their country," was proof that Communists wanted to "inflame racial and religious minorities . . . against the United States." The Jewish community, Schultz asserted, had its own Paul Robesons, but they were not typical, implying that the same applied to the African-American community. As he spoke, Schultz insisted at every turn that Jews in the United States were above reproach in terms of their loyalty to the country (though no one that day had said anything to the contrary), and that they were ever vigilant about the threat from Communists.

Later the same morning, the committee heard from Thomas Young, president and general manager of Guide Publishing, which put out Virginia's oldest and most successful black weekly newspaper. With a circulation of 65,000 in Virginia and neighboring North Carolina, the *Journal and Guide* was also one of the biggest black newspapers in the country. Young, a highly educated man, had been involved in the paper, with his father, who had founded it, for seventeen years, beginning in his college days. As one who was close to African-American public opinion, Young, who turned out to be an extremely eloquent and elegant speaker, had quite a bit on his mind about Robeson and his statement.

He began by claiming, as others had done before him, that the loyalty of the African American was not in question and that from the time the first black man had died for his country in the Revolutionary War up until the recent war, there had been nothing but admiration for the sacrifices of the black soldier. Unlike other speakers and, as he made clear later in his testimony, other newspaper owners and editors, Young did not think that Robeson or his statement could be so easily and cavalierly dismissed. Robeson's life, he reminded the congressmen, was "an inspiration to the humble people . . . it would seem highly improbable that Mr. Robeson could be unfaithful to his own people . . . his intemperate outbursts at Paris carried appreciable weight, however much we may dislike the notion."

Yet, and this was Young's main point, Robeson had lost touch with the common man, as it were, as evidenced not by what he said but by his persona and his concerns. Young was precise about what he meant: Robeson's "distant travels and his latter-day preoccupations with the affairs of the Soviets have broken the bond that he once held with the Negro mind." That was why "he no longer has *the opportunity to know* [my emphasis] nor the authority to speak about the aims and resolutions of this group." Robeson's gravest disservice, Young incisively argued, was to his people, not to his country.

Young was unforgiving in his criticism of Robeson. In his opinion, Robeson, by "advancing a foreign cause in which we have no real interest," was jeopardizing the democratic processes that were giving African Americans the rights they were entitled to. In conclusion, Young charged that "in the eyes of the Negro people this false prophet is regarded as unfaithful to their country, and they repudiate him."

Young's argument got to the heart of the matter and explained better than most that Robeson looking abroad for political solutions did not impress and indeed was particularly offensive to African Americans. Robeson's transatlantic character, rather than being something to admire, was, according to Young, an affront to his people.

With Thomas Young's testimony completed, the committee adjourned for the day.

The key witness next morning was Manning Johnson. His testimony ran the longest of any in the hearing: He had a lot to tell.

Over the next few years, Johnson, an African American, would prove a star witness in more than two dozen trials and hearings, both federal and state, because of his willingness to name names. Behind this willingness was the fact that he had been a member of the Communist Party and also, as he later explained (under oath), perjury was never a problem for him—just part of the job. For several years he was on the payroll of the Department of Justice and had enough material to make a living as a professional stool pigeon, one member of that select group of anticommunist warriors.

This hearing was one of Johnson's first appearances as a state witness. He was then in his early forties and identified himself as living in New York City, and working for a union representing clerks in the retail industry. This was his nineteenth year of involvement, as he put it, "in the labor movement."

Frank Tavenner, HUAC's counsel, led Johnson's questioning and soon got to the crux of his witness's usefulness. "During any part of that time [in the labor movement] have you been a member of the Communist Party?" "Yes," Johnson replied, "I was a member of the Communist Party for ten years." Questioned further, Johnson revealed that he had been with the Party through the whole of the 1930s, only severing his ties when it became clear that his and the Party's philosophies were growing apart—Johnson mentioned that he couldn't give up his religious convictions as the Party demanded; that he was against the creation of a Black Belt Republic; and finally that he disagreed with how the Communist Party was cynically using the Scottsboro Boys case for its own purposes. But, more than all these put together, Johnson claimed, it was the Nazi-Soviet Non-Aggression Pact of 1939 that finally tipped the balance; after that, he left.

Johnson described his years in the Party, paying special attention to his own advancement and the training he was given as a revolutionary, naming, along the way, his instructors and other prominent people he came across. Tavenner, who was still doing the questioning, had little need to prompt his witness, who, from the transcript at least, appeared to be perfectly comfortable in his position.

About one third of the way through the testimony, Tavenner got to the real business at hand. "In your vast experience in the Communist Party," he asked Johnson, "did you have occasion to meet Paul Robeson?" Johnson's answer, given without hesitation, dropped the bomb: "Yes. I have met Paul Robeson a number of times in the headquarters of the national committee of the Communist Party . . . during the time I was a member of the Communist Party, Paul Robeson was a member of the Communist Party . . . [he] has been a member for many years."

Because of Robeson's sensitive work, "highly confidential and secret"—this assignment, according to Johnson, was to influence artists and intellectuals, in connection with his concert tours, along Communist lines—Party members were told, under threat of expulsion, never to reveal his status. Robeson himself was under strict orders never to attend meetings of the national committee of the Communist Party.

And then, without any encouragement, Johnson offered his opinion on Robeson's psychological makeup. He had "developed a complex," Johnson explained, dropping another bomb, one perfectly calculated to bring fallout from the headline writers beyond the capital "He has delusions of grandeur. He wants to be the Black Stalin among Negroes."

It was now fast approaching 12:50, the appointed lunch break, so on that note, the morning session of the hearing was adjourned.

For most of the afternoon, Tavenner, who had resumed his role as chief questioner, prompted Johnson about Communist front organizations, specifically those concerned with African Americans, such as the American Negro Labor Congress and the National Negro Congress. Johnson explained how these organizations interacted with the American Communist Party and their relationship with Moscow, which was essentially doing whatever they were told to do. Soon, however, Tavenner brought Johnson back to the issue of Paul Robeson. "What is the attitude of the Communist Party to the recognized Negro leadership in the United States?" he asked. "Utter contempt," Johnson retorted. The Party considered those at the top of organizations such as the NAACP and the Urban League tools of the bourgeois state, but privately they feared them for the success they had already achieved. Nevertheless, the Party was intent on destroying these leaders and Robeson was "exploiting discrimination and other ills for that purpose."

Johnson was no fool and took the opportunity of this public forum to remind the committee that African Americans had a long way to go to secure their rights and that Jim Crow had to end. He asserted that in this respect the American government would be wise to support a "broad civil rights program ." That would not only give African Americans what they most wanted but would also deal a deathblow to Communism.

As might be expected, the very next day the *New York Times* headlined its take on Johnson's revelations "'Black Stalin' Aim is Laid to Robeson." Robeson, the article declared in its opening sentence, was a member of the Communist Party, and that knowledge was now firmly in the public arena. Speculations about Robeson's affiliation had been rife for a long time: both the FBI and MI5 believed Robeson had joined the Communist Party and had already assessed, but without definitive proof, when and how.

Now here, for the first time, was an eyewitness account from someone who had been high up in the Party bureaucracy. There was no further need for speculation, no need to resort to the kind of thinking used to "identify" Communists that was so perfectly reflected in committee member Harold Velde's pet saying: "If a person talks like a duck and walks like a duck and swims like a duck, he is a duck."

What more was there to say? What more did HUAC have up its sleeve?

# I Am a Radical

It was very likely Alvin Stokes who was behind getting HUAC to call up the hearing's star witness. It was an inspired move.

In the United States, Jackie Robinson was at least as famous as Robeson. He stood then, as he stands today, as the most significant figure in the desegregation of Major League Baseball, the first player to cross one of America's most difficult color lines, that of America's most popular sport.

Just like the military, which continued to remain segregated until the early years of the following decade, professional baseball had a strict color bar. African-American players before Jackie Robinson crossed the line could play only in their own leagues, which had come to mirror the structure of the white majors: the Negro National League and the Negro American League.

Before the end of World War II, attempts to integrate professional baseball had largely failed. Judge Kenesaw Mountain Landis, the first Commissioner of Baseball—a post he occupied for almost a quarter of a century, until his death in 1944—was vehemently opposed to integration, despite great pressure put on him by the African-American press. And as long as he remained steadfastly against integration, individual baseball club owners could hide their attitude behind his.

Robeson himself had tried his best to change this. In 1939 he had had a meeting with Landis, but nothing came of it. In December 1943, he was given another chance to influence the Major League's thinking about segregation when he was invited to address the club owners at their annual meeting. The owners apparently listened to Robeson's appeal, but then waited for a positive signal from Landis; his response was that any move was up to them. Frustratingly, they did nothing.

With the death of Landis in 1944 and the appointment of the Democratic senator from Kentucky, Albert Benjamin "Happy" Chandler, as the next Commissioner, the mood for change was clearly in the air. The return of African-American soldiers from the front and the sacrifices made by their dead comrades stepped up the pressure on highly segregated institutions like the military and sports. The clamor from the African-American press for an end to baseball segregation was swelled by the voice of Lester Rodney, who had been campaigning for integration in the sports pages of the *Daily Worker* for more than a decade.

On October 23, 1945, just days before Chandler took up his new role, Branch Rickey, general manager of the Brooklyn Dodgers, announced that he had signed Jackie Robinson, a twenty-six-year-old African American who had played during the previous season in the Negro American League, to play in the International League for a Dodgers-affiliated team.

Robinson, who had only recently come to baseball after excelling at other sports, made his debut with the Montreal Royals on March 17, 1946. The team, with more than a little help from Robinson, ended its season at the top of the league.

Shortly before the opening of the 1947 Major League Baseball season, Rickey announced that he had signed Robinson to play for his team, the Brooklyn Dodgers. On April 15, 1947, in front of a packed crowd at Ebbets Field, the Dodgers' home stadium, Jackie Robinson made his debut as the first African American to play for a Major League Baseball club. History had been made and, as far as the desegregation of baseball was concerned, there was no turning back, even though it would be more than decade before the last club to hold out ended its color bar.

~

Robinson had been scheduled to appear before HUAC on the opening morning of the hearings, on Wednesday, July 13. He had agreed to do this as early as July 8, according to a report in the *New York Times*. In the event, Robinson couldn't make the date, and his appearance was postponed until the morning of Monday, July 18. Robinson got up very early that day to catch one of the first flights out of New York for the nation's capital.

The session opened at 10:50 a.m. As a report in one newspaper described it:

> The small room, in which the hearing was held, was packed. People stood around the walls and outside in the hallway to get a glimpse and hear the star baseball player. Newsreel cameras were set up and an unusually large number of photographers were on hand. A wire recording was also made of Jackie's testimony.

Robinson, dressed in a fine suit and accompanied by his wife Rachel, entered the room and sat down at the desk in front of a microphone, the committee in front of him and the audience at his back. This was the hottest ticket in town and maybe even in the country. Photographers were normally barred from the committee's hearings, but an exception was made for this special day. The chairman, John Wood, claimed he was ill and couldn't attend. In his place, a subcommittee of four members assembled, together with the HUAC staff. Alvin Stokes, who had opened the proceedings the previous week, was to lead the questioning. However, there was to be no questioning. Instead, Jackie Roosevelt Robinson, born in 1919 in Cairo, Georgia, read a prepared statement.

He began with an apology, noting that although he was glad to accept the invitation to express his views, he didn't find it "exactly pleasant to get involved in a political dispute," as he earned his living in a field "as far removed from politics as anybody can possibly imagine." Many people, he told the committee, and not all of them Communists, he added, had urged him not to appear, but he had decided that he should out of a sense of responsibility.

Perhaps to the discomfiture of some of the members of the committee and a section of the American people, Robinson set out to remind everyone listening that the life of an African American, even one as privileged as he, could be "mighty tough." His crossing of the baseball color line was only a beginning. Out of almost four hundred Major League players in sixteen clubs, only seven were black players, playing for just three clubs. And baseball itself, according to Robinson, was just a start: There were many more fields to integrate besides sports fields.

African Americans, Robinson insisted, deeply resented racial "slurs and discrimination," and would go to any lengths to stop them. None of this had anything to do with Communism. And then Robinson, who had excused himself for being uncomfortable talking about politics, made one of the most political statements imaginable. He turned directly to the American public, represented by the audience behind him, and told them a single home truth. It is worth quoting him in full:

> The fact that it is a Communist who denounces injustice in the courts, police brutality, and lynching when it happens doesn't change the truth of his charges. Just because Communists kick up a fuss over racial discrimination when it suits their purposes, a lot of people try to pretend that the whole issue is a creation of Communist imagination . . . Negroes were stirred up long before there was a Communist Party, and they'll stay stirred up long after the party has disappeared—unless Jim Crow has disappeared by then as well.

Robinson had not been asked to discuss Jim Crow, but putting this vexed issue at the opening of his statement before coming to the real reason he had been invited was an excellent move. That done, Robinson gave his opinion on "Paul Robeson's statement in Paris," encapsulating his thoughts in the phrase "It sounds very silly to me." Though he respected Robeson as an artist and also respected his right to his own opinions, he, Jackie Robinson, personally had too much invested in "our country's welfare . . . and future to throw it away because of a siren song sung in bass."

And that was about it as far as Robinson's statement on Robeson was concerned. However, Robinson was not through yet; now he returned to his earlier theme. "I cherish America," he exclaimed, and then added, "but that doesn't mean that we're going to stop fighting race discrimination in this country until we've got it licked. It means that we're going to fight it all the harder because our stake in the future is so big."

Now Morgan Moulder, Democratic congressman from Missouri, reminded the committee that the loyalty of African Americans was not at issue: the committee was only interested in giving "an opportunity to you and others to combat the idea Paul Robeson has given by his statements."

A few minutes later, at 11:10 a.m. the chairman brought the hearing to a close.

Someone from the audience shouted, "Amen."

Lem Graves Jr., the Washington correspondent for the conservative *Pittsburgh Courier* and a distinguished war correspondent, was not, he claimed, taken in by the Washington hearings. Like many others before him, he maintained that African-American loyalty was not an issue—in all of the United States' wars there had never been a single instance of an African-American traitor and only "a minute proportion" of conscientious objectors. As for HUAC, most African Americans were suspicious of it because it had been mostly dominated by Southerners and had never investigated the Ku Klux Klan or "other Dixie fascist groups which have terrorized Negroes."

In his July 23 article, Graves called the July 18 session "pure window-dressing to make the hearing look like a full-scale, legitimate proposition." Its real purpose was getting Jackie Robinson to testify, so he would be seen to repudiate Robeson's Paris speech.

Certainly judging from the coverage given to the hearing in the American press, both white and black, there is no doubt that Robinson's appearance and testimony produced many more column inches than had all the other witnesses put together. The passage of time has tended to support Graves's cynical attitude toward HUAC.

Why, then, had Robinson agreed to appear? Was it his "sense of responsibility," or had there been other pressures?

It seems that at the end of December 1947, Alvin Stokes had contacted Branch Rickey about Robinson. Stokes was hoping that Robinson could help him identify and isolate black Communists in key positions of influence.

The reason why he thought so is that in June 1946 the newly founded United Negro and Allied Veterans of America—the only organization in the United States to assist African-American veterans, and which was not accredited by the much larger, more influential and decidedly white Veterans Administration—had appointed Robinson an honorary New York State commander. A year later, Tom Clark, the attorney general of the United States, listed the black veterans' organization as subversive. Both of these facts were entered in the FBI's folder on Robinson, although it was stated that at no time did the agency investigate him. Since the FBI was feeding HUAC with information, it is most likely that Stokes knew about Robinson's relationship with the alleged Communist front. This may have provided the leverage he would have needed to "convince" Robinson to testify.

Part of HUAC's power derived from encouraging American citizens to clear any suspicions that they were Communists themselves by "naming names," that is, by informing on their colleagues, who would then be given the chance to clear their own names in the same way. Alvin Stokes Jr. told David Falkner, one of Robinson's biographers, that his father could have had either Joe Louis, the great prize fighter, whose FBI file showed that he, too, had been honored by the United Negro and Allied

Veterans organization, not to mention that he had been a member of the organizing committee to celebrate Robeson's forty-sixth birthday; or the celebrated singer Lena Horne, but in the end he had fixed on Robinson. Both Louis and Horne, according to Alvin Stokes Jr., had been eager to clear themselves publicly, "to have the cloud lifted from them."

Stokes Sr. had apparently wanted Robinson to appear before the committee in the spring of 1948, but HUAC had been busy at the time with other high-profile hearings about Communism, regarding proposed legislation to curb the American Communist Party; espionage in the United States government; and investigations into Communist activities in connection with the atomic bomb. Where the committee might fit in an investigation relating to African Americans, whatever its terms of reference, was unclear. To complicate matters even further, after the general election that brought him to his seventh consecutive term in Congress, HUAC's then chairman, J. Parnell Thomas, was indicted on charges of conspiracy to defraud the government, bringing his political career to a close.

Still, despite the difficulty of scheduling Robinson's appearance, Stokes had maintained contact with him and with senior people in the Brooklyn Dodgers camp, including Branch Rickey and Arthur Mann, Rickey's assistant, throughout 1948 and the first half of 1949.

It must have seemed like a gift from the gods when in April 1949 the garbled quotation of Robeson's Paris remarks concerning the loyalty of African Americans in a war with the Soviet Union spread like wildfire through the American press. It would have become instantly clear to Stokes, at least, that Robinson was the perfect counterfoil to Robeson. How prescient he must have thought himself to have already lined up Robinson as a future witness, ready to be delivered with his club's blessing to the HUAC interrogators.

Branch Rickey would have listened carefully and obligingly to Stokes. Rickey was a fervent anticommunist and he was willing do everything in his power to stop the Communists from attempting to turn his radical step in integrating baseball to their advantage. So when Robinson received the telegram from John Wood, the new chairman of HUAC, to appear as a witness speaking against Robeson's statement, Rickey strenuously urged Robinson, who apparently hesitated, to accept the invitation. Rickey convinced Robinson that he was not going to Washington to defend African-American patriotism—the issue was his "sense of social responsibility."

As the day approached and Robinson continued to voice disquiet over his own grasp of politics—not to mention over the many letters sent to him from perfect strangers advising him not to go to Washington—Rickey took charge of drafting Robinson's speech. Even after enlisting Arthur Mann's help, Robinson was unhappy with the result. Years later, Rickey conceded that it was a tall order for two white men to write a speech for one black man repudiating the views of another.

In the end, it seems, a number of people put that speech together. Lester Granger, the Executive Director of the National Urban League, probably did most of the work. Granger, who had already testified in front of the Committee during the week that Robinson was scheduled to appear, did not hide the fact that he had little time for Robeson. Following the Rockland Palace rally, Granger had viciously attacked Robeson in Harlem's *Amsterdam News*, insinuating that he was a tool of the American Communist Party. "The Communist leaders here in America," Granger wrote in the paper's June 25, 1949 issue, "when they say their prayers at night and turn their faces toward the Moscow god whom they worship, must assuredly say a special prayer for the continued health and vitality of their current star attraction. They'd better for he's the last bit of glamour their raggedy party can produce these days."

Granger was not the only one involved in writing the final version of Robinson's statement. The hands of both Alvin Stokes and Rachel Robinson were visible in the final version—as the latter told a magazine writer, "Intent upon him, unconscious of the cameras, I was saying every word of his speech silently along with my husband."

After the hearing, Lester Granger, not surprisingly, was the first to congratulate Robinson. On the day after his appearance, Granger wrote to "Dear Robbie" that he was "inordinately proud" of his fellow African American—he had made a great impression on the American public. As proof Granger mentioned that after the radio and evening newspapers carried the story, he had mingled in New York "among bars, grills, sidewalk groups, and neighbors and friends" and all he heard was praise. "You have rendered a service to our people," Granger concluded, "which will be gratefully regarded for many years to come. On behalf of the National Urban League and the millions of Americans who believe in what we are trying to do, I want to thank you for your service." He hoped to "improve upon the friendship" in the future.

The mainstream American press echoed Granger's sentiments. Robinson, they agreed, had done as well in front of HUAC as he was doing at the plate. They concentrated almost entirely on the few words he said about Robeson and hardly mentioned his anti–Jim Crow statement.

On the day after Robinson testified the *New York Times* printed an article headlined "Jackie Robinson Terms Stand of Robeson on Negroes False," followed by a verbatim reprint of his statement. The next day, the paper returned to the now famous testimony with the headline "Communist Shut-Out." "Jackie Robinson," the article began, "scored four hits and no errors in his testimony in Washington on the relationship of Communism to the struggle for Negro civil rights. Simply and effectively, he made these points, which reveal that Jackie Robinson is a whole lot more than one of America's great baseball players." The article ended by affirming the liberal position that American democracy would see to it that the African-American struggle against race discrimination would be won, with no help from "false, self-serving, Communist support."

That was not the end of the paper's interest in Robinson, for a few pages further on readers learned that Representative Bernard Kearney, Republican of New York, had recommended Robinson to receive the Veterans of Foreign Wars gold medal for good citizenship. The next day, a fellow congressman from New York, Arthur Klein, proposed that Congress should print more than half a million copies of Robinson's statement to be distributed in schools, libraries and churches. "[It] should be read by all members of Congress," Klein added. Seven years later, Kearney would face Paul Robeson directly in another HUAC hearing.

The African-American press was less enthusiastic. Those papers, not surprisingly, were uncomfortable witnessing one famous black man attacking another when both had done so much for their people, and their reports were more ambivalent— indeed more so than their first reports on Robeson's Paris statement.

The furor and the publicity soon abated. Robinson returned to playing the game he knew best and for which he was best known. After he left the hearing, he got back to New York in time for a night game against the Chicago Cubs at home. The Dodgers won the game 3–0 and took a commanding position at the top of the league.

How did Robinson himself feel about his performance in Washington? One of his biographers referred to the episode as "one of the more embarrassing moments of his career," but that was probably long after the event. The record seems to suggest that embarrassment was not how Robinson felt for many years after his HUAC appearance. In the few examples we have where he referred to that day, he seems mostly inclined to defend his actions. In his acceptance speech upon being awarded the NAACP's prestigious Spingarn Medal in 1956, for example, Robinson made an explicit reference to Lester Granger and the help he gave him in preparing for the HUAC appearance. A year later, in an interview he gave to *Look* magazine, he declared, "Because of baseball I was able . . . to rebuke Paul Robeson for saying most of us Negroes would not fight for our country in a war against Russia."

Several years later, in 1963, Robinson defended what he said in Washington when he answered Malcolm X's charge that his white "bosses" had duped him. As the fiery leader put it in characteristic language, "It was you who let yourself be used by the whites even in those days against your own kind. You let them sic you on Paul Robeson . . . You let your White Boss send you before a congressional hearing in Washington, D.C. . . . to dispute and condemn Paul Robeson, because he had these guilty American whites frightened silly." To which Robinson replied, "I am proud of my associations with the men you choose to call my white bosses—Mr. Branch Rickey . . . I will not dignify your attempted slur against my appearance before the House Un-American Activities Committee some years back. All I can say is that if I were called upon to defend my country today, I would gladly do so."

This does not sound like embarrassment. However, years later, near the end of his life, Robinson, admittedly looking back almost a quarter of a century, did express regret for that day. As he told the author Alfred Duckett, who helped him with his autobiography, "I would reject such an invitation if offered now . . . I have grown wiser and closer to painful truths about America's destructiveness. And I do have increased respect for Paul Robeson, who over a span of twenty years sacrificed himself, his career, and the wealth and comfort he once enjoyed because, I believe, he was sincerely trying to help his people."

As for Robeson, we know what he said publicly in response to Robinson's HUAC appearance. On July 20, he held a press conference at Harlem's Hotel Theresa, which until the early 1940s had been a whites-only hotel. The press conference, organized by the Council on African Affairs, lasted two hours and was attended mostly by reporters from black newspapers and the *Daily Worker*: no mainstream press sent representatives.

Robeson began by issuing a short statement. In it, he argued that HUAC was attempting to drive a wedge between African Americans, turning the question of their loyalty into a subject for debate in order to deflect them from the struggle to get jobs, security, and justice. "I challenge the loyalty of the Un-American Activities Committee," Robeson hit back. Those congressmen, he insisted, had maintained an "ominous silence" when it came to lynchings, the Trenton Six, and other high-profile cases of injustice. The threat to peace and safety came not from the Soviet Union but from within the country. "Those who menace our lives," he maintained, "proceed unchallenged by the Un-American Activities Committee." He would not, he concluded, "be drawn into any conflict dividing me from my brother victim of this terror."

The assorted press corps tried, nevertheless, to draw Robeson into precisely the conflict with Robinson that he flatly rejected in his statement. Robeson repeated, "I have no quarrel with Jackie." That didn't stop them trying again, but they failed every time. When one reporter asked whether Robeson thought that Robinson had done a "disservice" to African Americans, Robeson retorted, "Yes, because it helped the Un-American Committee." He added that all African Americans should demand the right to testify on what they felt about their conditions, implicitly arguing that the deal that they were getting was un-American. "Would you like to testify?" a newsman asked. "You bet your boots I would, and I demand that Mr. Wood from Georgia be there." Robeson reminded the assembly that Wood had excused himself from the hearing with Robinson because of illness, but he, Robeson, had an alternative explanation: "Wood wasn't there because he doesn't want to call Jackie 'Mr. Robinson' . . . We cannot forget that John S. Wood . . . once called the Ku Klux Klan an American institution."

Robeson called on African Americans to seize this opportunity to improve their situation—the best chance that they had had to do so for a long time. "They must be militant, and they will succeed," he insisted.

Two days later, at a meeting sponsored by the Civil Rights Congress in Newark to free the Trenton Six, Robeson threw down the gauntlet and unequivocally declared his political position. "I am a radical," he said, "and I am going to stay one until my people get free to walk the earth. Negroes just cannot wait for civil rights. This year it's a ball player; next year we'll have a professional basketball player. And that's only the beginning."

# 8

# Peekskill

Robeson had first been asked to perform near Peekskill, in New York's Westchester County, in 1946, when he received an invitation from the association of residents of Mohegan Colony. Located on the southern shore of Lake Mohegan, north of New York City and several miles east of Peekskill, the Mohegan Colony had been established in the 1920s as a permanent settlement adhering, broadly, to an anarchist philosophy. Lewis Mumford, the famous social planner and cultural thinker, laid out the colony's infrastructure in 1930. The resulting community, which included a school and a makeshift theater, was intended for year-round living but soon became a summers-only destination for the 300 families who had bought lots.

During the war and after, Mohegan residents invited top-notch musicians to perform in the summer months, including the famous flamenco guitarist Carlos Montoya, a number of highly rated string quartets from New York City, Woody Guthrie and Leadbelly, and a string of dancers and comedians. In 1946, the committee responsible for musical entertainments decided to invite Robeson.

On that occasion hundreds of people arrived—many more than expected, many of them by car, and many of them without any connection to Mohegan Colony. The colony was swamped, but the concert was a great success.

The following summer, in anticipation of an even larger crowd, Robeson gave a concert in Peekskill Stadium, a baseball field on the edge of the town. Four thousand people attended, according to the *Peekskill Evening Star*, the town's major newspaper. All the seats in the grandstand were filled and the overflow, estimated at 1,500 people, was accommodated in a hurriedly provided area of the infield.

On the Monday following, the *Peekskill Evening Star* reviewed the concert in glowing terms but also pointed out that few permanent residents of Peekskill attended. The report provided no explanation of this, but the low turnout from Peekskill may have been because the local post of the American Legion had asked residents to boycott the performance on the grounds of Robeson's communist sympathies.

It was true that the majority of the concertgoers had little to do with Peekskill. They had been drawn from the substantial population of summer residents who vacationed in the surrounding area. Most were working-class Jews from New York City, affiliated to trade unions and distinctly left wing. They and their families looked forward to spending their summer break from the heat and grime of the factory and the city in a pleasant and clean environment. Most of them stayed in basic bungalows attached to a "camp" or "colony," and many of these settlements provided entertainment in one form or another, as well as child care and educational or vocational opportunities. It was a worker's paradise.

The summer residents in the camps and the permanent population in town inhabited different cultural and political worlds: left-wing, unionist and frequently communist on one side, conservative and Republican on the other; Jewish on one side, Protestant and Catholic on the other; concerts in aid of progressive causes on one side, Chamber of Commerce dances on the other.

The success of the 1947 concert, the proceeds of which went to the Committee to Aid the Fighting South (an organization founded to support African Americans facing political and economic oppressions such as lynching and barriers to unionization) prompted

Robeson to return, in August 1948. This time, the local paper did not review the performance, as it had done in the previous year, but simply noted in a short report that two youths had thrown apples at the stage but had been quickly ushered away.

The apple-throwing incident was brief and quickly handled, but what lay behind it was something more serious. Robeson was experiencing mounting criticism because of his politics, and his appearances were either being cancelled or subjected to specific conditions.

In April and May 1947, first in Peoria, Illinois, and then in Albany, capital of New York, Robeson concerts that had been arranged and for which tickets had already been sold were cancelled without warning. A month later, a scheduled appearance in Toronto was allowed on condition that Robeson agree to sing but not speak. What seemed to prompt these actions was that HUAC had recently, in the course of its campaign to outlaw the Communist Party, cited Robeson, along with many others, as a supporter of the Party and its front organizations.

HUAC's citation had led the Peoria city council to adopt a resolution stating that it disapproved of "bringing in any speaker or artist who is an avowed and active propagandist for un-American ideologies," and this was enough to convince the sponsor of Robeson's concert that the singer would not be welcome. Robeson took no notice of the cancellation and traveled to Peoria anyway. "Since when in America does a city keep an artist out because of his political beliefs?" he told a reporter. He did not get to sing in any public space. Instead, he attended a reception held for him in the home of a supporter, at which some thirty people were present. His next engagement, in nearby Davenport, Iowa, was also canceled. Robeson let that one go by. The concert in Albany did finally get authorized, but not before the New York State Supreme Court issued an injunction that forced the city's board of education to allow it. However, the judge ruled that the performance should be limited to a "musical concert and no more." Although veterans' organizations called for a boycott, more than a thousand people, it was reported, turned out to listen to Robeson's program and "warmly applauded" it.

The Peekskill concert of August 1949 was planned on a bigger scale than any of the previous events. An extensive site, the Lakeland Acres picnic grounds, a few miles to the northeast of Peekskill in the adjoining town of Cortlandt, was rented from its owners. The date was set as Saturday, August 27, and the concert was to be an evening event, beginning at 8 p.m. Paul Robeson and Pete Seeger were both scheduled to appear. The proceeds from ticket sales would go to help the Harlem chapter of the Civil Rights Congress.

All of the arrangements for the concert were made by an organization called People's Artists, which had just been launched as a separate endeavor, spun off from a larger, more ambitious organization, People's Songs, that had been formed at the end of December 1945 in Pete Seeger's basement apartment in Greenwich Village. The purpose of People's Songs was to promote the distribution and performance of folk and protest music in the United States. The group produced song sheets and books and staged concerts and hootenannies—the folk equivalent of jam sessions in jazz. Its board of directors included the leading proponents of American folk music—Pete Seeger, Woody Guthrie, Lee Hays, and Alan Lomax. The organization's sponsors included Leonard Bernstein, Oscar Hammerstein, Aaron Copeland, and Paul Robeson.

People's Artists had staged hootenannies in Greenwich Village, but its first big event was the Peekskill concert. Pete Seeger recalled that it was not scheduled to be anything more than a lazy, quiet affair, beer and sandwiches in the open air. He was certainly, as he remembered, very casual about it. He had recently purchased a plot of land about ten miles to the north of Peekskill. He was planning to sing no more than a few songs. On the evening of the concert, he packed his banjo in the car and, together with his sixty-year-old mother, headed south, just as Robeson was heading north from New York City on a train.

On Monday August 22, the *Peekskill Evening Star* carried a number of pieces concerned with the forthcoming concert. The first article, appearing on the newspaper's front page, set the tone. "Robeson Concert Here Aids 'Subversive' Unit." The article played directly on the word *subversive* in a way that was calculated to drive a political wedge between Peekskill residents and the summer visitors.

Over the next few years Americans would hear that word frequently, and everyone, Robeson included, would be defined by it in one way or another. The newspaper described Robeson as "an avowed disciple of Soviet Russia." His outing by Manning Johnson in Washington, D.C., a few months earlier was mentioned, particularly the phrase "the Black Stalin," and Jackie Robinson's comments were repeated once again. In addition, the article mentioned that People's Artists had been branded a Communist front in 1948 by the California Un-American Activities Committee. As for the Civil Rights Congress, it, too, was subversive, "dedicated not to the broader issues of civil liberties, but specifically to the defense of individual Communists and the Communist Party." The article concluded by reminding its readers that in 1947 Peoria's city council had effectively prevented Robeson from performing, implying that Peekskill's citizens should do the same.

The newspaper's editorial, under the banner "The Discordant Note," continued the theme of the front page. Robeson was described as a great talent—"his magnificent voice, which thrilled millions, opened a brilliant career for him"—but politics had poisoned that: "If the Robeson 'concert' this Saturday follows the pattern of its predecessors, it will consist of an unsavory mixture of song and political talk by one who has described Russia as his 'second motherland.'"

The editorial did not advocate any specific action but ended with an open-ended challenge: "The time for tolerant silence that signifies approval is running out. Peekskill wants no rallies that support iron curtains, concentration camps, blockades, and NKVDs, no matter how masterful the décor, nor how sweet the music."

The correspondence section of the same issue ran a letter from Vincent J. Boyle, who was identified simply as a local veterans' leader but who was later revealed, in an interview with the New York State Police, as the "Americanism Chairman" of the American Legion post at nearby Verplanck. Boyle, like the editor, stopped short of calling for a specific action, but his letter went much further than the editorial or the front page in calling for a reaction to "Robeson and his Communistic followers," referring to Communism as an epidemic as serious as the polio epidemic that was sweeping the nation.

To draw readers further into his sense of outrage, Boyle reminded them that the concert was scheduled in the picnic area located directly opposite the town's two main cemeteries: "Yes . . . across the street from the resting place of those men who paid the supreme sacrifice in order to insure our democratic form of government." He then asked readers to join with the American Legion and other veterans' organizations in opposing the appearance of Robeson and his friends, to "leave no doubt in their minds that they are unwelcome around here whether now or in the future." He was not, he stated, "intimating violence" but neither would he rule it out: "I believe that we should give this matter serious consideration and strive to find a remedy that will cope with the situation."

On the day of the concert, the *Peekskill Evening Star* reported that the veterans' organizations had agreed to march to the site in protest. There would be three divisions, although no one was prepared to estimate how many men that might be—they hoped for as many as 5,000. The police, for their part, were making no special arrangements for the picnic grounds. The state police would be sending no extra details, and there would be no Peek-skill city police presence, either.

Robeson had certainly heard the rumors of possible disturbances at the concert. He might also have read the article in that morning's *New York Times* about the telegrams sent from Westchester County residents to the state district attorney's office protesting the growing anti-Robeson hysteria, which they said was being stoked by the *Peekskill Evening Star* and veterans' organizations.

Robeson was worried. When he got to Grand Central Station, before taking the train to Peekskill, he phoned his old friend Helen Rosen, who with her husband Dr. Sam Rosen had a country house in Katonah, about a dozen miles to the east of Peekskill, where Robeson was planning to stay for a few days after the concert.

Rosen, who did not want Robeson to take any chances, phoned her close friend Sid Danis, an accountant who worked in New York City and who also had a holiday home near Peekskill. Danis agreed that he and three other friends would arm themselves with wooden sticks, and meet Robeson at Peekskill station. Helen Rosen also planned to drive there. When Robeson arrived, he got into the backseat in Danis's car and sat between two of Danis's friends. The two-car cavalcade then set off, Rosen's taking the lead. The idea was to drive the back roads, which Danis knew well, to the concert site, and then Robeson would proceed to the stage area.

Despite the potential for trouble—even if only a fraction of the projected 5,000 protesters arrived, that number, together with the almost 2,000 concertgoers who had already bought tickets, would make for a very large crowd—the entire police presence was only eight men, four of whom, from the state police, were on "political detail."

The veterans' march started out from Peekskill around 7:30 p.m. and reached the concert site close to 8 p.m., just before the time that the performance was supposed to begin. The marchers did not disburse, but instead took up positions along the road leading to the entrance of the grounds. Concertgoers who braved the protest line were subjected to vicious verbal abuse, including shouts of "You dirty Jew!" "Lynch the fucking niggers!" and "Hitler was a good man. He should have killed all the Communists and Jews!" Traffic jams, deliberately planned, kept most concert-goers' cars from getting to the site. Many of the cars that did manage to get through were attacked and several of them were overturned.

Only about 200 concertgoers actually made it to the audience area in front of the stage where more than 2,000 chairs had been neatly arranged. A burning cross some six feet high loomed ominously a few hundred yards beyond the stage.

At 8:45 p.m., half an hour after the scheduled start, a large group of protestors advanced to the stage area, some of them yelling, "Where's Robeson?" They began throwing chairs, ripping up the stage and attacking audience members. Probably in an effort to control the situation, someone turned off the overhead lighting, which produced even more panic. Stones and rocks could be heard in the darkness whizzing past the heads of the concertgoers: some were hit, but none seriously. The fighting stopped as both sides headed away from the area, though some protestors remained behind and began burning whatever they could lay their hands on. At 10 p.m., the police turned up with an ambulance and took away three injured concertgoers. The rest of the audience, under police protection, left in a state of utter disbelief.

The few audience members who had managed to get near the stage area thought the concert was expected to go ahead as planned. They had no idea that Robeson and Seeger never reached the picnic grounds, though in Robeson's case, it was not for want of trying. As Sid Danis told the story:

When the car was approximately maybe an eighth of a mile from the picnic grounds, a matter of two or three city blocks in distance, we were stopped by some people . . . who advised us that the crowd of veterans [were] looking into every car . . . and where there were people . . . who were Black, attempts were made and occasionally successful to rock the car so far that [it] turned over on its side and sometimes completely turned over . . . We were informed that Paul Robeson should not be seen by these vigilante groups.

Seeing what was happening, and at this point there seemed no alternative, the car's other occupants tried to convince Robeson that he should sit as far down on the floor as he could manage, while others covered him with their bodies so that he couldn't be seen by anyone peering in. According to Danis, Robeson resisted this tactic. He wanted to face his would-be assailants. He wanted to get to the platform and "speak and voice his feelings."

Instead, Danis turned the car around and drove Robeson back to the train station and the safety of New York City.

The reaction to the riot at the picnic grounds was swift. The Rosens put out a call for a protest meeting to convene on their property. At least 1,500 people brought their cars and sat on the grass listening to speeches from the newly (and hastily) formed Westchester Committee for Law and Order. Robeson should return to Peekskill, the committee decided. Union representatives pledged their support and offered to help protect performers and concertgoers at the rescheduled concert. Meanwhile, at a press conference held at the Hotel Theresa in Harlem, Robeson demanded that Governor Thomas Dewey order an investigation of the riot.

The Civil Rights Congress announced that it would be holding a protest meeting (one leaflet called it a rally against the Klan; another bore the banner "The Swastika Behind the Fiery Cross"), at the Golden Gate Ballroom, on Lenox Avenue, August 30 at 8:30 p.m.

Alvin Stokes, the professional HUAC investigator, who had been at the committee's July hearings most concerned with Robeson's Paris speech, was among the huge crowd that filled the vast ballroom that night. Estimates of the number present vary, but Stokes, who was very meticulous, reckoned that there had to be at least 3,000. Every seat was taken, and people standing lined the walls. At the entrance there were at least 1,000, and Sergeant Davis of the Bureau of Criminal Investigation of the New York State Police, who was also at the rally, reported that 7,000 people thronged the area outside the ballroom.

The rally went on for three hours, with speeches and pep talks from various members of Harlem's African-American community, and music from Pete Seeger. Robeson was the main attraction, and his songs (including "Ol' Man River") and his fiery, defiant speech did not disappoint the enormous gathering. He was not going to be shut down:

> We're going to have our concerts across this land, and we'll see that our women and children are not harmed again . . . we'll protect ourselves . . . I want my friends to know, in the South, in Mississippi, all over the United States, that I'll be there with my concerts, and I'll be in Peekskill too.

Though the focus of the evening's rally was the aborted Peekskill concert, Robeson did not forget the bigger picture and reminded his audience of the great task ahead, a challenge brought into sharp relief by events north of Harlem. "The Negro People say, give us some freedom! Give us some democracy." A torchlight parade down Lenox Avenue completed the evening.

Two days later came the announcement that People's Artists would be organizing a return Peekskill concert, scheduled for the afternoon of September 4, a Sunday. Stephen Szego, the sympathetic owner of a property adjoining the Lakeland picnic grounds, agreed to rent his land out for the concert. The Joint Board of Fur Workers called upon all fur workers in New York City to mobilize and protect the concertgoers—those who were veterans themselves were told to wear their uniforms and decorations. Admission to the concert was free.

As soon as the date was announced, the heat intensified. Signs began to appear in and around Peekskill, on the sides of cars, nailed to trees and in shop fronts—"Wake Up America—Peekskill Did!" In the middle of the night, shots from a .22 rifle were fired into the wall of Szego's house, which was also attacked over the next few nights by arsonists. A newly formed organization, the Associated Veterans' Group, representing fourteen Hudson Valley veterans' organizations and chaired by Vincent Boyle, called an emergency meeting for the evening of September 2, to decide how to respond to Robeson's return—they had already been granted a permit to parade.

On September 3, the day before the scheduled concert, the *Peekskill Evening Star* estimated that as many as 50,000 people might be there: as many as 30,000 marchers were expected to turn out for the parade—"the biggest Americanism demonstration in the history of Peekskill"—and People's Artists, according to this report, were projecting 20,000 concertgoers.

On September 4, the weather was perfect: a cloudless sky and temperatures in the mid-80s Fahrenheit. Veterans from the Fur Workers' Union were the first to leave New York City, assembling at 6 a.m. in Midtown Manhattan. When they got to Peekskill, they and members from as many as fourteen other unions, 2,500 in all, together with some 500 volunteers—most of them veterans—from the surrounding summer residences and camps, formed themselves into a huge ring around the concert site, providing a buffer between the public roads behind them and the parking and stage area in front of them.

Leon Straus, thirty-two years old, a vice-president of the Furriers International Union, decorated for his service as an army lieutenant in World War II and currently in the Infantry Reserve, was in charge of defending the concert. He and some dozen other men organized the young veterans into their positions. Straus was also responsible for protecting Robeson. He provided a truck, on which Larry Brown was to sit at a baby grand piano, under a large oak tree and surrounded by veterans, including Straus. Some would stand; others would sit on the back of the truck. Robeson would take his usual position beside the piano; he would be flanked by two American flags.

The protective circle was in place by 10:30 a.m. The police arrived a half hour later and took up their positions. There were 900 officers altogether, drawn from Westchester County towns and the New York State Police. Around midday, concertgoers began to arrive. The veterans' march, which actually numbered only 1,000 people, had already made its way to the entrance, and these, together with the demonstrators who lined the roads leading to the dirt track into the hollow where the stage had been erected, welcomed the largely New York crowd with volleys of verbal abuse: "Go back to Russia!" "Go Back to Jew York City!"

Robeson was still in Harlem, waiting to be picked up. Heshie Marcus had been selected from the furriers to be one of two guards personally responsible for Robeson's safety. It wasn't easy to find someone who matched Robeson's stature but Marcus certainly did. At six feet, four inches, the 225-pound Marcus was taller than Robeson by an inch or two. He had been warned that there might be trouble, that there were rumors of people armed with rifles who were going to take up positions in the high ground surrounding the concert area. He was not afraid, Marcus said. All he was given in the way of instructions was to sit in the backseat of the car on one side of Robeson while someone else sat on his other side; if necessary he and his partner would push Robeson down on the floor and cover him with their bodies.

Sol Silverman, a member of the furniture makers' union and a large man himself, drove the car that morning from his union headquarters in Manhattan to the pickup address in Harlem. When Marcus looked around, he saw at least two other cars carrying a number of people. Robeson, Marcus recalled, was the only black man to get into his car. He "got in . . . and shook hands all around."

The concert began on time, at 2 p.m. with the singing of the "Star Spangled Banner" and then continued through a program that included two pianists playing short classical pieces, Hope Foye singing Negro spirituals and Pete Seeger concluding the warm-up with a selection of American folk songs.

Then Robeson, who had been told to stay in the car until the coast was clear, stepped onto the truck, took the position that Straus had planned for his best protection, and began to entertain the audience. For his program he had chosen a number of spiritu-als, including "Go Down Moses"; the "Song of the Warsaw Ghetto"; and, of course, "Ol' Man River."

From the stage everything seemed to be going well. Leon Straus, however, had a problem on his hands. Word came to him that concertgoers were being attacked on the road outside the site. Interviewed thirty years after the day of the concert, Straus recalled what happened:

Paul Robeson was given a signal when to end his perform-ance . . . the people [on the platform] responsible . . . told him absolutely what had to be done. They were going to move him out especially and early and secretly before they did anything else . . . Robeson became part of a line of cars, not the first car and not the last car. In a small advance force . . . A number of cars had been prepared to leave the grounds first before the announcement that the concert was over and he would be in this grouping. It was about nine or ten cars.

Robeson was told to lie down in the car. The two union men covered his body and blankets were draped over the passenger windows. The convoy pulled out of the site at speed, all the while pelted by rocks and stones and occasionally hit by bats and clubs. When the caravan regrouped outside of Peekskill to take stock in relative safety, they saw that every car had been damaged. Once the drivers were certain that there were no ambushes ahead, the caravan continued to New York and Harlem, where Robeson was dropped off.

Robeson got away unscathed, even though his situation must have been extremely frightening. Others, however, were not so lucky. Outside the concert area all hell had broken loose. Many would-be concertgoers had been attacked on their way to the area and prevented from getting there. Those who did make it were attacked when they attempted to leave and return home. And according to these victims, their attackers were aided and abetted by the police.

About 150 buses had been hired to take people up to Peekskill from throughout the greater New York City area. Compared with cars, buses were easy targets, and there was considerable damage both to the vehicles and the people.

According to the *New York Herald Tribune*, more than 200 people were injured, six of them seriously. About a third of the buses were attacked and damaged, their windows and windshields smashed into fragments. The newspaper did not estimate the damage to private vehicles, but we know that cars were pelted with large stones and their windows, too, were smashed. Many cars were also viciously rocked and some actually overturned.

In his deposition to the Civil Rights Congress, which he drafted and signed in front of a notary public two days after the concert, Daniel Fanshel explained what happened after he and many others were told by the police to disembark from their bus when they came within sight of the concert area:

> [We] proceeded to file in columns of two past the area where
> a large, hostile crowd was gathered. Many police were lined
> up . . . the crowd was shouting angry, vile, and obscene

epithets . . . we were separated from the couples in front of us. Just then a bottle was thrown from this crowd, missed us . . . At this moment the crowd came surging through the police line. The police became angry and headed toward the Negroes who had been following in columns of two behind us. At that time, one of the mob spit in my wife's face several times and she was unable to see . . . I looked around for a way to escape with her.

Right in back of us, I saw the police turning upon a Negro in a white shirt. Gray-clad policemen were hitting him violently over the head with nightsticks. I saw him fall down.

"The following day, I saw a photograph on the first page of the *New York Herald Tribune* and saw a picture of a Negroe [sic] being hit on the head by a policeman . . . He was identified as one Eugene Bullard. This scene was seen by me; I was only a few feet in front of him holding my wife.

Some of the most terrifying experiences and some of the day's worst injuries happened when the audience was leaving. One of the ugliest scenes and most terrifying ordeals was described by Archie Lipshitz, a passenger on Bus 212, which had brought in residents from the Bronx and Brooklyn.

Once they reached the concert ground, many drivers, fearing an attack, had abandoned their buses, and volunteers commandeered these to get the people out. Bus 212 retained its original driver. Lipshitz described the violence that was inflicted on the concertgoers and also how the police turned a blind eye to it:

As the bus pulled out of the grounds, the police told the bus driver to slow down and, as he slowed down, rocks began to crash against the windows. This went on for about one-half mile, and all the time the police was slowing down the driver and the rocks were being thrown at us, with the police standing by and seeing them throw it.

Marshall Marotta from Brooklyn was also on the bus and also commented that the police did nothing to stop the rock throwing.

Sid Marcus, brother to Heshie, who had been in the car with Robeson, had been asked by Straus to join the security team. Because of his size and strength he was detailed to stand about ten yards from the stage between Robeson and the audience to protect the women and children nearby. When the security detail heard rumors that violence was brewing at the exit, Straus told Marcus to get as many women and children as possible into bus 212. He also told Marcus to sit at the front of the bus in case the attackers tried to board it. As the bus tried to get away, ordered by police to keep to a slow pace, "a big rock came through the right side of the front windshield." Marcus was convinced the rock was aimed at him deliberately—it certainly hit him.

"I noticed the crack in the windshield," Marshall Marotta said. "Sid Marcus started to jump and kick in his seat . . . Sid became uncontrollable. A few of the fellows had to hold him down. Top shirts were used to keep the blood from spitting out. The driver stopped to pick up a policeman on the road. He refused to escort us to the hospital. I noticed two rocks in the bus near the driver's seat."

Marcus's face was shattered with glass from the bus windows. The rock had hit him in the face on his cheekbone with such force that it had dislodged his eye. He was holding it in his hand. He was bleeding profusely and kept losing consciousness. He remembered people screaming at the sight, of women ripping up their slips in order to cover him to stem the bleeding. He then went totally blind and a tremendous sensation of pressure on his brain overtook him. As he put it: "every nerve in my body was on fire . . . these bastards were inside of me with little daggers cutting me up." Marcus was lucky to be alive. After a long course of treatment he was left with only one eye, and his nightmares continued for decades.

He said later, "They were out to kill. There was no question about that, and it wasn't just dirty commie Jew, or nigger loving bastards. There wasn't any of these epithets anymore. These people were there to do a job on us."

The day after the Peekskill concert, Robeson led fifteen witnesses into "a hot, congested room filled with the white glare of photographers' lights." Some of these witnesses were bandaged. They had assembled here in the library of the Council on African Affairs offices on 26th Street in Manhattan for a press conference, to protest against police brutality and to argue that black people had been singled out for punishment.

One of the speakers was Eugene Bullard. He said that he had been knocked down and beaten by state police as he was trying to enter the concert grounds. According to the report in the September 10 *Amsterdam News*, printed with a photograph showing Bullard being beaten (this is the same photograph that Fanshel saw in the *New York Herald Tribune*), Bullard had been attacked by the police after he spat back at a man who had spat at him.

Bullard was an African American in his fifties who had run a successful nightclub in Paris for years. He had also received the Croix de Guerre for his bravery at Verdun and had flown twenty missions in the Lafayette Flying Corps in the First World War— he was the first African American to qualify as a military pilot. He was not someone to accept being spat at without retaliating.

Bullard's injuries were not serious. The newspaper reported that he had sustained several bruises and a cut on his left elbow. Others who attended the concert, especially when they were leaving the performance, were not as fortunate.

Where were the police when they were not attacking the concertgoers or allowing others to attack them? Well, at least during the concert, members of the Bureau of Criminal Investigation of the New York State Police were cruising the parking areas taking down license plate numbers and then checking the car owners' names against lists of what were called "subversive organizations," provided to further their work in identifying Communists. They had done the same on August 27.

Accusations and counteraccusations followed immediately. Newspapers, national, as well as local and black, got swiftly off the mark. So, too, did ordinary citizens, who barraged the authorities with letters and telegrams: The editor of the *Peekskill Evening Star* received a fair share, as did Westchester's district attorney, George Fanelli, and Governor Dewey. Even President Truman received hundreds of telegrams from concerned citizens across the country.

On the same day that Robeson held his press conference at the Council on African Affairs, when he laid the blame for the attack on the police, Fanelli, who had been in charge of law enforcement at the concert, praised the officers, claiming that "there would have been mass killing if they hadn't kept control at the danger center in the concert area." The governor's office stated that Dewey had no comment to make until he received a report from Fanelli and Westchester County Sheriff Fred Ruscoe.

A few days later, the newspapers stated that Governor Dewey had received the report but at this point would only release the text, reserving comment until the superintendent of the New York State Police, John Gaffney, had also reported.

The main points of Fanelli's report, which was printed in full in the *New York Times* on September 8, would not have surprised either his supporters or his critics. Once he had detailed the arrangements he had made and described the day's events, Fanelli lavished praise on the various police forces, commending them on the "patience, tact, and efficiency they displayed under the most trying circumstances." The "damage and trouble" he attributed to teenagers who had no connection with veterans' groups.

On September 11, Superintendent Gaffney produced his version of events, in which he exonerated his force and laid the blame for the "disorders" on both sides, which he described as

Robeson and his followers and "irresponsible youths . . . scattered along roads some distance from the scene of the concert."

Governor Dewey still made no public comment, but three days later, he called Fanelli, Ruscoe and Gaffney to his office for a meeting. Four and a half hours later, the governor held a press conference announcing that he was asking District Attorney Fanelli to conduct a special grand jury investigation, but not before he expressed his own opinion that even though the right of free speech and the right of assembly were inalienable, "the disorders were provoked deliberately by Communist sympathizers of Mr. Robeson." Dewey's instructions to look at Communists as the source of the trouble was, quite clearly, the agenda of the conservative faction in New York State. Two weeks after Dewey spoke, Ralph Gwinn, a Republican congressman whose district included Peekskill, gave a speech in the House titled "The Communist Military Raid on Peekskill," in which he referred to the concertgoers as "invaders . . . armed for trouble."

The grand jury was sworn in at the beginning of October. During the eight months that it took evidence—from almost 250 witnesses, whose testimony filled almost 6,000 pages—other organizations rushed to get their reports in print and out to the general public. First off was "Eyewitness: Peekskill USA," published under the auspices of the Westchester Committee for a Fair Inquiry into the Peekskill Violence.

This pamphlet, a blow-by-blow account of the period between the concert date of August 27 and September 4, 1949, using eyewitness statements and photographs taken at the scene, laid all blame on the protesters' mob and the police who aided and abetted them. The violence they rained on the innocent concertgoers constituted a denial of the latter's civil rights and was, to the authors of the report, clear evidence of a growing fascist tendency in the United States that had to be stopped.

The American Civil Liberties Union (ACLU), in their report "Violence in Peekskill," which came out soon afterward, took a broader view of the riots. ACLU investigators had spent more than a month in the Peekskill area interviewing almost one hundred people, in a quasi-scientific attempt to canvas as representative a cross-section of the community as they could.

In coming to their conclusions, the ACLU investigators stated that they were convinced that the rioters were acting out of a sense of patriotic duty—that they were doing what the federal authorities expected of them when it came to denying voice to a political and dangerous minority—Communists—and that the nation would applaud them for their actions.

With this in mind, the ACLU authors stressed that there was an important difference between those who had protested Robeson's appearance and those who had violently attacked the concertgoers. The former had been voicing their opposition to Communism; the latter, who had caused the trouble and inflicted the injuries, the authors argued, were driven by anti-Semitism, directed mostly at the Jewish summer residents. The local press was not without blame: They had inflamed "Peekskill residents to a mood of violence." As for the issue of protection, this, too, was complicated: The state police, in the authors' estimation, had done their job while "the county police fraternized with the rioters." The concertgoers were entirely blameless. They had been the victims of planned violence.

The ACLU report was virtually ignored by the American press. More than half a year later, in the middle of June 1950, the grand jurors wound up their investigation of the Peekskill riots and filed a 9,000-word statement. Its contents were just what might have been expected given that Attorney General Fanelli had been in charge of the hearings and Governor Dewey had put the issue of Communism at the heart of what he wanted to see investigated.

There were two underlying causes of the outbreak of disturbances at both concerts, the jurors concluded. One was "the growing awareness on the part of the American people of the dangers of Communism to the United States." The second and more specific cause was the statements Robeson had made during the year leading up to that summer—"These statements . . . derogatory to his native land and favorable to Communist Russia," the report said, "served to emphasize in the public mind Robeson's position as a Communist leader . . . Paul Robeson in 1949 became a symbol of Communism itself."

Unlike the ACLU's report, the grand jury's dismissed the suggestion that the violence had been planned and found nothing inflammatory about the *Peekskill Evening Star*'s comments. These only "served to bring to the surface and intensify the latent sentiment against Communism which already existed in the community." Neither had the violence anything to do with anti-Semitism or "anti-Negro" sentiments, but instead had grown out of resentment of Communism and of Robeson as its spokesman. By contrast, the "Communist" organizers' strategy had been "to foment racial and religious hatred." New York's *Daily Worker* had also inflamed this sentiment.

Violence, the grand jury concluded, was un-American, unwarranted, and lawless. The perpetrators should be subject to the laws of the land. But the target of this violence, Communism and its ideological ambitions, was the real threat and nothing could mitigate that conclusion. The grand jury's report made this very clear to its readers:

On that day [September 4] Westchester County was used by the Communist Party as a proving ground to test its machinery for mobilizing its forces, manipulating public opinion, and, more important, for rehearsing its strong-arm forces . . . the shock troops of a revolutionary force which is controlled by a foreign power and committed to methods and ultimate ends incompatible with our constitutional system.

In Robeson's FBI file there is an internal memo that offers an intriguing hint as to where the grand jurors might have got the idea that the Communists had orchestrated the racial hatred displayed that day and that the security team assembled by the concert organizers was a "quasi-military force." The memo, from the special agent in charge in Detroit to J. Edgar Hoover, refers to the appearance in the Detroit office of someone (name blacked out) bearing copies of two reports, "Inquiry Concerning Quasi-Military Forces Organized by the Communists" and "Inquiry on Racial Incitations Practiced by Communists." The reports had been commissioned by New York State for the grand jury. Their author, a "trustworthy Legionnaire with several years top level communist experience," had been paid $200 a week for the six-week period it took to complete them. They had been released by the American Legion's National Americanism Commission, a pillar of the Legion's educational program, and were being distributed to American Legion posts throughout the United States, and the caller wished the FBI to have the copies he'd carried into the office.

Both documents relied heavily on quotations from prominent American Communists and spokespeople for the Communist International. And whatever else one may say about them, both reports were founded on the belief that one could not make sense of the Peekskill riots without understanding the history of Communism within the United States and in the Soviet Union. In the report on "racial incitation," for example, the author is at pains to point out that Moscow had been using the issue of African Americans since the time Comintern had lent its support to the idea of a free Black Republic in the south.

The similarity between the reports' conclusions and the grand jury's make it clear that the latter relied very heavily on the former. There is some internal evidence about the author's identity; most likely he was Karl Baarslag, who had spent most of the interwar period as a union organizer for radio officers. In the course of this work he became very familiar with Communism, only to become one of the most fervent and important anti-Communists in the postwar period.

In 1947, he was hired by the American Legion to head the Sub-Committee on Subversive Activities, a new department within the National Americanism Commission. His duties included publishing a monthly newsletter, *Summary of Trends and Developments Exposing the Communist Conspiracy*, which in 1952 became the biweekly *Firing Line*.

In his unpublished autobiography, Baarslag explained how he further developed a system, first learned during his time in Naval Intelligence, of recording the activities of Communist interests in the United States. He boasted that he had amassed some 60,000 cards on which were entered references to such activities. For Robeson, he proudly recorded, he had more than 250 such citations, as he called them. Baarslag's associations with the grand jury in the Peekskill case, the FBI and, in time, Senator Joe McCarthy, and his knowledge of Communism made him a key and highly respected figure in a wide network of private intelligence gathering on suspected Communists.

Unlike the ACLU's, the Peekskill grand jury's conclusions were reported in the American mainstream press, under headlines such as "Robeson Riot Red Rehearsal" in the *Chicago Herald Tribune* and "Jury Warns on Reds' Rise" in the *New York Times*. And that was about it. As far as the press was concerned, there was little more to say. Peekskill soon disappeared into the recesses of collective memory.

Less than ten days after the grand jury's report, Americans found that they had something new to worry about, of greater significance than Peekskill, though not on an altogether different theme. On June 25, they learned, North Korea had invaded South Korea, and on June 27, President Truman pledged naval and air support to South Korea. The Korean War was under way.

# PART III

# JIM CROW'S WORLD

# 9

# Strike Three

From the publication of the American Civil Liberties Union report to the New York State Grand Jury presentment on the Peekskill riots, a period roughly covering the first half of 1950, Paul Robeson's name hardly appeared in the US mainstream or African-American press. That relative silence, which one might think came as a welcome relief to Robeson, was shattered on several stinging occasions. Although white commentators were giving him a wide berth, one powerful voice from the African-American political community was reminding him and others who cared to listen that Robeson was not off the hook.

Asa Philip Randolph was a few years older than Robeson and, like him, the son of a minister in the African Methodist Episcopal Church. When he was in his early twenties, Randolph, already a committed member of the Socialist Party of America and an ardent follower of W.E.B. Du Bois' ideas on the situation of African Americans in the United States, moved from his home in Florida to New York City.

In 1917, Randolph, together with Chandler Owen, a close friend and fellow Socialist, launched the *Messenger*, a radical monthly magazine, published in Harlem, that advocated a wide range of basic rights for African Americans, including the right to equal treatment under the law, equal employment opportunities, and the right to organize into unions. The magazine added a powerful Socialist voice to the African-American political landscape, accusing America of denying black citizens the rights that white ones had and took for granted, and for brutalizing them through lynchings and race riots.

The *Messenger* was part of the Harlem Renaissance, that great flowering of African-American cultural life in New York during the 1920s and 1930s. But even though it published early essays and stories by black writers who would achieve fame beyond Harlem, the magazine suffered from financial problems and finally folded in 1928.

By then, however, Randolph had become more directly involved in another cause: labor organization, an issue that had interested him early on and was frequently discussed in the *Messenger*'s pages. In 1925, a group of porters who were employed by the Pullman Company approached Randolph, hoping to convince him to head a new union, the Brotherhood of Sleeping Car Porters. It was the policy of the Pullman Company, which built and operated railway sleeping cars in the United States, to hire only African Americans as porters. At the time of the meeting between the porters and Randolph, Pullman was the largest employer of black men in the United States, with more than 12,000 porters on its payroll.

Randolph accepted the challenge and became the union's first president. He placed the *Messenger* at the union's service, using its pages to lambast the company's policy toward its black employees. The battle Randolph had let himself in for proved to be bitter and protracted. The Pullman Company had earned a reputation as a tough and unyielding negotiator. The notorious 1894 Pullman Strike, a nationwide dispute over a cut in wages announced unilaterally by the company, had been broken up by US troops and marshals and many strikers were killed or wounded.

Ten years after Randolph took charge of the union, it finally succeeded in becoming the legally mandated voice of its members. Two years later, after years of intransigence, the Pullman Company agreed for the first time to negotiate a contract improving the terms and conditions of employment for sleeping car porters. This victory not only helped the porters but also inspired black workers in other industries to unionize and press for better conditions.

Randolph's work with the porters' union won him national fame: One journalist hailed him as the "major Negro prophet in the realm of labor organization." In 1936, Randolph and other African-American leaders joined forces to launch the National Negro Congress, an organization composed of disparate trade union, religious, and civic groups committed to militant grassroots activism.

Randolph served as the organization's president, but at its annual convention in 1940, he turned on the delegates, accusing them, especially those who were members of the Communist Party or sympathetic to their ideology, of selling out to Moscow. "I consider the Communists," he stated in a newspaper interview, "a definite menace and a danger to the Negro people and labor because of their rule-or-ruin and disruptive tactics in the interests of the totalitarian Soviet Union." Randolph's convention speech effectively ended his ties with the organization, and he refused to stand for office again. In a couple of years' time, Max Yergan would take his place.

That speech heralded a new chapter in Randolph's political career; he had become a vehement and unrelenting anti-Communist, but without abandoning his belief in grassroots activism. While retaining his association with the Brotherhood of Sleeping Car Porters, Randolph fixed his sights on discrimination in the military and defense industries, in 1941 launching the March on Washington Movement. Though the movement did not actually lead to a march on Washington, through it Randolph managed to step up the pressure for desegregation of the US military.

Randolph's interest in the issue was not new. In 1918, an editorial, probably written by Randolph, in the *Messenger* had bluntly proclaimed, "No intelligent Negro is willing to lay down his life for the United States as it now exists. Intelligent Negroes have now reached the point where their support of the country is conditional." Now, with the Second World War over and without any sign from above that segregation of the military would be abolished, Randolph resumed the rhetoric of civil disobedience.

Knowing that Truman's chances in the 1948 presidential election depended on the black vote, Randolph stepped up the rhetoric on what African Americans might or might not do if the military was not desegregated. In a visit to the White House in March 1948, Randolph reported to Truman that he sensed the mood among African Americans was hesitant when it came to joining the service. "In my recent travels around the country," he said, "I found Negroes not wanting to shoulder a gun to fight for democracy abroad unless they get democracy at home."

When, several weeks later, Randolph, as national treasurer of an organization called the Committee Against Jim Crow, which he helped to found, testified in front of the Senate Armed Forces Committee, he told its members in no uncertain terms that he would lead a civil disobedience campaign against a military draft unless racial segregation and discrimination were eradicated, and that he would personally "advise Negroes to refuse to fight as slaves for a democracy they cannot possess and cannot enjoy."

When Wayne Morse, the Republican senator from Oregon, reminded him that in a time of war such action would be considered treasonous, Randolph answered that that would be a price worth paying in return for equal rights. When Morse pressed him further on whether he would take such a stand if America were attacked, Randolph ducked and answered simply that it was time the government made fundamental changes.

One might have expected Randolph to sympathize with, or at least to understand, Robeson's Paris speech as it had been reported, but actually it had annoyed him to no end. Randolph explained, "The Communists would sacrifice America, the Negro people and heaven and earth for Soviet Russia." That Robeson was a Communist sympathizer was not the problem: Randolph insisted that Communists had the right to be heard like anyone else—or, as he put it in a 1947 article, "No free speech, freedom of the press or assembly for republicans or democrats, if Communists are denied the same rights."

Randolph, unlike some of the other African-American leaders, had not lashed out at Robeson in the days immediately following the Paris speech. Indeed, it would seem that he held back his opinions, publicly at least, until after the Peekskill riots, when he wrote a letter to the editor of the *New York Times*, published on October 9, 1949. The purpose of this letter was to explain to as wide an audience as possible that Peekskill and what had happened there had nothing to do with "the cause of the Negro and his fight for liberation." The rioting had not been racial. Those who had tried to stop the concert—the American Legion and the Veterans of Foreign Wars, aided and abetted by a police force that at best had turned a blind eye to what Randolph called "a travesty upon democracy and an unutterable disgrace and outrage"—were, he argued, demonstrating against Communism and Robeson.

At this point, Randolph left Peekskill behind and turned instead on Robeson himself, taking as his point of departure the Paris speech. Robeson, he said, echoing other commentators, "had no warrant to speak as the voice of the Negro people of America." But Randolph did not argue for loyalty, as had so many other black leaders who had distanced themselves from Robeson. Randolph himself had said that in his view, African-American men would not lay down their lives unconditionally for the United States—a point that was not so different from Robeson's.

Instead, he took Robeson to task for daring to speak for African Americans without having earned the right to do so. "The right to become the responsible voice of an oppressed group," Randolph maintained, had to be earned the hard way by struggling beside that group for a long time. The right could not be appropriated overnight.

Randolph then told the readers that although Robeson was a great artist, to be sure, famous chiefly through his work on the stage and in the movies, he was "practically unknown to the

Negro liberation movement as a seasoned participant." In his association with left-wing movements he had had "little, if any, contact with the Negro masses." In short, Randolph concluded, Robeson was a "Johnny-come-lately to the cause of the Negro."

Not long after this letter was published, Randolph spoke at a meeting at the Second Baptist Church in Los Angeles, where he again referred to the Paris speech and repeated that Robeson had no authority to speak on behalf of African Americans. Randolph took this opportunity to explain further how Robeson had disqualified himself: He had spent very little time with African Americans, preferring the company of Europeans.

Several months later, in February 1950, Randolph was on a nationwide tour spreading his "gospel of anti-Communism," summed up in the phrase "Communism, Number One Enemy of the Negro People." In Richmond, Virginia, in front of a largely black audience at the Ebenezer Baptist Church, he once again attacked Robeson. This time he didn't simply refer to the Paris speech; instead, he made it the focal point of his address billed for all to see as "Should Negroes Fight for the USA in a War With Soviet Russia?" Reinforcing the characterization of Robeson that he had been shaping in earlier remarks, he added that Robeson was further disqualified to speak for African Americans because he was a wealthy man and had not had to struggle. Pointing his finger directly at Robeson, Randolph answered his own question: "Anyone who says the American Negro would not fight in a war with Russia simply does not know the Negro."

On this speaking tour, Randolph spread his anti-Communist and anti-Robeson message wherever he went. He was not alone in refusing to let the Paris speech rest. He was joined by the *Negro Digest*, a monthly magazine modeled on the format of *Reader's. Digest* and the first magazine of its kind to target an African-American audience. The first issue had appeared in 1942, carrying a wide variety of articles, essays, and poetry; there was one intriguing recurring article, "If I Were a Negro," that the editors invited prominent white people to write.

The cover of its March 1950 issue was mostly taken up by a candid photograph of Robeson singing to an audience. To the right of his head was the title "Paul Robeson: Today's Most Controversial Negro."

Regular readers of the magazine knew what this was all about, for in the February issue the editors had prepared them for what they billed as the highlight of next month's publication. "No issue affecting the Negro problem in the last quarter century," they announced, "has aroused as much controversy as famed singer Paul Robeson's political stand as regards the cold war between the US and Russia. Although it is almost a year since Robeson declared in Paris that Negroes would not fight against the Soviets in any war, the verbal battle over his statement continues."

Departing from its normal *Reader's Digest* practice of mostly reprinting material that had appeared elsewhere, for the March 1950 issue the editors had specifically invited two distinguished African Americans to debate Robeson's Paris speech: W.E.B. Du Bois for and Walter White, the head of the NAACP, against.

Neither man needed an introduction within the broad African-American community. Du Bois was not only a friend of Robeson's—they had known each other since the 1920s—but had been a member of the American delegation to the World Peace Congress in Paris and had been present when Robeson spoke.

Du Bois was under no illusions: He knew that these facts had associated him in the public mind not only with Robeson but also with Communism and that he had already paid a price for this. On April 29, 1949, Martin Jenkins, president of Morgan State College, a black college in Baltimore, Maryland, withdrew an invitation he had made to Du Bois in late March and, ironically, confirmed the day after Robeson's speech, to deliver the commencement address to the graduating class. In his notice of cancellation, Jenkins pointed out that Du Bois, although one of

America's greatest black scholars, had not only appeared in Paris with Robeson but afterward had failed to "condemn his treasonable statement . . . If you were to speak at Morgan State College . . . it would give the appearance of our being in sympathy with your general views," Jenkins explained. He concluded, "I think that Mr. Robeson's views and approach are to be severely condemned."

Du Bois began his piece for the *Negro Digest* by describing the scene in Paris on that April evening in 1949 when Robeson entered the auditorium and all present rose to their feet and cheered. He pointed out that although Robeson was there among great and famous people—he singled out Picasso and Joliot-Curie—"none of these received so tumultuous a tribute." Du Bois then offered readers his own interpretation of Robeson's words that evening: "And so he declared that American Negro victims of color prejudice, serfdom, slavery and race hate, if in their right minds, would never fight a country which alone among nations opposes these crimes against civilization."

As far as Du Bois could see, the US mainstream press and a large number of African-American leaders had ignored what was being said at the Paris Peace Congress. Instead they had focused exclusively on Robeson's words, repeated them endlessly and contemptuously, dismissing them as dangerous and treasonous. At no point had they debated their meaning. Du Bois added that when he wrote to several white and black newspapers expressing his absolute agreement with Robeson's position, his words were not reported—certainly not by the mainstream papers. The illusion had been created that Robeson stood alone in his views and isolated from the people he claimed to speak for.

Du Bois claimed that Robeson had more support among African Americans than was being admitted and said that the effort to gag him would fail. The American Legion, Du Bois maintained, knew that, and it was for this reason that they had tried to stop him appearing in Peekskill. Robeson's voice would rise above those who preferred to hear him sing and not talk, because, as Du

Bois wrote in closing his essay, it stood for "Peace and Free Speech to Fight War and Poverty."

White, who had been in the vanguard of Robeson's critics and who had provided the State Department with information meant to discredit Robeson, diplomatically did not engage with the Paris speech. Instead, he began by portraying Robeson as a lost soul, as someone who has undergone fundamental changes in "his mental and emotional processes." Gone, White lamented, were those heady days of "gaiety and intellectual stimulation": Robeson had now surrendered to the "vagaries, reversals, contradictions and plain downright dishonesties of the Communist Party line." Given this opening, it is perhaps not surprising that the bulk of White's essay attacked the Soviet Union and the American Communist Party, directly and through the supposed opinions of Robeson, though these were never spelled out. White insisted that African Americans would "be insane to cast their lot with the Communists." As for Robeson, White concluded that he was "wrong, naive and unrealistic in believing and advocating that communism can cure the ills [of capitalist exploitation]."

There is no way of knowing how this debate was received, but it is interesting that, as Du Bois outlined and predicted, African-American leaders—and White was right in the forefront of them—did not want to engage directly with Robeson, even when they were given, as White was, adequate space and time to do so.

What happened in these pages of the *Negro Digest* was typical. Robeson could not shake off the Paris speech, and the Peekskill episode, though Robeson's antagonists had been widely condemned for their violence, did not help matters. As the widely reported New York State Grand Jury presentment put it, the Peekskill riot was an expression of the country's reaction to Communism. The fact that it got out of hand did not change what had caused it in the first place.

The depth of feelings aroused by Robeson came to the surface over and over again. On the afternoon of Sunday, March 12,

1950—in the same month that the *Negro Digest* debate appeared, the television program *Today with Mrs. Roosevelt* aired as usual. Over the years since Franklin Roosevelt's death, Eleanor Roosevelt had made a name for herself internationally as a champion of human rights and of institutions promoting them, especially the United Nations. Early in February 1950, the National Broadcasting Company (NBC) aired for the first time a half hour discussion program hosted by Mrs. Roosevelt. Her first guests included J. Robert Oppenheimer and Albert Einstein (who appeared via a film), who were invited to discuss the hydrogen bomb and atomic energy. The reviews of this pilot program were generally positive, and future broadcasts, which most commentators agreed would make a useful bridge between popular and specialist programming, were welcomed.

At the end of the March 12 broadcast, an announcement was made that the following week Mrs. Roosevelt would take as her topic "The Position of the Negro in American Political Life" and that a number of prominent African Americans, including Paul Robeson, would be appearing. The idea was to give the audience a taste of the different views on this subject held respectively by Democrats, Republicans, and Progressives—the third party that in 1948 had run Henry Wallace, Roosevelt's vice president during the war years, against Truman and Dewey in the presidential election. On the show, the Progressive Party would be represented by Robeson.

As soon as the program was announced, there was a public eruption. NBC's viewer mail survey clocked all incoming letters and phone calls concerning all of its broadcasts, and as the letters came in over the next few days, it became clear that the overwhelming number who wrote protested Robeson's appearance; a smaller proportion of those who phoned in felt the same way. By far, most of the protests came from individuals representing veterans' organizations, especially the American Legion and the Veterans of Foreign Wars—the groups implicated in the Peekskill riots.

he Progressive Party. Robeson, however, had a few words to
ay, and although they were not widely reported in the main-
tream press, they appeared in the *New York Times* on March 16.
Robeson denounced the company, but not Mrs. Roosevelt—"I
m sure," he was reported as saying, "that all Americans who
vork for these goals [civil liberties] will resent the arbitrary action
f NBC and will raise their voices in protest."

As for Mrs. Roosevelt, she had little to say on the matter in the
ress apart from remarking that many people had "misunder-
:ood" the nature of her program, but she did not explain this
:mark any further. She later added that the purpose of the
rogram was to give equal time to the invited speakers. The
iisunderstanding stemmed from the fact that some people
iought Robeson would be given unlimited time. Had the
rogram gone ahead on March 19 as originally envisioned, it
vould have been Robeson's first major television appearance.
lowever, needless to say, the program was never rescheduled.

n appearance on Eleanor Roosevelt's program was just one of
.any invitations that Robeson had accepted during the first half
f 1950. He traveled widely in the country, speaking at functions,
tending rallies, joining picket lines as far away as Baltimore,
hicago, and Los Angeles.

Then, on May 28, a day after he had picketed in front of the
Vhite House, Robeson boarded a plane in New York for London.
t London Airport, immigration officers allowed him to land
.ly on the condition that he would leave the country within one
eek. He told the authorities that he had a return ticket for June
MI5 learned of his arrival and Special Branch of the Metropoli-
n Police reported that three men, "none of whom was
cognized," met Robeson at the airport; the four left in two cars
r the Euston Hotel.

Robeson was in London as a guest of the British Peace Commit-
:, a national organization that had been established in the wake
the Paris Peace Congress in April 1949 to continue the work of

Whether it was on the basis of this reaction or
after the March 12 broadcast and announceme
week's lineup, a meeting was held between the pro
ers, Elliott Roosevelt—Mrs. Roosevelt's son—an
They decided, or so it was reported, to postpon
That same day, Charles Denny, general counsel f
a statement confirming the decision and statin;
agreed that Mr. Robeson's appearance would lead
derstanding and confusion, and no good purpose
in having him speak on the issue of Negroes in
Roosevelt and Martin Jones, though they were a:
ment by several newspapers, added nothin
announcement.

Veterans groups used the pages of the Hearst-c
*Journal-American*, which had broken the stor
cancellation, to voice their approval of the decisi
number, the state commander of New York's A1
alleged that Robeson's appearance "would hav
and bigotry."

Nevertheless, there were also protests at the N
Almost half of those who phoned the network c
the action. Charles Baldwin, executive secretary
sive Party, reacted with a harshly worded stater
"When the owners of a great radio chain," he
pretext of a few protests to impose censorshi]
attempt to silence the voice of a great Ameri
behalf of civil rights for his people, then the der
all Americans are placed in jeopardy."

Baldwin demanded in a telegram to Elliott tha
rescheduled and that he should be advised im
new date of broadcast. The Progressive Part
release to that effect on the Sunday that the s]
aired, but, realistically, there was little hope of a

Baldwin's reactions, not surprisingly, appea
black newspapers. The mainstream press repor

the Partisans of Peace on the home front. The British Peace Committee was hosting a meeting of the World Peace Movement on May 30–31 at a hotel in Bloomsbury to plan for the Second World Peace Congress, provisionally scheduled to be held in Italy in October. Robeson would be attending that meeting, representing the American delegation along with O. John Rogge, leader of the Trenton Six defense, who had also been in Paris in the previous year.

The UK government was concerned about the meeting, as they believed it to be another ploy in what they cynically described as the Soviet Peace Offensive. The Foreign Office considered what steps they could take to refuse entry to some of the delegates. A list of fifteen people of interest was compiled, and Robeson's name was among them. They agreed that his visit would be seen as being of "propaganda value to the Communists," but no good grounds for his exclusion existed. Besides, they added, "a howl about racial discrimination would probably outweigh any advantages in excluding him."

The meetings took place as planned. About two dozen dignitaries, from countries as far apart as China and Finland, were present. Missing, although not because the UK authorities did not allow him in, was Frédéric Joliot-Curie, who had only recently been removed from his post as chairman of the French Atomic Energy Commission because of his political views. Aside from discussing how to further the aim of international peace, the delegates came to the firm decision that the Second World Congress should take place in Genoa beginning on October 15.

On the evening following this meeting, June 1, the British Peace Committee hosted a peace demonstration at Lincoln's Inn Fields. Robeson was at the top of the bill and was given a rapturous reception as he spoke of peace and exploitation and sang favorites like "Joe Hill" and "Ol' Man River." The *Daily Worker*, which covered the evening's "Cry for Peace" in graphic detail on its first and third pages, announced that the "surging throng" was estimated at 20,000. The Foreign Office report put the figure at a sober 6,000, and Cominform's official magazine upped it to 25,000. Whatever the size of the crowd—and photographs of the evening do show a throng of people jammed into the square— apart from the *Daily Worker*'s story the event went largely unreported in the British press.

As he had told the UK immigration officers he would, Robeson boarded a plane for his return to New York on the day after the Lincoln's Inn Fields demonstration. He must have been looking forward to continuing his work for international peace.

That peace, though, came to a shattering end when President Truman ordered air and sea forces to aid South Korea after it had been invaded from the north. On June 28, 1950, 18,000 people attended a rally at Madison Square Garden where Robeson was the keynote speaker. He did not hold back in his denunciation of Truman and his decision to sacrifice the lives of American airmen and sailors for what Robeson and other critics saw as a corrupt puppet government in Seoul. But Robeson was less intent on criticizing American foreign policy than on reminding his audience what this commitment meant to African Americans, and on that issue, he was absolutely clear. He cried out from the podium: "I have said before, and I say it again, that the place for the Negro people to fight for their freedom is here at home—in Georgia, Mississippi, Alabama and Texas—in the Chicago ghetto, and right here in New York's Stuyvesant Town!"

Robeson often spent his nights in New York staying with Harold (Gig) and Bert McGhee, fast family friends for a quarter of a century, in their apartment on Manhattan's Upper East Side. The night of July 26 was, according to information received at the New York field office of the State Department's Internal Security Division, one such occasion. At 7:30 p.m., special agents Clare and O'Hanley spoke to someone at the McGhee apartment, but that person, a woman, did not know whether Robeson was staying over. For the next five and one-quarter hours the special agents remained outside the apartment until Mr. McGhee arrived home. Clare and O'Hanley questioned him before he entered the apartment, but all they could get out of him was that Robeson had left in the morning before he himself had arisen and that he had no idea what his guest's plans were.

Next day, Clare and O'Hanley called in at the offices of the Council on African Affairs looking for Robeson and found instead Louise Patterson, who was the Council's secretary and the wife of William Patterson. She was not able to help them but next day, July 28, she phoned the field office at 3:30 p.m. to tell O'Hanley that Robeson was in the office and could be seen in half an hour. O'Hanley and special agent Richard Sabra hurried to the Council's offices and arrived at the appointed time.

O'Hanley now takes up the story. "Robeson had with him Nathan Witt, his attorney . . . I told Robeson that I was there at the request of the passport division to ask that he surrender to me his passport. Without replying, Robeson looked at Witt, who said, 'It's all right, Paul, they can do that to people they don't like' . . . Robeson said he did not have the passport with him but that he would have it for me at 10 o'clock the following morning . . . [he] again gave his assurance that the passport would be there at 10 o'clock the following morning."

At that, the "two flatfeet" headed back to their field office. O'Hanley again: "I was at the Council on African Affairs . . . at 9:50 a.m. on Saturday, July 29, but it was not until 10:15 that one W. A. Hunton came in and said that he had a message for me to call Mr. Witt at his home . . . Witt told me "Mr. Robeson and I gave it further thought and decided that we would not surrender the passport, and leave the next move up to you."

Several days later, the State Department canceled Robeson's passport and told immigration and customs officials to stop him if he tried to leave the country.

Strike three.

# 10

# But Not Out

The FBI eagle eye caught the small notice in the New York *Daily News* of November 27, 1950. Others would have missed it altogether, but the New York special agent read in Ed Sullivan's regular tittle-tattle column "Little Old New York" that Paul Robeson was booked on the Cunard liner *Media* for Southampton. He fired off a memo to J. Edgar Hoover, but not before he'd investigated the matter further. After all, the FBI had Robeson under surveillance and their vigilance had intensified once the State Department had informed other agencies that he could not leave the country.

The FBI agent contacted Clare, the special agent who had gone to the McGhees' apartment to demand Robeson's passport. Clare checked the passenger list; it was true that someone called Robeson had booked passage, but his first name was Peter; he had been born in Canada and now lived in England. Customs officials confirmed that Paul Robeson was not on the ship.

To make sure that Robeson's status had not changed, Clare spoke to the Passport Division of the State Department. Nothing had changed, he was told: "Under no conditions would *Paul Robeson* be issued a passport." And they meant it. It would be almost eight years before the State Department reversed their decision. For now, they could not even be drawn to give a reason for their action. They were prepared to state merely that Robeson's actions abroad had not always been in the country's best interests. Only later would the real motive for Robeson's containment be revealed.

~

Although the term "McCarthyism" has come to signify in the popular mind the era of political repression in the United States that lasted for much of the 1940s and 1950s, the state machinery of this repression did not come from or indeed have anything to do with Senator Joseph McCarthy. It had been created and put into action across a broad range of governmental agencies; one of the first of these was put into place on March 21, 1947, when President Truman signed Executive Order 9835. This presidential directive established what came to be known as the Truman Loyalty Program, a set of procedures intended to insure that current employees and applicants for positions in the civil service were loyal to the United States. Information affirming a person's loyalty was drawn from a variety of sources, including FBI files. Evidence of disloyalty, which was also to be taken into account, included "membership in, affiliation with or sympathetic association with any foreign or domestic organization, association, movement, group or combination of persons, designated . . . as totalitarian, fascist, communist or subversive."

The responsibility for designating which organizations were disloyal to the country fell to the attorney general, Tom Clark. The compilation of these became known as the Attorney General's List of Subversive Organizations. Former attorney general Francis Biddle had drawn up an earlier list in 1942, during the Roosevelt administration, but Clark's differed from it in significant ways. It was almost twice as long as Biddle's and, reflecting changed political circumstances, consisted mainly of Communist or Communist "front" organizations.

A thick blanket of secrecy, the details of which have only recently emerged, covered the whole process behind Clark's list—how it was compiled, the criteria used in its compilation and the reasons why none of the listed organizations were notified that their names had been added. Today it is clear that both the FBI and the US Justice Department committed huge resources to producing the list and that the FBI was the sole agency that provided information for it, but many other key questions remain unanswered.

Though some officials, such as J. Parnell Thomas, chairman of HUAC, branded Clark's efforts as farcical—Parnell was reported as saying that his committee knew of more than 300 Communist front organizations that Clark did not mention—most press coverage welcomed the list. And even though Communist and Communist-front organizations made up only part of it, they and only they were very quickly equated with the word *subversive*. As an example of the extent to which *communist* and *subversive* had become fused, and that fusion made authoritative, one can cite the report that heralded Attorney General Clark's list when it was published in Washington, D.C.'s *Times-Herald*. Of the dozen organizations the list highlighted, all but one of them, the Ku Klux Klan, were, according to the article, Communist fronts. Among them were the National Negro Congress, American Youth for Democracy, the Civil Rights Congress, the Joint Anti-Fascist Refugee Committee, and the Veterans of the Abraham Lincoln Brigade. "This partial list of anti-American groups," the article continued, "fronts, fifth column units, and so on, has now been issued, and it is official, and the list constitutes a guide to all loyal Americans who want to combat these subversives in proper American ways."

The attorney general's list was not meant for any use beyond that stipulated in Truman's executive order. However, once the full list was published in the *Federal Register*, in March 1948, it provided the public with a blueprint definition of *subversive*, and that definition was "Communist." And once the list was public, there was no control over who would use the list or how. As the historian Robert Goldstein put it, the attorney general's list amounted to an official blacklist—one that was absolutely author-itative, since its author was the government's chief lawyer: "Once published [it] was quickly adopted by a wide variety of public and private groups, including state and local governments, the mili-tary, defense contractors, hotels, the Treasury Department . . . and the State Department (in making passport and deportation deci-sions), to deny employment or otherwise discriminate against

listed organizations or persons alleged to be affiliated with them."
To that catalog can be added the press, when seeking background
for stories about individuals and groups, and the FBI itself, whose
files, after 1947, incorporated the list into the reports of its own
surveillances of individuals and organizations.

Although the attorney general's list had an air of authority, it
did not have any legal or instrumental status. It was entirely up
to the users of the list to decide how to make it serve their
purposes. For example, in late 1950, the Columbia Broadcasting
System began to demand proof of patriotism from more than
2,500 of its regular employees. Individuals were asked to fill in a
simple form, answering three questions regarding their political
affiliations and associations with a "yes" or a "no." The third
question, regarding association with subversive organizations,
directed the individual to the back of the form, where the attorney general's list was reproduced for guidance as to what
constituted "subversive."

After the list was published, many left-wing speakers who
had found on college campuses a sympathetic platform for their
ideas saw their appearances being barred and cancelled, on the
grounds that they were somehow associated with a "subversive" organization.

Two years after it had been published in the *Federal Register*,
the list was given legislative teeth. On September 23, 1950,
Congress passed the Internal Security Act, or McCarran Act,
named for its author, Pat McCarran, the seventy-four-year-old
Democratic senator from Nevada, a veteran of Capitol Hill who
had first been elected in 1933. It was not an entirely original piece
of legislation; it was based on an earlier proposal drafted by Richard Nixon, then a Republican congressman from California, and
Nixon's colleague Karl Mundt, a Republican from South Dakota.
Their bill had passed the House but not the Senate.

Despite the fact that Truman disliked McCarran's bill and,
indeed, vetoed it, it passed easily through Congress. The first
significant piece of anti-Communist legislation on the statute

books since the outbreak of the Korean War, the act required the American Communist Party and its affiliates to register with the attorney general's office, and further required that a Subversive Activities Control Board be established whose job it was to identify those groups in the United States which, in the board's estimation, were Communist front organizations and subject to surveillance. Here, as it did on the attorney general's list, *subversive* meant Communist, pure and simple.

And *registration* meant a far-reaching and detailed disclosure of the names of the officers of the organization in question, its finances, operations, means of disseminating information, and the names and addresses of all of its members. As Karl Mundt put it, registration would "bring out of the black night of seductive secrecy the operations and activities of those conspiring to change the American way of life by stealth."

On April 22, 1953, the Subversive Activities Control Board filed a petition to have the Council on African Affairs register with the attorney general as a Communist front, one of twelve organizations (and among those, one of three black organizations) ordered to do so. Since its formation in 1937, the Council on African Affairs had become the largest organization in the United States devoted to the issue of African solidarity and to the independence of peoples of that continent who were still colonial subjects. By 1953 it had been under close FBI surveillance for more than ten years.

Under the chairmanship of Paul Robeson and the vice chairmanship (since 1947) of W.E.B. Du Bois, the Council on African Affairs was a formidable voice for African Americans as well. While advocating for African freedom, whether against colonialism or apartheid, the Council always aligned the struggles of African peoples with those of African Americans. Its publication, *New Africa*, launched in 1942 and renamed and redesigned as *Spotlight on Africa* in 1953, was the most comprehensive monthly newsletter on African affairs in the nation. In the twenty or so pages of each issue, readers found a wealth of news and analysis hardly matched by any other publication worldwide.

In response to a letter he received from a Mr. Marks, an African-American citizen of Memphis, asking him why he should worry about racial conditions in Africa while "we as a minority group catch Hell here in the USA," Alphaeus Hunton, the secretary of the Council on African Affairs, explained in simple yet very convincing language why it mattered. In doing so, Hunton made one of the clearest cases possible for the importance of the Council to African Americans:

> If you say that what goes on in the United States is one thing, quite different from what goes on in the West Indies or Africa or anywhere else affecting black people, the answer is that you are wrong. Racial oppression and exploitation have a universal pattern and whether they occur in South Africa, Mississippi or New Jersey, they must be exposed and fought as part of a worldwide system of oppression . . .

This answer would not have come as much of a surprise to Mr. Marks, but Hunton then made a second point, citing Paul Robeson as a source, that was less self-evident. He said that African Americans should aid Africans not only out of the spirit of a "humanitarian concern for their welfare," though that was clearly important, but also because by helping Africans achieve freedom "we further the possibility of their being able to help us in our struggles here in the United States . . . Can you envision what a powerful influence a free West Indies or a free West Africa would be upon American democracy?"

Instead of registering immediately, as they had been ordered to do, the Council on African Affairs responded with a strongly worded eight-page denial of all the charges levied at it by newly appointed attorney general Herbert Brownell. The Council asked for and was granted an extension, but when they had not registered by the end of September, the Subversive Activities Control

Board began preparations for a hearing, scheduled to begin in early November.

The assistant attorney general wrote to J. Edgar Hoover asking him to have the FBI prepare the case for the Department of Justice. Collecting documentary evidence of the alleged Communist leanings of the Council and the alleged Communist affiliations of its officers—copies of *Spotlight on Africa*, countless letterheads, newspaper clippings (mostly from New York's *Daily Worker*), and other bits and pieces—was easy: after all that was what the agents of the FBI did. But this material was not enough, because none of it stood as evidence that the Council on African Affairs operated as a "Communist front."

For that, the FBI had to come up with reliable witnesses who were prepared to state under oath to the Department of Justice's lawyers that they were present when such and such a decision was made. The FBI had a stable of reliable witnesses (often shared with other investigative units, such as HUAC) who were brought out to testify, but the credibility of some of these was doubtful. So, using its nationwide network of agents and informers, the FBI trawled political meetings all over the country, looking for individuals willing to inform.

The going was tough. Months passed, and though many people were interviewed, most could not claim to know anything more about the Council on African Affairs than what they had gleaned from its publications. A few, who said they knew more, did not want to appear for one reason or another.

In the end, every deadline the Department of Justice handed to the FBI passed; 1953 became 1954. In a separate development, Hunton received a subpoena to appear before the Grand Jury of the United States District Court in Washington, D.C., on October 7, 1954. The Department of Justice, Hunton was informed, regarded the council's work in sending aid to South Africans as "grounds for possible prosecution under the Foreign Agents Registration Act." This law, passed in 1938, required that agents in the United States who represented the interests of foreign powers in a "political or quasi-political capacity" needed to disclose the nature of that representation and any financial relationship that ensued from it. A few years earlier, W.E.B. Du Bois had faced a jail sentence when his Peace Information Center was charged with disseminating propaganda as an agent of foreign governments. The case had been dismissed for lack of evidence.

The Council on African Affairs had had close a relationship with both the African National Congress (particularly with Nelson Mandela) and with the South African Indian Congress; on two occasions, in 1946–47 and 1952–53, the Council had sent money to South Africa. Hunton's subpoena ordered him to bring an enormous cache of documentation on the Council's relationship with the South Africans, including all correspondence, publications, and financial records over a nine-year period. As it turned out, at the grand jury hearing Hunton was mostly questioned about the extent to which the South African opposition leaders were "Communist or Communist-controlled."

What the Department of Justice made of all this evidence we don't know; in any case, it took no action. The issue of registering with the Subversive Activities Control Board was still pending, and the FBI was still having difficulties finding witnesses. Another deadline passed. It was now 1955, and the January deadline for a grand jury hearing went by. The hearing was rescheduled once more, for June 15, and for the first time looked as though it might actually take place, when a group of lawyers from Washington, D.C., prepared to travel to New York to interview the individuals who had agreed to testify—in whom the FBI secretly did not have much confidence.

The lawyers never made the trip. On June 20, an FBI agent working on preparing the case noticed an article in the *Daily Worker* with the headline "African Affairs Council Dissolves, Directors Say Others Continue Pioneering Work, Harassment by Government Hampers Activities." The meeting that led to this decision had taken place on June 14. Hunton explained to the Council's executive board that the Council had no option but to dissolve: the pioneering work of the council was now being carried out by other organizations; the various investigations to date had strained the council's precarious finances to the breaking point; and neither the council nor its officers could sustain the full onslaught of the Subversive Activities Control Board.

A few days after learning that the Council had been dissolved, Hoover wrote to William Tompkins, the assistant attorney general, asking him to clarify his position under the circumstances. "An early reply to this request would be appreciated," Hoover added, "in order that no unnecessary investigative efforts in attempting to develop additional witnesses are expended by this Bureau."

Tompkins already knew of the dissolution, since it had been reported in the *New York Times*, but instead of affirming that the case was closed, he told Hoover that the most recent date for the hearing, July 11, 1955, was being kept open pending the results of an investigation. He ordered the FBI to investigate whether the dissolution was "bona fide" or was "being used as a subterfuge to avoid the provisions of the Internal Security Act of 1950."

Hoover, perhaps reluctantly, followed orders and found two "reliable" informants who confirmed that the Council on African Affairs was no longer in business and provided evidence to that effect. *Spotlight on Africa* had published its final issue in May; the council had canceled its mail contract with the post office and there was no activity at the council's offices in Harlem. On September 15, Tompkins, apparently satisfied with this information, told Hoover that the case was closed.

Before it disbanded, the Council on African Affairs had moved from their previous address to 53 West 125th Street. The FBI noted that the entire building was a hotbed of radicalism. On the fourth floor was the Harlem chapter of the Civil Rights Congress (on the attorney general's list); on the third floor was the Harlem Trade Union Council (also on the list). On the second floor was a loft where regular meetings of the Committee for the Negro in the Arts (on the list) were held.

The Council on African Affairs was on the same floor, and in fact shared premises with a monthly newspaper called *Freedom*, a joint venture planned by Du Bois and Robeson and a key undertaking of Robeson's recently established Freedom Fund, whose aim was to encourage and support those projects that would help African Americans achieve full rights.

*Freedom*'s first issue had appeared in November 1950, and since then the paper had proved to be a remarkable catalyst and intellectual melting pot for the black radicalism advocated by Robeson and Du Bois. It attracted to itself some of the brightest and most talented minds in the community, and they wrote and worked for the publication throughout its career.

Getting *Freedom* off the ground had been the responsibility of the editor, Louis Burnham, a native New Yorker who had worked as an activist in the South for more than a decade before returning to his hometown. Burnham's last political position there had been executive director of the Southern Negro Youth Congress, a movement that grew out of the National Negro Congress and shared its objectives of jobs, health, education and citizenship for African Americans. While in the South, Burnham had come under the influence of Du Bois's ideas, and through his work as Southern organizer for the Progressive Party he had become acquainted with Robeson. He was also very close to two couples, Augusta and Edward Strong and Esther and James Jackson, who moved to New York during Burnham's editorship of *Freedom* and would continue to foster black radicalism into the 1960s and 1970s.

*Freedom* was explicitly designed for an African-American readership. As Burnham outlined in an interview printed in the first edition, it was a black newspaper, one of many in the United States but with a very different set of characteristics from the others: It took a working-class line and supported the labor movement; it advocated third-party politics; its coverage of news

and its editorials focused on the issues of world peace, the anticolonial struggles in Africa and Asia, and human rights in Latin
America.

*Freedom* became a platform for Robeson; each issue included
an article from him on current concerns. In this series, called
"Here's My Story," Robeson covered all manner of topics—
some personal but with wider consequences, such as his passport
case, and some on the really big issues. Civil rights was frequently
on the agenda, along with peace, Africa, China, and Indo-China.
W.E.B. Du Bois and Albert Einstein were celebrated, and Senator Joseph McCarthy was severely criticized.

Besides politics, the newspaper carried a wide range of cultural
material, including books and theater reviews, stories, poetry,
and a regular column, "A Conversation from Life," contributed
by Alice Childress, whose first play, *Florence*, appeared off-
Broadway just before *Freedom* was launched. Adding her voice to
both cultural and political pages was Lorraine Hansberry, best
known for her play *A Raisin in the Sun*, who began working for
the newspaper first as an assistant to Burnham but eventually as
associate editor. Essie Robeson also contributed material of her
own, while bringing in writings from promising authors whose
work she tried to convince Burnham to publish.

No one associated with or working for *Freedom* was there by
accident. They had been drawn by Robeson and Du Bois and eventually by the paper itself as it became a platform for many exciting,
vibrant and daring ideas about politics and culture, labor activism,
and anticolonialism. African Americans within the Freedom
Family, as it was called, struck sparks from each other in much the
same way as had the makers of the Harlem Renaissance.

Writers and thinkers such as John Henrik Clarke, Robert F.
Williams, Yvonne Gregory, Vicki Garvin, and Beah Richards
contributed to *Freedom*. And through these people and the organizations to which they were attracted—the Harlem Trade Union
Council, the National Negro Labor Council, the Committee for
the Negro in the Arts, the Civil Rights Congress, the Council on

African Affairs—new political alliances were forged that nurtured a Harlem-based black radicalism in direct opposition to, and in defiance of, mainstream America's virulent anti-Communism.

One example of how these alliances worked in action was the call to arms for African American women from across the country to meet in Washington, D.C., and demand redress for their grievances from the Department of Justice. There they formed Sojourners for Truth and Justice, whose initiating committee consisted of a number of the Freedom Family—Lorraine Hansberry, Alice Childress, Beah Richards, Louise Patterson, Essie Robeson, and Shirley Graham Du Bois (a member of the editorial board)—as well as other black women, notably Bessie Mitchell, who had personally experienced injustice from the courts and government authorities in the case of the Trenton Six. At the organization's founding convention in Washington, more than 130 African-American women from fifteen states met to promote a "black left feminist human rights agenda."

Unlike the other tenants at 53 West 125th Street, neither *Freedom*, nor Freedom Associates, nor the Freedom Fund (later called the United Freedom Fund) ever made it on to the attorney general's list. Whether they were asked to register by the Subversive Activities Control Board is less certain. The FBI thought so, but no evidence has yet come to light to support this.

Nevertheless, *Freedom* did not get an easy ride. As far as the FBI was concerned, Freedom Associates, the umbrella organization, was a Communist front, "primarily operated for the purpose of giving aid and support to the Communist Party, USA." As for the members of its editorial board, they were, according to the FBI, either past, or present members of the Party.

"HELP!" cried the front page of the March 1955 issue, "Unless we get immediate help from you, FREEDOM will die." Printers and mailers would no longer give the newspaper credit; half of the subscriptions had lapsed; the editors were begging for donations no matter how small. *Freedom* had been in financial difficulties for some time. A project to expand readership in the South—by having a car, named the "Freedomobile," travel around the Southern states for six weeks, introducing potential readers to the newspaper—never materialized; and though the paper also tried to sell copies and entice subscriptions through sympathetic union associates, readership hardly went beyond New York.

Money from Robeson's concerts gave the newspaper some breathing space but, as for so many organizations targeted by state, federal, and security bodies, the onslaught was too much to cope with. *Freedom*'s final issue was the July-August 1955 edition.

The Freedom Family, according to Lorraine Hansberry, was much larger than readers ever imagined. "*Freedom* continued to attract a battery of frequent contributors without whom the total effectiveness of the paper would certainly have been much less," she wrote. "These gifted artists, journalists and photographers included Charlotte Dorsey and Yvonne Gregory, Inge Hardison, Ollie Harrington . . . and Moneta Barnett, an exceptional young artist who contributed some of *Freedom*'s most successful editorial cartoons. And there have been dozens and dozens of other people who have at one time or another worked freely in the cause of Paul Robeson's newspaper."

# 11

# Lynching, Southern Style

*Lynching* is a word associated in most people's minds with mob violence and the murder of blacks, typically in the South. In 1892, the Tuskegee Institute (now University) in Tuskegee, Alabama, which served the African-American community, began to collect statistics on lynching in the United States, by race. In that first year, the data collectors reported that 230 people had been lynched and that more than two-thirds of them were black. Although there were also white victims, as the Tuskegee data revealed, their numbers after the turn of the century were small, and in most years from the end of the First World War onward, no whites at all were lynched. In contrast, during these same years, about twenty-five blacks, on average, were lynched every year.

Lynching was a shame on the nation. Over the years, the government had tried on many occasions to step in and make it a federal offence. Seven presidents petitioned Congress; 200 antilynching bills were introduced in Congress and three of them passed the House, but none ever made it through the Senate. Controlling this sorry history and standing in the way of legislation was a powerful group of white Southerners, mostly senators but also representatives. Supported by their white voters, these congressmen wielded an enormous, dispro-portionate power, which ensured that Washington could not blast Jim Crow out of existence.

During the 1930s, when the NAACP and the Association of Southern Women for the Prevention of Lynching had campaigned vigorously against the practice, it seemed that lynching was in decline, that progress had been made.

But in 1945, when many African Americans returned from combat expecting that the country they had fought for would reward them with improved civil rights, their hopes were disappointed. Southerners saw them as "uppity negroes" who should be punished for their claims. Lynching was not yet history.

One case, in Georgia in July 1946, made front pages across the United States.

"Two Wives Die With Mates in Mass Lynching," read the banner in the *Chicago Herald Tribune*; the *Boston Globe* led with "Federal Investigation in Lynching of Four Georgia Negroes," and the *Chicago Defender*, which devoted many pages to the lynching, chose a headline that referred as much to the paper's crusading position as to the case itself: "Defender Vows to Fight Until Lynch Evil Dies; Victims of Southern Insanity; Four Negroes Murdered by Georgia Mob; Horror Sweeps Nation."

The details of the case were indeed horrifying. Two African-American couples, in their twenties and thirties, had been lined up and shot on a secluded roadside near the town of Monroe, Georgia. They had been riding in a car driven by Lloyd Harrison, a local white farmer; the car was ambushed on Moore's Ford Bridge over the Appalachee River by a group of about twenty white men. According to Harrison, these men started dragging away only the two black men, but when the wife of one of them cried out to one of the abductors, whom she apparently recognized, to stop, the two women were grabbed as well. The mob drove away with their captives and Harrison reported what had happened to the police in Monroe. When the bodies of the two couples were recovered, they had been shot more than sixty times. One of the victims had been a veteran of the Second World War.

The story appalled the American public. The newspapers kept a close eye on events in Georgia, irate citizens sent federal and state authorities messages of disgust at Southern brutality, and throughout the country protesters met and made their voices heard and raised funds to help track down the killers. Foreign newspapers carried the story as well; some Soviet papers carried front-page accounts.

As chairman of the Council on African Affairs, Robeson swiftly sent President Truman a telegram demanding federal action to "apprehend and punish the perpetrators of this shocking crime and to halt the rising tide of lynch law." He reminded Truman that the mass lynching in Georgia took place just a few hours before the president sent a message to Congress directing their attention to a recent recommendation by the International Labor Organization for minimum working and living standards in colonial countries. Robeson called this a tragic irony. "Only when our government has taken such action toward protecting its own citizens," Robeson pointed out, "can its role in aiding the progress of peoples of other countries be viewed with trust and hope."

Less than two weeks later, more than 1,000 people gathered in Harlem to hear Robeson repeat the message he had sent to the president.

Aside from expressing his disgust at the murder and ordering Attorney General Tom Clark to use federal resources at his disposal to bring the perpetrators to justice, President Truman did very little about the tragedy in Georgia. Certainly he did not bow to any of the mounting pressure on him as chief executive to take general action on lynching. Attempts by protest groups to gain an audience with Truman failed repeatedly.

At a rally to raise funds for the Democratic Party held in Madison Square Garden on September 12, 1946, and attended by an estimated 20,000 people, Robeson was the only speaker to refer to the Georgia lynchings. In his speech he lambasted the federal government for its inaction, wondering why the leaders of the country had no problem calling on the army and navy to deal with troublesome workers but did nothing to stop the lynchers. "What about it, President Truman?" Robeson exclaimed.

"When will the federal government take effective action to uphold our constitutional guarantees?"

By the time he faced this crowd, Robeson had already been at work on a plan to confront Truman. Robeson wanted effective antilynching legislation and he thought he knew how he could force Truman to get it passed.

Robeson had been friendly with Albert Einstein since they had met in Princeton, in 1935. Einstein saw racism as a disease of white people and didn't pull any punches when writing or speaking on the topic:

> Your ancestors dragged these black people from their homes by force; and in the white man's quest for wealth and an easy life they have been ruthlessly suppressed and exploited, degraded into slavery. The modern prejudice against Negroes is the result of the desire to maintain this unworthy condition.

Einstein was an obvious candidate for Robeson to invite to join in his American Crusade to End Lynching and act as its co-chairman. Then, enlisting W.E.B. Du Bois and the prominent white lawyer Bartley Crum, Robeson began drumming up support. By the time he was ready to put his plans into action, he had managed to get a broad section of America's influential and well-known people, both black and white, behind him. The list of his sponsors included musicians Artie Shaw, Frank Sinatra, Lena Horne, and Larry Adler; actors Gregory Peck, Gene Kelly, Orson Welles, and Canada Lee; and composers Yip Harburg and Oscar Hammerstein II. There were also religious leaders, scientists and politicians.

What Robeson had in mind was a hundred-day program, scheduled to begin on September 22. The first step in direct action was for all crusaders to assemble on that date in Washington, D.C. for a day of antilynching activities. A meeting with President Truman was scheduled for 11:30 a.m., when a delegation would make its case to the president for federal action. This would be followed by a conference, and in the evening a mass meeting would be held in front of the Lincoln Memorial, where eyewitnesses to lynchings would relate their experiences. Robeson would round off the day with a concert.

The following day they would launch their intensive campaign to get the federal authorities to act. The aims of the crusade included the apprehension and punishment of every lyncher; the passage of a federal antilynching bill; and the exclusion of known Klan members from holding seats in Congress. The program's official starting date and its length were both symbolic: They fit precisely Abraham Lincoln's own program for the emancipation of slaves, which began on September 22, 1862, with his preliminary announcement of the emancipation and ended on January 1, 1863, when the proclamation went into effect, officially freeing slaves in all Confederate states still at war with the Union.

The crusaders of 1946 would have to be patient, however, because the entire House and half of the Senate were up for midterm re-election on November 5. The political shape of the new Congress would determine the chance of an antilynching bill becoming law.

The call went out to churches, schools, and civic and labor organizations as well as individuals to gather in Washington for the first day of action. Veteran groups were especially invited, specifically because since the end of the Second World War black veterans had been targeted, particularly in the South. They had returned home after proving their willingness to sacrifice themselves for their country, expecting their country to give them something in return: civil rights.

On the appointed day, September 22, 1946, 3,000 black and white people joined Robeson on a crusade to end lynching. Einstein, who should have been there, was ill and unable to travel. At 11:30, as scheduled, Robeson and eight delegates—representing newspaper proprietors, church groups, and the National Negro Congress—met with Truman. Reports of the meeting, including Robeson's own, suggest that Truman was irritated by the delegation. They presented him with letters, including one written by Einstein. Robeson began reading out a prepared statement, which Truman interrupted, saying that the wave of lynchings concerned him but it was not the right political moment to do anything.

Mrs. Harper Sibley, president of the National Council of Church Women, and Robeson both asked the president how the United States could take the lead at the Nuremberg war crimes trials, sentencing Nazis for their actions in Germany, when at the same time African Americans were being lynched. Truman insisted that domestic matters had to be kept separate from foreign ones; Robeson characteristically responded that he could not see how the two could be kept apart.

When Truman told the delegation, "You of all people ought to stand behind this country—the United States and Great Britain are the last refuges of freedom in the world," Robeson shot back, "The British Empire is the greatest enslaver of human beings in the world."

Robeson told Truman that returning veterans were showing signs of unrest and were determined to get the justice at home that they had fought for abroad. "I asked the president," Robeson recalled, "to call a national emergency to deal with mob violence." Truman shook his fist and said Robeson's words sounded like a threat; he added that he could not call a national emergency.

The meeting ended. Outside the White House, David Niles, a presidential assistant and unofficial adviser on African-American affairs, tried to soften Truman's harsh stance for the gathered newsmen. "The president," he said, "feels that this is a political matter and that the element of timing is important."

The rest of the crusaders' day went according to plan and culminated in the evening when Robeson, standing at Lincoln's feet, issued a new emancipation proclamation, one for the present time, a proclamation of an America free of lynching.

~

The NAACP did not support Robeson's initiative. Its National Office of Organization actually instructed all of its branches not to participate. When he heard that Du Bois had lent his support to Robeson, Walter White wrote to him on September 19, 1946, saying that the fight against lynching was an integral part of his association's work and that Du Bois' participation in a separate effort had complicated the situation. Du Bois, who was still connected to the NAACP, answered White, "I gladly endorsed the Robeson movement which asked my cooperation. This did not and could not interfere with the NAACP program. The fight against mob law is the monopoly of no one person, and no one organization."

On the same day he wrote to Du Bois, White led his own delegation, the National Emergency Committee Against Mob Violence, to Truman and urged the president to call a special session of Congress to pass laws against mob violence. White pointed out to Truman, as Robeson would several days later, that mob violence at home "was making a mockery of the efforts of American representatives" in the United Nations "to create a world of peace based on human freedom and justice."

Meanwhile, the FBI, which had been gathering information on the American Crusade to End Lynching, concluded from a report in a weekly military-intelligence summary, "This crusade has all the earmarks of another Communist attempt to instill racial friction."

Meanwhile the American Crusade to End Lynching continued its 100-day campaign, writing to prospective candidates for Congress to say that the crusade's followers would be supporting only candidates who would make antilynching legislation a priority. Once the elections were over, the organization sent out letters to every new Congressman asking these members to support, sponsor and vote for antilynching legislation. Finally, at the end of the one hundred days, supporters of the crusade were asked to reconvene in Washington for the conference that would bring the campaign to an end.

~

As the Tuskegee Institute went on collecting statistics, it became clear, after the mass lynching in Monroe, Georgia, that 1946 was going to be a very dark year in race relations. By the end of the year the institute would report that six lynchings had officially taken place and many more murders were being investigated to see if they fit the institute's criteria defining lynching. The last year that had seen this many lynchings had been 1942, and before that 1938.

Truman was under intense pressure to act. The Georgia lynchings, in particular, were hardly ever off the front pages of the press; both white and black groups held protest meetings throughout the country. The South, however, remained complacent and Southern Democratic senators were preparing to filibuster the next proposed antilynching bill; meanwhile in Georgia no arrests had been made.

On December 5, 1946, Truman issued an executive order creating the President's Committee on Civil Rights, charged to investigate the status of civil rights in the country. *To Secure These Rights*, the report of the fifteen-member committee—made up of distinguished leaders from labor, law, education, and the church—was published in October 1947 and made a number of important recommendations. However, the committee was disbanded in December, and that was about it. Although the American Crusade to End Lynching had managed to get pledges from twenty-five representatives and two senators in favor of antilynching legislation, the legislation was never passed. Several months later, on February 2, 1948, armed with his committee's report, Truman asked Congress for an antilynching law, but the Southern Democrats managed to kill it dead.

In 1951, frustration with the inability of the machinery of government to put a halt to mob violence and the lynchings that had continued each year after 1946 led Robeson and William Patterson, now national secretary of the Civil Rights Congress, to a bold move. Sponsored by the Civil Rights Congress, they decided to petition the United Nations to charge the United States with genocide.

This was not the first time that an African-American organization had tried to go through the United Nations to expose African-American grievances. On June 6, 1946, the National Negro Congress had delivered a petition to Trygve Lie, the secretary general of the UN, to end the oppression of African Americans. The document argued that African Americans, who were mostly concentrated in the Southern states, were being kept in an oppressed economic, political, and social condition, while Southern politicians blocked their right to vote and resisted any attempt at effecting antilynching legislation. The United Nations, the petition argued, was "the highest court of mankind" and its members would understand the plight of the African Americans.

The United Nations sidestepped the issue, asking for more documentation on local human rights abuses, but by the time the National Negro Congress complied, in February 1947, building a case showing that "America's 'Negro question' . . . had international implications," they had run into such financial difficulties that they weren't able to complete the task. By the summer of that year, the organization was on its last legs, and a few months later what was left of it was incorporated into the Civil Rights Congress.

Next to step into the vacuum was the NAACP, whose leaders had watched the difficulties experienced by the National Negro Congress from the sidelines and believed that "the congress had stumbled onto a great idea." In August 1946, the association asked Du Bois, as its research director and foreign policy expert, to consider the possibilities of a UN petition and to take charge of drafting one. Du Bois took a more scholarly approach and, with the help of several contributors, prepared a lengthier and more detailed case than had the National Negro Congress. On October 23 the long, many-sectioned document, "An Appeal to the World," was ready and was accepted by John Humphrey, director of the UN Commission on Human Rights.

The NAACP's petition had greater success than its predecessor, in that it did reach a final form, but it fell early in its trajectory through the United Nations bureaucracy. In December 1947, when the petition came before the organization's Sub-Commission on the Prevention of Discrimination and the Protection of Minorities, the United States vetoed it. In the following year, 1948, the NAACP gave up struggling for human rights in the international arena and concentrated instead on achieving civil rights at home. As it distanced itself from the big issues of colonial independence and human rights, issues that were being increasingly painted as "red," the NAACP also formally severed its long association with Du Bois.

It was the Civil Rights Congress, therefore, that made the third attempt at getting the African-American issue debated in the United Nations, and they took a radically different approach.

On December 9, 1948, the United Nations General Assembly, sitting in temporary accommodation in Paris at the Palais du Chaillot, adopted the Convention on the Prevention and Punishment of the Crime of Genocide. It was the first UN treaty on human rights. The convention consisted of nineteen articles, but for the purposes of Robeson and Patterson's petition, only Articles I, II, and III were germane. In these articles, *genocide* was defined as acts committed in times of either peace or war that were intended to "destroy, in whole or in part, a national, ethnical, racial or religious group." The convention defined five acts of genocide, but only three of them applied to the petition. These were: killing members of the targeted group, causing them physical or mental harm, and "deliberately inflicting on the group conditions of life calculated to bring about its physical destruction in whole or in part." Genocide, the convention went on, was punishable, as were conspiracy, attempt and incitement to commit genocide, and complicity in genocide.

The United States had signed the convention, and Truman believed in it, but when he sent the treaty to the Senate for ratification, on June 19, 1949, it met with strong opposition, mostly stirred up by the American Bar Association, and it died there.

Although the United States had not ratified it, the convention came into force in January 1951 as a component of international law. Robeson and Patterson believed they could make a case that the government of the United States had committed genocide against its African-American population and had therefore violated international law. So, during the summer of 1951, they began drafting a petition that was published in October 1951 in its final form: a 240-page book with the arresting title *We Charge Genocide*, subtitled *The Historic Petition To the United Nations for Relief From a Crime of the United States Government Against the Negro People*.

The petition was carefully crafted using the definitions laid down in the convention's main articles. It began with a review of the case and gave a sense of the scope and history of the American genocide, mentioning many famous lynchings and the activities of such groups as the Ku Klux Klan. It related incidents of murder, of legal lynching (cases where an African American had, according to the petition, been a victim of a gross miscarriage of justice), mental harm, and the denial of the right to vote. It then went on to argue why individuals had the right to petition the United Nations in cases where their human rights were not being protected by their own government, and why they were indicting the United States for racial crimes. Then, in the longest section of the petition, Robeson and Patterson provided readers with details of specific acts of genocide from the beginning of 1945 until June 1951, arranged by the appropriate articles of the convention, beginning with "Killing Members of the Group." So, for example, on page 64, there was an entry for July 25, 1946, which told of the gruesome lynching of the two African-American couples near Monroe, Georgia. It continued in this vein with incidents proving mental and physical harm, examples of the inflicting of intolerable conditions of life—economic, civic, and social—and documented ways in which the United States had attempted, incited, and conspired to and been complicit in committing genocide.

Robeson and Patterson managed to find almost 100 people to support their petition. Most of them were African Americans, many of them were associated with Robeson in the organizations he headed—the Council on African Affairs and Freedom Associates—and several of them were relatives of victims of illegal and legal lynchings. The white petitioners included academics and writers, among them Howard Fast and Jessica Mitford.

Once the book was available, it was widely distributed through the networks created by the Civil Rights Congress and was ready for presentation to the United Nations. That meant traveling to Paris, but because Robeson was still without a valid passport—he applied to the Passport Office for permission to travel to France and was flatly denied it—Patterson would take the petition to the General Assembly at the Palais du Chaillot while Robeson presented it to the United Nations' secretariat in New York.

Robeson arrived at the secretariat accompanied by a fourteen-person delegation, including two widows, Amy Mallard and Josephine Grayson, who claimed that their husbands' deaths— the cases were documented in the petition—had been a direct result of the genocide. The delegation handed over copies of the book to an official, and that was that—a completely straightforward procedure. Patterson's experience was altogether different and showed up in stark detail how political realities had changed between the drawing up of the NAACP's petition and the publication of this one.

Patterson arrived in Paris on Sunday, December 16. The FBI had placed informants there to keep Washington up to date. Patterson personally carried twenty copies of the book on the plane and shipped sixty copies in advance to Paris—he feared that his baggage might be deliberately placed on a different flight. On Monday, the next day, as planned, and simultaneously with Robeson's arrival at the UN building in New York, he presented the petition to the secretary general of the United

Nations and the president of the General Assembly. Patterson then spent the rest of the week lobbying delegates and making himself available to newsmen. He got a particularly warm reception from French left-wing newspapers, notably *Action* and *L'Humanité*.

Patterson suspected that his visit to Paris was being monitored by the State Department, and his suspicions were exacerbated by the behavior of Ralph Bunche, the prominent African-American academic and diplomat who had received the Nobel Peace Prize in the previous year. Bunche, who had been closely involved in drafting the United Nations Charter, was politically opposed to Patterson and now seemed to be deliberately avoiding him. *We Charge Genocide* was anathema to Bunche.

Bunche was not the only African-American diplomat in Paris. Truman had appointed two others to the United Nations as alternate delegates. One of them was Edith Sampson, a prominent lawyer; the other was Channing Tobias, an important civil rights activist. They and Rayford Logan, a historian and sometime adviser to the NAACP on international affairs, had been selected by the State Department to defend their country's racial policies by lecturing on the subject and giving as many interviews as possible.

In anticipation of Patterson's trip to Paris—which had become public knowledge in mid-November of the previous year when the Civil Rights Congress's plans for presenting the petition were broadcast on national radio—the State Department had prepared for a counterattack; these famous African-American leaders were part of its arsenal. The department also enlisted the help of the NAACP to denounce the petition, but the association was cautious about doing this, since most of the evidence in it came from their own research department. Instead, the association assisted the State Department, through the department's propaganda arm, the United States Information Agency, in publishing a counterbook, *The Negro in American Life*, which painted a positive, progressive portrait of African-American history since emancipation.

These actions were intended to undermine Patterson's mission, but the State Department had a more direct weapon. Shortly after Christmas, the American embassy in Paris contacted Patterson and demanded his passport. Patterson refused and understood immediately that he needed to get out of the country as quickly as possible. As he described it to a newsman, "They told me they would visit me in my hotel. I didn't wait till they came." He bought an air ticket to Budapest, stayed for a few days and then moved on to Prague, speaking in both cities and giving press interviews.

On January 17, 1952, Patterson arrived in London but found that the Americans had asked British authorities to deny him entry. After detaining him for seventeen hours, immigration authorities yielded to a request from the London-based National Council for Civil Liberties and gave Patterson leave to remain in the UK for five days. He spent the time speaking to the press, trade union leaders and Communist Party officials, many of whom knew Paul Robeson when he had visited the country two years earlier.

Patterson then returned to New York, arriving at Idlewild Airport on January 23. When he stepped off the plane, Customs Service and State Department officials were waiting for him. He was taken to a private office and subjected to an examination. Patterson reportedly described it as a "personal search." State Department agents then seized his passport. Further travel by Patterson, the State Department told reporters, "would not be in the best interest of the United States"—an echo of how they had explained their similar treatment of Robeson. One hundred supporters were waiting to cheer Patterson when he was done with officialdom.

Several days later, Patterson was treated to a welcome-home rally at Rockland Palace in Harlem. Two thousand five hundred well-wishers were there to hear him speak. Robeson sang.

~

Robeson and Patterson's petition was never debated by the United Nations General Assembly, and once Patterson was back in the United States, it was forgotten. Using the "highest court of mankind" to kick the US federal government into action to end its race problem had now failed three times. It would not be tried again.

# PART IV

# PASSPORT CONTROL

# 12

# The Longest Undefended Border

At 1 p.m. on Thursday, January 31, 1952, Paul Robeson was riding in a car owned and driven by Ted Cochran of Tacoma, Washington, a representative of the International Union of Mine, Mill and Smelter Workers. John Gray, an unemployed union official from Chicago who was acting as Robeson's secretary, was sitting in the backseat. Cochran's vehicle was in the middle of a cavalcade of three cars organized by the Seattle branch of the National Negro Labor Council. Robeson had arrived earlier that morning in Seattle after a long train journey from New York. Now Cochran was taking Robeson to Vancouver. The car was stopped, however, in Blaine, Washington, at the border between the United States and Canada.

The American-Canadian border is the longest undefended land border in the world; in 1952, it was also one of the easiest to cross. Formalities were minimal; for Canadians, in particular, a visit south to the United States was more common than travel in Canada itself. Crossing the border, for both Americans and Canadians, involved not much more than stating your name, place of birth and purpose of visit. Robeson had no reason to think that his crossing would be any different to that of any other American. But Robeson was not just any American.

It was no secret that Robeson would be crossing the American-Canadian border. The Special Branch of the Royal Canadian Mounted Police (RCMP), who were responsible for political surveillance and monitoring in the country, had learned about his visit well in advance. Their source had attended a planning meeting of the Western District of the International Union of Mine, Mill, and Smelter Workers (less cumbersomely known as Mine Mill) on January 11, 1951, in Vancouver, where members decided that the Canadian national convention would be held in the city in late January and early February and that Paul Robeson should be invited as the main guest, to sing and to speak.

Special Branch immediately cross-referenced this information; they had been keeping tabs on Robeson since 1937 and grew nervous whenever he visited Canada. When they learned, for example, that he was scheduled to give his first-ever Vancouver concert on October 31, 1940, they had immediately contacted Immigration Department officials, because "in view of ROBESON'S definitely anti-British feeling . . . the Immigration Department may wish to give some consideration to his entry into this country."

Once the Cold War began, the rhetoric changed: fear of anti-British statements became fear of pro-Communist speeches. Both American and Canadian intelligence officers tracked Robeson's 1947 Canadian trip very closely, reporting especially on his relationship to Canadian Communist groups. Soon Canadian authorities became alarmed by Robeson's presence. In December 1948, the Canadian secretary of state for external affairs received advice from officials in his department that it was in the country's best interests to prevent Robeson from making political speeches. On the basis of the American attorney general's list, the Canadian government had also decided that Robeson was a Communist and that according to a cabinet decision taken in March 1948, he could be refused entry into the country for that reason. In the event, Canadian authorities, this time, did not bar Robeson from entering Canada. As one official put it, "I would be reluctant to see Robeson, the singer, refused entry to Canada but it is going to be difficult to separate him from Robeson, the political propagandist."

Several days after Special Branch learned that an invitation would be going out to Robeson to appear in Vancouver, the

*Vancouver Daily Sun* printed an article confirming the union's plans; other Vancouver newspapers followed suit. Robeson's projected visit to Vancouver was now public knowledge.

On January 18, the *Vancouver News Herald* ran the completely surprising headline "US to Ban Paul Robeson from Concert in Vancouver." In the story, the paper reported that the State Department had told Robeson that he could not leave the United States to appear at Denman Auditorium on the evening of February 1. It also quoted a State Department source as saying that if Robeson "should slip through the hands of US Immigration border officials, Canadian authorities have already been alerted to halt him."

The newspaper was correct that Canadian immigration officials had agreed to stop Robeson at the Canadian side of the border should he manage to get through the American side. But the item about the State Department having informed Robeson that he could not leave the United States to appear in Vancouver was not true.

American officials had learned of Robeson's plans to perform in Vancouver almost as soon as had Special Branch. Everett J. Strapp, the officer in charge at the Blaine crossing, reported to John Boyd, district director of the Immigration and Naturalization Service in Seattle, and Strapp's superior, that he had heard on the radio that Robeson was scheduled to appear in Vancouver on February 1. Everett also reported that his "watch-for card" told him precisely what to do should Robeson appear. On the basis of the information, a few days later Boyd contacted all district directors at the major American-Canadian entry points in case Robeson decided to cross into Canada from another state than Washington.

Meanwhile, in Washington, D.C., someone from the Canadian embassy had phoned the Immigration and Naturalization Service to tell them that Robeson was due in Vancouver in the near future. Whoever received the call that day entered the details of what happened next in a file memo dated January 17. The memo writer stated that he had phoned the Passport Division, who told him that the orders to prevent Robeson from leaving the country were still in force, that his passport had expired and would "not be renewed under any circumstances."

In Seattle, Boyd received orders from the State Department's Enforcement Division on January 21 to be on his guard. The written notice prohibiting the visit, which the Vancouver newspaper reported had been sent to Robeson, had in fact never left Washington. An internal check on January 28 revealed that the State Department still had the notice in its offices.

Ruth Shipley, chief of the Passport Division, had already anticipated the possibility that Robeson might try to leave the United States, even before his passport had been made "null and void" at the beginning of August 1950. On July 26, 1950, she had written to Argyle Mackey, the acting commissioner of the Immigration and Naturalization Service, informing him that Robeson should be prevented from leaving "the continental limits of the United States," on the grounds that "his departure would be prejudicial to the interests of the United States." Mrs. Shipley added that officers of the Immigration and Naturalization Service, should they be confronted by Robeson, could detain him under certain provisions, which she quoted in the memo. Very soon all ports of entry, including those along the Canadian and Mexican border, were on high alert, as if Robeson were a wanted criminal.

Waiting to greet Robeson on the afternoon of January 31 was a welcoming party from Mine Mill—some of them had crossed into the United States and others were waiting on the Canadian side of the border—and a press contingent, from Vancouver's several newspapers. But when Robeson arrived, instead of answering a few simple questions and then driving across to Douglas, British Columbia, like hundreds of thousands of Americans annually, he found himself being asked to leave the front seat of the car and report to the Blaine immigration office.

There he found Inspector Everett J. Strapp, the officer in charge of the American side of the border crossing, sitting at his desk. "[He] nervously informed me," Robeson recalled, "though no passport was needed, a special order had come through forbidding me to leave the country. If I did, it might mean five years, and a fine! . . . John Gray . . . was with me, and he did go across the border into Canada for a few moments to establish his right to do so."

That was the order that Mrs. Shipley had referred to in her letter to Acting Commissioner Mackey. By the time Robeson arrived at Blaine, immigration officers at all American ports of entry had been given a copy of this order.

And now Robeson had it, too: Everett handed him a copy of the written notice that he should have received in New York. Robeson was asked to read and then sign the notice, which he did. The order stated that the State Department was prohibiting Robeson's departure from the United States in accordance with an act of May 22, 1918, which President Franklin Delano Roosevelt had reissued as a presidential proclamation on November 14, 1941. Both the 1918 act and the 1941 proclamation had been wartime measures designed to control departure and entry into the United States by those people whose activities abroad or presence in the country were deemed to be against American interests.

The penalty for violating the order was a maximum fine of $5,000 and/or a maximum prison sentence of five years. Roosevelt's 1941 proclamation, invoked as part of the state of national emergency, was still in force when Robeson was in Blaine because, strictly speaking, the United States and Japan were still at war and the national emergency still in force. Nobody knew then, and certainly not Robeson, that the state of emergency would be lifted in just three months.

For now, Robeson had no choice but to sign the notice and remain in the United States. After an hour in the immigration office, he emerged and spoke to reporters from the Vancouver press. "I shall continue to fight to be free to visit friends in Canada," he said. And then he continued, "An act such as this virtually puts me under domestic arrest. I have not been brought to court, nor have I been warned, except to the extent that my passport was taken from me . . . I had been told in New York that a passport was not needed for American citizens to enter Canada. I would not have made the long trip had I suspected that extraordinary measures would be used to prevent me crossing the border."

During the hour that Robeson had spent with Officer Strapp he had insisted that Strapp should clarify the situation by phoning his superiors. The written notice handed to Robeson was the result of that call. Robeson got back into Cochran's car and returned to Seattle. The union honor guard that had planned to escort Robeson to their convention returned without him. When news spread to Vancouver of what had happened in Blaine, Harvey Murphy, Western regional director of Mine Mill, who had been the one to invite Robeson, incensed at how his guest had been treated, led sixty union officials to the offices of Robert Smyth, the US consul-general in Vancouver, to protest. Murphy and his men got nothing out of Smyth, who was unwilling to discuss the matter.

No doubt immigration officials felt they had scored a significant victory in having Robeson acquiesce to State Department orders. But Robeson would not go quietly. The invitation to sing and speak in Vancouver still stood, and Robeson was not about to cancel.

When Robeson got back to Seattle, he was met by three members of the National Union of Marine Cooks and Stewards, who found him "tired from the trip and the ordeal at the Immigration Station." Robeson and Gray wanted a place to stay in the city's black community, and this was arranged.

Between them, Robeson in Seattle and Murphy in Vancouver decided on a radical rebuttal to the State Department's action.

Murphy asked George Gee, a colleague from the Electrical Workers Union, to connect the Denman Auditorium's telephone line to its public address system. At the appointed time, 8:48 p.m., Robeson, who was in the Seattle headquarters of the National Union of Marine Cooks and Stewards, of which he was an honorary member, phoned Murphy in Vancouver. Murphy answered the phone and Robeson's voice was broadcast throughout the hall. Over 2,000 delegates sat there spellbound.

For seventeen minutes Robeson spoke and sang. Special Branch Constable A. E. Thomas was in the audience that evening. Murphy, who suspected the presence of the security service in the auditorium, had earlier put forward a resolution to send a protest to what he called the Civil Rights Committee (he meant the Human Rights Commission) at the way Robeson had been treated at the border. Thomas described the moment: "He requested all those in favor of the resolution to stand. It appears that everyone stood up, whereupon xxxxx (blackened out) requested that anyone opposed to the resolution should stand up—no one did so."

Thomas listened carefully to Robeson over the public address system. He reported that Robeson had said that it was not the American people, but their government, who had barred him from leaving his country, and that he could not be silenced. Robeson concluded the transmission by singing "I Dreamed I Saw Joe Hill Last Night."

Al King, president of a local chapter of the union in Trail, British Columbia, was also in the audience. Robeson's "Joe Hill," King recalled, "brought the house down." And then, when Robeson had finished his program, Murphy told Robeson over the phone for all in the auditorium, including King and Constable Thomas, to hear: "This summer," Murphy said, "and for every summer after that until they let you pass freely, Mine Mill will meet you at the Blaine border. We'll have a truck and sound and you can sing and speak to the people on both sides of the border. Together we'll beat this boycott."

During his unintended stay in Seattle, Robeson was looked after by three union members, who arranged a press conference and prepared for the phone call to Vancouver. They and their wives also had dinner with Robeson before driving him to the train station for the trip back to New York City.

One of the men, Jerry Tyler, recounted all of this is in a letter he wrote to the secretary treasurer of the union at its national headquarters in San Francisco, Eddie Tangen, in whose house Robeson had once stayed. "Just told like that," Tyler apologetically explained in the letter, "it doesn't sound like much." And then he went on to give a moving account of what it meant for him to be with Robeson, even for a short time:

> But how in the hell can you put into words the feeling you get from knowing that in even a small way you helped make history by assisting one of the most powerful speakers and fighters for peace and labor? How can you describe the thrill and inspiration of spending hours helping a REAL man, a man big physically, mentally and morally? How can you paint a word picture of the impact on yourself of a man so full of warmth and love that he stands like a giant, yet makes you feel, without stooping to you, that you too are a giant and hold the power of making history in your hands as well?

No date had been set for the boycott-breaking concert at the time, but the Vancouver press reported that the executive board of the union had agreed to Murphy's offer and to the date of May 18. Within two weeks, both the US Immigration and Naturalization Service and the FBI had learned the details of the forthcoming event.

On the day of the concert, officers from the FBI and the RCMP joined the crowds. The FBI men brought filming equipment and the RCMP officers recorded British Columbia license plates; officers from the State Department did the same on the American side.

As a freshman, Robeson became the first African American on Rutgers's football team. In late 1917, when this photograph was taken, Robeson was the hero in a crucial 14–0 shut out against Newport Naval Reserves.

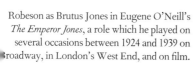

Robeson as Brutus Jones in Eugene O'Neill's *The Emperor Jones*, a role which he played on several occasions between 1924 and 1939 on Broadway, in London's West End, and on film.

744-42

Robeson's most famous dramatic role was as the stevedore Joe in Kern and Hammerstein's *Show Boat*, in which he sar "Ol' Man River." He is seen here in a still from the 1936 film of the show, directed by James Whale.

Paul with his wife Eslanda (Essie) Robeson in Southampton, July 10, 1939, arriving in Britain after a short stay in New York. The Robesons would soon return to the United States following the outbreak of World War II.

Henry Wallace (far left) launched his presidential campaign in the 1948 general election as the Progressive Party candidate. Robeson (far right) was a staunch supporter. With Robeson and Wallace is Frank Kingdon (right), and all of them are attentively listening to Albert Einstein, a close friend of Robeson's.

Robeson relaxing after his speech at the World Congress of Partisans of Peace on April 20, 1949. Peter Blackman is his right and W.E.B. Du Bois on his left.

An effigy of Robeson, hanging from the rear of a tow truck parked near the site of his September 4, 1949 concert. It was the sort of image that greeted the thousands who came to hear Robeson, before they were attacked by demonstrators.

Union members from New York City were determined to protect Robeson during his September 4, 1949 Peekskill concert. This photograph shows part of the protective ring around the concert site.

Eugene Bullard, here being beaten by police at the Peekskill concert, was the first African-American military pilot and earned the French Croix de Guerre for his bravery during World War I. He spent almost twenty-five years in Paris where he built up a successful career as a musician and nightclub owner.

On May 18, 1952, Robeson gave the first of what turned out to be four annual concerts in Peace Arch Park, a public space between the Canadian (British Columbia) and the American (Washington State) border crossings. At the exact middle of the park, straddling the international border, stands the Peace Arch. Robeson, who was not allowed out of the United States, sang to the Canadian and American audience one foot from the Canadian side of the Arch.

'I Came to Sing

PAUL ROBESON

PEACE ARCH
PROGRAM

Sponsored by
THE
INTERNATIONAL UNION
OF
MINE, MILL
AND
SMELTER
WORKERS
UNION

Jackie Robinson giving evidence at a hearing of the House Un-American Activities Committee, July 18, 1949, an occasion on which he criticized Robeson's 1949 Paris Peace Congress speech. Robinson was America's most famous African-American sportsman, the first to play in baseball's Major League and a man spearheading the process of its racial integration.

Robeson appearing in front of the House Un-American Activities Committee hearing on the "Unauthorized Use of United States Passports," June 12, 1956. Unlike other witnesses before and after, who buckled before the committee, Robeson defiantly stood up to his inquisitors, teaching them a lesson they would not forget.

Robeson returned to London in July 1958 after his eight-year-long battle with the State Department to get back h[...]
passport. Robeson threw himself into British political life immediately. In this photograph he is seen addressing [...]
crowd of some 10,000 people, assembled in Trafalgar Square on June 28, 1959, demonstrating against nuclear weapons[...]

It was Harvey Murphy's brilliant idea to stage the concert at the Peace Arch. The concrete and steel arch, topped on one side with the American flag and on the other with the Canadian, sits in the middle of a grassy area straddling the boundary between the United States and Canada, about halfway between the two border crossings. A few meters to the west of the arch is the Pacific Ocean, and to the east, the edges of the two American and Canadian border communities. Running directly on either side of the Peace Arch are two roads—one southbound, carrying mostly Canadian traffic to the American border post, and the other northbound, doing the same for American traffic heading to the Canadian border post. The Peace Arch Park is effectively in both countries, and Americans and Canadians can enter it from their respective sides without reporting to either immigration service, and can move around freely on both sides of the international border. It is both physically and symbolically a liminal zone. The park had already been used for a Canadian-American Peace Rally in the early summer of 1950, which Murphy had helped organize.

Robeson was technically not planning to leave the United States or to enter Canada on this occasion, and there was nothing authorities on either side of the border could legally do to interfere with his appearance on the American side. On the Canadian side, however, word came down from Ottawa that should Robeson try to go beyond the confines of the park and enter Canada, he would not be allowed in.

John Gray, the man who had been in the backseat of Robeson's car when it was turned back in Blaine, took charge of the cross-border planning. He arrived in Seattle several days before the concert date and liaised with Terry Pettus, a prominent left-winger and Northwestern editor of the *Daily People's World*, a newspaper closely associated with the Communist Party. It was no secret that Pettus was a member of the Party. Gray also traveled to Vancouver to discuss arrangements with Harvey Murphy at Mine Mill.

Murphy took charge of arranging for a truck, a piano, and loudspeakers for the concert. This equipment was positioned exactly halfway into the park, at the east-facing side of the arch.

Robeson flew into Seattle on the day before the concert. He arrived at the park without incident and the free concert, which also featured Larry Brown at the piano, began at 2:30 p.m. "The Star Spangled Banner" and "Oh Canada" were piped over the loudspeakers, and then Harvey Murphy took the stage, that is, the back of the truck, and welcomed the huge audience of Americans and Canadians—many of the latter had come on a fleet of more than twenty buses chartered in Vancouver by Mine Mill—to the event, which the union billed as the largest public gathering in the history of the Northwest, with as many as 40,000 men, women and children attending. "We are happy," Murphy yelled out, "that we are the means of bringing you together, but I know that Paul Robeson—that name—what that stands for is what every decent man and woman in the world stands for."

The crowd burst into applause. Then Robeson mounted the truck, joining Murphy, several others from Mine Mill, and Larry Brown at the piano. He was careful to remain on the American side of this strategically positioned stage, to avoid technically violating his confinement and becoming subject to the fine or imprisonment or both on his return to the border post.

After thanking Murphy and Mine Mill, Robeson turned to the audience and began to speak in the familiar defiant vein. "I stand here today under great stress," he began, "because I dare—as you do, all of you—to fight for peace and a decent life for all men, women and children wherever they may be. And especially today I stand fighting for the rights of my people in this America in which I was born." He insisted that this was a historic occasion and one that would enable him "to sing as I want to—to sing freely without being stopped here and there."

And then he launched into "Every Time I Feel the Spirit," a spiritual more than one hundred years old. "Ol' Man River," "Joe Hill," and several more spirituals followed, all of them to rapturous applause. He recited excerpts and sang songs in Chinese, Russian, and Yiddish, underpinning his vision of a united humanity and its expression through music. "Traveling about the world," he said, "I have seen and experienced the oneness of mankind. Not the differences but the likenesses—the common human spirit that we see in the various people's songs."

The concert lasted for two hours. Robeson promised to return the following year for another Peace Arch concert, and then exclaimed, "I'll see you soon; I'll be in Vancouver in a few months." Then he left. Slowly the people surrounding the Peace Arch got up, bundled their belongings and returned to their respective sides of the border. The FBI agents stopped filming. They had taken four rolls of 16 mm movie film, one roll of Super XX, and three rolls of Super X. Everyone came away with something special from this unique event.

However, only the Vancouver press covered the concert; newspapers on the American side of the border were mostly silent. Those few that did carry the story gave it very little space and estimated the crowd at only 4,500. The *New York Times* account gave the impression that the audience had been entirely Canadian.

Robeson kept his first promise: The following year, and for two more years after that, he traveled to Peace Arch Park and sang and spoke under the auspices of Mine Mill, always remaining on the American side. But although the state of national emergency was lifted in April 1952, when hostilities with all other nations had come to a legal end, at the end of June 1952, despite a presidential veto, it was extended, and Robeson never made it to Vancouver.

# 13

# A Political Meddler

It was unpleasant to have the State Department splashing the announcement of its revocation of his passport all over the country's newspapers, as it had on August 4, 1950. But Robeson refused to give up the document. For several days after his encounter with the special agents of the State Department's Internal Security Division, Robeson tried to get Washington to explain what it had done. This was not easy, but over time, explanations did emerge, and they were very revealing.

The word had gone round in Washington, at the State Department and the FBI, that Robeson was planning a Western European trip in late August 1950 and that on this trip he would attend a few meetings and give a few concerts. Internal documents show that the State Department was especially concerned about Robeson's plans for Italy. The US embassy in Rome had alerted Washington that they were uneasy about Robeson's participation in "an upcoming Communist meeting." This "Communist" meeting was a scheduled meeting of the Italian National Council of Peace Partisans in Rome. An outgoing telegram from Washington to Rome at the beginning of August advised the embassy to enlist the aid of Italian authorities to prevent Robeson's entry into the country.

The American authorities had every reason, given their attitude to the peace movement as it was defined in Paris in April 1949, to feel jittery about Robeson going to another peace meeting. The Paris Peace Congress and Robeson's speech were still exciting bitter criticism. But the Paris meeting had been only the beginning of what the Americans and British preferred to label the Soviet Peace Offensive. Peace activities were being stepped up across Europe.

At the conclusion of the Paris Peace Congress, a permanent committee of the Partisans of Peace had been established to coordinate national peace movements. One of its first, dramatic, and ambitious ventures resulted from a meeting in Stockholm in mid-March 1950. Initiated by Frédéric Joliot-Curie, this meeting launched a worldwide appeal to ban atomic weapons unconditionally. Known as the Stockholm Peace Appeal, the petition was distributed throughout the world and hundreds of millions signed it.

Also in Paris, a resolution had been passed to hold a second congress of the Partisans of Peace in the following year. At the end of May 1950, a meeting of the World Peace Movement in London, at which Robeson was present, decided that this Second Congress would be held in Genoa in mid-October.

No sooner had this plan been launched than it ran directly into a major stumbling block. In June, Count Carlo Sforza, the Italian foreign minister, declared that he would not be granting visas to foreign delegates. Hastily the executive committee of the Partisans of Peace changed the venue to Warsaw and the date to September. That decision, however, did not stand; when the committee met in Prague in the middle of August, the members decided that London, which the British Peace Committee had offered as a venue, would suit the peace movement better.

November 13–19 was provisionally set as the week of the conference. Then London was dropped in favor of Sheffield, but that plan, too, had to be changed when the British government sabotaged it by refusing visas to a number of key delegates. When it became clear that "more than two-thirds of the foreign delegates and the entire foreign leadership of the World Peace Council" would be excluded, the organizers decided to cancel the Sheffield meeting. Eventually, Warsaw was reconsidered, and the Second World Congress of the Partisans of Peace was finally held in the Polish capital between November 16–22, 1950.

Robeson would have been aware of this bumpy organizational ride to Warsaw and so would the US State Department. Robeson had an invitation to Prague as well as to the Second World Congress and he had every intention of participating in the latter. The State Department knew all this and revoked his passport to stop him from attending. Of course the State Department's action did not go unnoticed in Warsaw. Every American delegate there praised Robeson and criticized the State Department. Not surprisingly, given the politics of the peace movement, Robeson was elected in absentia to the Presidium of the World Congress as a member of the American delegation.

Of course, Robeson was not told at the time that the reason he was being prevented from leaving the United States was because the State Department did not want him going to international peace meetings. The letter sent to Robeson telling him that his passport had been revoked did not give any reason at all. But when Nathan Witt, Robeson's attorney, wrote to Secretary of State Dean Acheson for an explanation, the reply, from Mrs. Ruth Shipley, simply stated, "Paul Robeson's travel abroad *at this time* [my emphasis] would be contrary to the best interests of the department." And, for the time being, that explanation was all that was available.

Nathan Witt kept on at the State Department, trying to get them to meet with Robeson, to give him an explanation as to why they had asked for his passport and why they had revoked it. Finally the State Department agreed to a meeting, though they told Witt, "the Department feels that no useful purpose would be served by your proposed trip to the Department to discuss Paul Robeson's case."

On that point they were right. The meeting took place on August 23, 1950. Witt packed his side with a judge, an attorney and the dean of a law school. Robeson asked his friend William Patterson, himself a lawyer, to come along. Two officials from the Passport Division, Ashley Nichols and Willis Young, the acting chief, represented the State Department.

Witt accused the State Department of an arbitrary action that violated Robeson's rights. Why had they done this? he asked. No straight answer was forthcoming, but Nichols gave a pretty strong hint of what lay behind the State Department's decision when he asked Robeson for a statement that if he went abroad he would not speak. According to the press release from the Council on African Affairs, in which the details of the Washington meeting were reported, Nichols went further and specified that unless Robeson would agree to "refrain from criticizing the treatment of Negro Americans and the American government's foreign policy during his travels abroad," the State Department would stand put on its cancellation of his passport."

Robeson's answer to that was typically honest—and defiant. The news release reported that Robeson "expressed his deep and abiding loyalty to America," and at the same time remained resolved "to continue to criticize those acts emanating from foreign and domestic policy which in any way curtailed the constitutional liberties and human rights of the Negro people. He contended that this was in keeping with his duty as a loyal American citizen and consistent with his constitutional rights."

Robeson's legal team agreed with him and said so. After two hours, the meeting ended. The State Department stood its ground. No statement, no passport.

So, it was not only Robeson's advocacy of peace that disturbed the State Department. Added to that was their concern that Robeson would go around the world criticizing America's policy toward its black population. This, they contended, had to be stopped, and passport revocation was their weapon of choice.

Robeson's legal counsel, and that included the eminent men who had sat at his side at the State Department meeting, agreed that talking directly with the authorities was pointless. The court was their only recourse.

For the next few months, Nathan Witt prepared the case. On December 19, 1950, Robeson sued Dean Acheson, the secretary of state, in the US District Court in Washington, D.C., petitioning the court to "correct this unwarranted violation of [his] citizenship rights by the Executive branch of government." Specifically the argument was that the State Department was depriving Robeson of his constitutional rights of freedom of speech and the right to own and procure property—in particular, his right to earn a living was being violated, as the State Department's actions forced him to cancel scheduled concert appearances abroad.

It was a good gambit, but on April 21, 1951, the court upheld the State Department's actions by claiming to have no jurisdiction in the case. Robeson appealed immediately.

The case dragged on. In a brief to the court submitted in the early part of February 1952, the State Department made an incredible statement in justification of its position. In simple terms, their argument was that Secretary Acheson's actions were his business and not the court's. In the words of the brief, "the exercise of the Secretary's discretion in matters involving foreign affairs is non-reviewable."

So, what was there in the combination of Robeson and foreign affairs that the State Department was so exercised about? It is worth quoting their remarks more fully, both their statement and the footnote they appended to it. In the statement, the brief reminded the court that Robeson had alleged that Dean Acheson had acted as he did because, in his judgment, Robeson's travels abroad were contrary to the national interest. "[The Secretary of State] disapproved of the political ideas previously expressed by [him], and disapproved of [his] association abroad with persons of a similar political bent; and, further, because [he] is recognized as a spokesman for Negroes, for other minorities, and for the working classes. Obviously the Secretary weighed and judged the facts . . . It is true that [he] alleges [he] is a loyal citizen whose political activities are guided by the Constitution . . . But the Secretary thought otherwise, that he had evidence which satisfied him that [Robeson] was a dangerous anarchist, or that he was conspiring with citizens of one foreign nation to overthrow by force and violence the government of another."

The footnote added to this answered a hypothetical technical point, but toward the end of it, the State Department revealed what really infuriated them about Robeson. It stated that Robeson had "been for years extremely active politically on behalf of the independence of the colonial peoples of Africa," then came to the nub of the problem: "Though this may be a highly laudable aim, the diplomatic embarrassment that could arise from the presence abroad of such a *political meddler* [my emphasis], traveling under the protection of an American passport is easily imaginable. After all, 'the President is the sole organ of the federal government in the field of international relations.'"

So that was it. Robeson was a political meddler. At about the same time, MI5 in London was referring to Robeson as a "first-rate nuisance." Since the independence of colonial peoples was an ongoing process without any clear timeline, the United States government could, if it continued to abide by this argument, keep Robeson imprisoned forever. No wonder they insisted in internal memos that they would never grant him a passport.

Needless to say, these revelations, although they were public property, were not broadcast through the media. Only a few people knew about the disclosure in the footnote. Robeson made sure his *Freedom* readers were kept abreast of his fight with the State Department; he also made sure that the audience at the second Peace Arch Concert, in 1953, knew all about his status as a political meddler.

Robeson's appeal was argued on March 13, 1952. On August 7, 1952, the court decided to deny the appeal on the grounds that since his passport had already expired (January 25, 1951), "the case was moot." Robeson was stuck, and the impediments thrown in his way, even between the time of the appeal's argument and the court's decision, were getting tougher and would continue to grow.

~

The legislative framework around passports and the right to travel was set by the Internal Security Act of 1950, the McCarran Act, which became law on September 23, 1950. Its preamble set out the political context explaining the need for such legislation. Communism, it argued, was a "world-wide revolutionary movement whose purpose it is, by treachery, deceit, infiltration into other groups, espionage, sabotage, terrorism, and any other means deemed necessary, to establish a Communist totalitarian dictatorship in the countries throughout the world through the medium of a world-wide Communist organization." One of the vectors for the penetration of Communism in the world was "the travel of Communist members, representatives, and agents from country to country."

Americans, the preamble continued, "who participate in this world Communist movement are effectively discounting themselves as Americans: [they] repudiate their allegiance to the United States, and in effect transfer their allegiance to the foreign country in which is vested the direction and control of the world Communist movement." Communism presented "a clear and present danger to the security of the United States" and it fell to Congress "to preserve the sovereignty of the United States as an independent nation . . . to enact appropriate legislation recognizing the existence of such worldwide conspiracy . . . and to prevent it from accomplishing its purpose in the United States."

Besides requiring suspected Communists to register with the attorney general, and establishing the Subversive Activities Control Board, the act legislated against the travel of suspect people. In particular, Section 6 of the act made it unlawful for a member of an organization registered with the attorney general to apply for a new passport or to renew an existing one. In effect, as one commentator on passport regulations of the period has put it, "From the perspective of the United States Government, if a passport was desired by a Communist, he or she was welcome to seek one from his or her de facto sponsor: the Union of Soviet Socialist Republics."

Robeson would have known that had the Council on African Affairs registered with the attorney general, he would not have been able to renew his passport when it expired at the end of January 1951. The organization, as we have seen, sat back and waited for the Subversive Activities Control Board to come to it, which it finally did in April 1953.

Thus, although others seeking passports fell foul of the McCarran Act, Robeson escaped its reach. His passport problems did not come within the act's terms of reference. But that was not true of the next round of legislation, in which Pat McCarran teamed up with Francis Walter, a long-serving Democratic representative from Pennsylvania and staunch anti-Communist whom Robeson called "whining and fame-seeking," teamed up to attack the Communist threat from another angle.

The McCarran-Walter Act, also known as the Immigration and Nationality Act, came into force on June 27, 1952, despite President Truman's attempt to veto it. Among a welter of legislation concerned with rules on immigration, naturalization, quotas and eligibility, there were specific sections dealing with the notion of undesirability in certain immigrants and visitors to the United States; about what steps the attorney general could take to deport undesirables; and about passports.

The part of the act that referred to passports was in the section "Travel Control of Aliens and Citizens in Time of War or National Emergency," which declared it unlawful, in times of war or periods when the president had proclaimed a national emergency, for any American citizen to leave or enter the United States without a valid passport. This section of the act reiterated a feature of American passport policy that had been in existence throughout the twentieth century, namely that passports were instruments of travel that only became truly relevant under very specific circumstances. Anyone reading this part of the Act might easily have thought, "It makes sense," but how many of them would have realized that when the act went into force, the country had already been in a state of national emergency for more than a year, as President Truman had proclaimed one on December 16, 1950, and would remain in force for more than two decades? (It was lifted on September 14, 1978.) From that period onward, every American citizen had to have a passport to leave and reenter the country.

Whether it was in anticipation of the act or whether for other reasons is unclear, but on May 24, 1952, Secretary of State Dean Acheson set out a new department policy on passports. In making the announcement—which came through a State Department press release and was picked up the next day, May 25, by the *New York Times*, among other papers—Acheson noted that he was revisiting passport policy because, in his opinion, another, and new, class of undesirables had to be included among those already ineligible for a passport. The Passport Division had routinely refused passports to fugitives from justice, mentally ill persons, and persons likely to become a public charge abroad. It had also refused passports, Acheson added, "to persons . . . [who] had, on previous trips abroad, engaged in political activities in foreign countries." The connection between Acheson's argument and Robeson's passport problem is obvious.

Now, Acheson argued, it was time to add a new undesirable to the list: the Communist. His justification was the conviction of the eleven members of the Communist Party who had been arrested under the Smith Act in 1948, and specifically the Court of Appeals' statement that it was satisfied that these men engaged in a conspiracy that was "a clear and present danger to the United States." The State Department believed that the worldwide Communist movement was spread by disciples traveling freely and preaching revolution.

In this new political climate, Acheson's passport policy would be guided by the following general principle:

It would be inappropriate and inconsistent for the Department to issue a passport to a person if information in its files *gave reason to believe* [emphasis in original] that he is knowingly a member of a Communist organization or that his conduct abroad is likely to be contrary to the best interests of the United States.

A passport entitled the bearer to protection and help from American diplomatic offices abroad, and this, Acheson argued, was "correlative with the obligation to give undivided allegiance to the United States." Someone, therefore, who either at home or abroad promoted the interests of a foreign country to the detriment of the United States "should not be the bearer of an American passport."

Well, though he had managed not to be caught by the regulations of the McCarran Act of 1950, this policy statement would have hit Robeson square between the eyes. In his press release, Acheson admitted that although these regulations were new to the public, they were not new to the department, which had been following them since February 1951—in other words, around the time that Robeson's passport had expired.

This news was bad enough, but worse was to come. On September 2, 1952, the State Department, building on its earlier policy statement, announced that a few days before, on August 28, a new set of codified passport regulations had been adopted that specifically covered those cases involving "questions of possible subversive activities on the part of the applicant."

This greatly incensed Leonard Boudin, general counsel for the Emergency Civil Liberties Committee, founded in late 1951 by a group of progressives, including several lawyers, to defend the constitutional rights of individuals, particularly suspected Communists. Boudin, who had taken over Robeson's case from Nathan Witt in 1952, noted that this was the first time in the country's history that the State Department had issued "political regulations . . . restricting the right to travel."

And those political regulations were very specific as to whom the State Department defined as Communists: present members of the Communist Party or past members who were still, according to the department, acting to promote the Party's interests; persons not affiliated or ever affiliated with the Party but who supported the Communist movement; and persons "as to whom there is reason to believe, on the balance of all the evidence, that they are going abroad to engage in activities which will advance the Communist movement."

It was a very wide net, indeed. But the regulations made a further and even bolder move in nailing down those whom they termed Communists. The last section of the new regulations, section 51.142, sought to flush out Communists by making them incriminate themselves:

> If it is deemed necessary, the applicant may be required, as a part of the application, to subscribe, under oath or affirmation, to a statement with respect to present or past membership in the Communist Party. If applicant states that he is a Communist, refusal of a passport in his case will be without further proceedings.

Though nowhere in the policy statement or in the regulations did the State Department use the term *un-American*, an idea of un-Americanism was certainly there in all but words. How close the department came to that word and, therefore, to the House Un-American Activities Committee, would be revealed in time.

Once his passport had expired in 1951 and the courts had failed him in 1952, Robeson tried the more direct way of getting a passport, by simply applying for a new one. His first attempt was after he had been awarded the Stalin Peace Prize on December 22, 1952. On January 30, 1953, he applied to the Passport Division for a passport to attend the prize-giving ceremony in Moscow. He was denied. That would not have come as much of a surprise; the *New York Times*, had published an article on December 27 reporting that the State Department would not be granting Robeson a passport to go to the Soviet Union. On July 29, 1953, Robeson tried again, this time after receiving an invitation to play Othello in London. Once again he was turned down.

On that occasion, Robeson got a letter from Ruth Shipley telling him that he was denied on the basis of information possessed by her office that he was a Communist and that he had "manifested a consistent and prolonged adherence to the Communist Party line on a variety of issues . . ." The letter ended by noting that it was incumbent upon Robeson to demonstrate to the State Department, to their satisfaction, any deviation from the Communist Party line that might incline them to favor his application.

Robeson complained bitterly, then and on many occasions following his January 1953 application to travel to Moscow, that he was being singled out to sign the oath regarding present or past membership of the Communist Party that the State Department had added to its passport regulations in September 1952.

Robeson argued that half a million US citizens annually received passports without executing such an oath. That may have been true, but the oath was discretionary. According to the regulations, a demand for it was only applied if the State Department felt it was necessary. In Robeson's case, it did.

On each occasion that he applied for a passport, Robeson was presented with the oath, which he resolutely refused to sign. The State Department's file on him, he found out later, consisted of his participation in or mere sponsorship of a number of organizations that had either appeared on the attorney general's list or had come under the scrutiny of the Subversive Activities Control Board, and casual messages or even intended messages to organizations and meetings deemed Communist. The list, by no means exhaustive, referred to more than thirty such markers of Robeson's Communist sympathies. This so-called evidence of Robeson's affiliation with the Communist Party was precisely what was going the rounds at the FBI.

Robeson made a fourth application on July 2, 1954, in order to tour Britain, Israel, and continental Europe. The State Department met it with the same response. No oath, no passport.

Robeson's many attempts to gain a passport had made no impact on the State Department. And then, when all of his and Boudin's avenues seemed to have been exhausted, the atmosphere around passports changed abruptly and positively. The bolt from the blue came on March 15, 1955 when Judge Henry Schweinhaut, of the District of Columbia Court of Appeals, ordered the State Department to grant Otto Nathan, an economist who had taught at Princeton among other places and had been an adviser to the American government, a hearing on his passport application. Nathan had applied for a passport at the end of December 1952 and had heard nothing about his application since then. He had agreed to sign the affidavit concerning his Communist activities, declaring that he had none.

Leonard Boudin had taken up Nathan's case. On his client's behalf he had filed a complaint against the secretary of state in August 1954, and Judge Schweinhaut's order was the result of that filing. When, on June 1, 1955, the judge had not heard back from the State Department, he ordered them to grant Nathan a hearing on or before June 7. The waiting game started again, but just as they were expecting the State Department to begin a hearing, instead, on the day before the deadline, Boudin received a note from the attorney general saying that Nathan now had a passport and was free to go abroad, specifically to go to Europe to attend to the estate of his Princeton friend Albert Einstein, who had died in April; Einstein's will had named Nathan his executor.

The Nathan case showed clearly that the State Department's hand could be forced. They could, under some circumstances, be made to change their mind and, as several commentators pointed out, they apparently did not like hearings.

And then it got even better. Toward the end of June, a court of appeals ruled in the case of Max Shachtman, chairman of the

Independent Socialist League, who had been trying to get a passport for three years, that the State Department could not claim "exclusive discretionary powers in deciding who shall be allowed to travel abroad." Shachtman, the State Department had argued, was affiliated with a subversive organization, one on the attorney general's list. For more than six years, the court remarked, Shachtman had been trying to convince the State Department that his organization was anything but subversive, that it was vehemently anti-Communist and that he could prove it if they would only grant him a hearing. This the State Department never did.

The judges' opinion was written by Charles Fahy, who had served under Roosevelt during the president's third term and who was noted for his advocacy of workers' rights and the right of American citizens to belong to the American Communist Party. Fahy wrote that membership in an organization on the attorney general's list was insufficient reason to withhold a citizen's passport. This was the first time that judicial doubt had been cast on the status of the list. Fahy further claimed that the State Department could not refuse a citizen a passport without due process of law, and, even more importantly, that "the right to travel, to go from place to place . . . is a *natural right* [my emphasis] . . . A restraint imposed by the Government of the United States upon this liberty, therefore, must conform with the provision of the Fifth Amendment—No person shall be deprived of liberty without due process of law."

Full of optimism, Shachtman pressed the State Department again for a hearing. Little more than a month later, the State Department decided not to contest the Court's decision and handed Shachtman a passport.

In the meantime, a slew of similar cases came up in district courts; passports appeared as if by magic. Martin Kamen, a physicist who was teaching at Washington University, St. Louis, was first refused a passport in 1947 when he applied for one following an invitation to lecture at the Weizmann Institute of Science in

Tel Aviv. He finally got his passport in early July 1955. At about the same time, Clark Foreman, the director of the Emergency Civil Liberties Committee, who had been trying to get a passport since 1951, suddenly succeeded after a federal district court judge ordered the State Department to grant him a hearing. And then it was the turn of Joseph Clark, a foreign correspondent for the Communist Party's organ, the *Daily Worker*.

When news of Clark's success got out, I. F. Stone, the inveterate left-wing investigative journalist and essayist, commented in his self-published newsletter, *I. F. Stone's Weekly*:

> As a writer for the *Daily Worker*, he is ineligible for a passport under half a dozen provisions of the departmental regulations: he follows party line, advances party aims, has associated over the years with Communists, etc., and he failed to sign an affidavit swearing that he is not a Communist. If a Communist can get a passport without signing this humiliating affidavit, it is time non-Communists refused to sign it, too.

The first half of 1955 established new precedents in the history of the American passport. Court cases, for one, had demonstrated that the State Department could be made to reverse its decisions, and some of these cases, like Shachtman's, were historic. Added to that was the happy day (to many) April 30, when Ruth Shipley, whom I. F. Stone referred to as the Czarina, retired as director of the Passport Office. She had been in this post since 1928, serving under five presidents—including Roosevelt—and nine secretaries of state. She notoriously had reviewed each application personally, though at its peak her office had a staff of more than two hundred. She had had, in the word of a Supreme Court advocate, "limitless discretion."

Even Dean Acheson, Shipley's boss between 1949 and 1953, had been in awe of her. He referred to her office as the Queendom of Passports and once noted that she wielded "almost absolute power to decide who might leave and enter the country."

Describing her thinking, he continued, "Mrs. Shipley was alert to the dangers inherent in the travel abroad of Communists and other subversives and steadfastly adhered to the policy of refusing a passport . . . to Communists."

Stone was right to characterize Shipley as a Czarina: Everyone who had been denied a passport between June 1928 and May 1955 had been denied one by her.

With Shipley safely out of the way and her post filled by a new recruit from within the State Department, Frances Knight, everything was looking up. Boudin had succeeded with Nathan and now the time appeared ripe to get Robeson's case back on track.

On July 8, 1955 Boudin struck. He telegrammed the secretary of state demanding that Robeson be issued a passport, in line with those granted to Kamen, Foreman, and Clark. Receiving no reply, and knowing that the State Department had avoided submitting itself to a hearing in all of the passport cases that had come up before the court during the year, Boudin requested an appointment with Frances Knight to discuss Robeson's application. To his delight and surprise, Knight agreed to a meeting, which was scheduled for the morning of Monday, July 18.

Just before the meeting was about to begin, Boudin received a telegram from Frances Knight saying that she could not attend the meeting personally because she was required to appear at a Senate subcommittee hearing and that Raymund Yingling, a State Department legal adviser, would stand in for her. Robeson, Boudin, and several others met with Yingling, but to their surprise, he knew nothing about the Robeson case and had no idea what the meeting was all about. In his recollection of the day's events, Boudin said that he requested a meeting with those who knew what they were talking about.

Later that afternoon, the meeting took place as originally planned when Frances Knight reappeared. With her was her superior, Scott McLeod, the administrator of the Bureau of Security and Consular Affairs; her deputy director, Ashley Nichols, whom Robeson and his then counsel Nathan Witt had met with on an earlier occasion; and Loy Henderson, the undersecretary of state for administration, a high-ranking post with an impact on departmental policies, including passport policies. Yingling attended, too.

It was, Boudin recalled, a cordial and productive meeting. Knight took the exact same position that her predecessor had, namely, that Robeson's passport application remained incomplete since he had never signed the affidavit. Boudin argued that if a passport was a natural right, as was concluded in the Shachtman case, then it could not be conditional upon an affidavit. When Henderson asked around the table whether there was any legislative support for the affidavit, Yingling said he didn't know and Knight thought that a Senate committee had recommended it.

So much for policy. Boudin then turned to the question of Robeson being prevented from leaving the United States for those parts of the world where a passport was not required. Henderson had never heard of such a restriction and said he would look into it immediately. As to the passport, though, "that would take some time for the Department to consider."

Boudin did not express any opinion on the day's proceedings in his memorandum. If he had entertained any optimism that a new director at the Passport Office might signal a change of direction, he was sadly mistaken. He may or may not have known that the new Czarina had been handpicked by Ruth Shipley.

The day after the meeting, Boudin got a telephone call from Ashley Nichols. Robeson, he said, was free to go to Canada. Boudin telegraphed Nichols to confirm the conversation, stating that it was his "understanding that Mr. Robeson could now travel to any place for which a passport was not required."

The wire back simply restated that Robeson could go to Canada.

# 14

# A Cruel, Criminal Libel

In 1955, Robeson was fifty-eight and had been without a valid passport for almost five years. For an artist with a vast international following, this was, as no doubt the State Department intended it to be, a cruel state of affairs. Darting to and from Washington, D.C., appearing at a hearing and attending courts, filling in passport applications and meeting with his lawyers, all took up a lot of time as well as money. Robeson did what he could to make a living through concert appearances within the continental United States. Sometimes he met with bans and rejections, but mostly, he continued to sing and speak. His huge following in the large urban centers—Chicago, New York, San Francisco and Los Angeles—as well as on many college campuses guaranteed that at least he would not be forgotten.

But he was still without a passport. Despite the tireless work of his legal team and a concerted effort by representatives of peace organizations, cultural, civil rights, and labor groups and many individuals, who came together collectively in 1954 to form a pressure group, the Provisional Committee to Restore Paul Robeson's Passport, nothing, it seemed, could persuade the State Department to relent.

Still, they had lifted their restriction on his going to Canada and that, at least, was some kind of victory. Now, at the beginning of July 1955, Robeson prepared for his fourth Peace Arch concert and, for the first time since 1952, he was able to cross the border out of American territory without fear of punishment or penalty.

The decision to go ahead with another Peace Arch concert had been made in April, after Robeson had arranged a concert tour of California and the Pacific Northwest. The date of Sunday, July 24 was set. The truck, the piano, and all the sound equipment would be coming from the Canadian side and all arrangements handled by Mine Mill, as had become customary.

The crowd was smaller than it had been in 1952, but at least 10,000 people were there to hear Robeson sing and thank them for their support. The concert program contained a few classical pieces by Beethoven and Mussorgsky, folk songs from Europe, and a number of "Songs of Struggle," including a French-Canadian piece and the always expected "Joe Hill" and "Ol' Man River."

Robeson's speech was full of optimism and hope—"We have reached a turning point," he told the crowd, "and the onrush of events—from Bandung to Geneva—is an invincible tide against the Cold War and the threat of atomic holocaust. Here in the United States we see many hopeful signs of a changing political climate, and democratic peoples of all lands rejoice to see that McCarthyism is being rebuffed increasingly by the American people." The newspapers that carried reports of the concert all agreed that it was a resounding success and that Robeson was in great form.

Whether McCarthyism, as Robeson proclaimed, was indeed in retreat and being replaced by a new political climate was debatable, but it was true that Joseph McCarthy's reign as the leading anti-Communist in the Senate was over. On December 2, 1954, the Senate, by an overwhelming vote, censured the senator from Wisconsin for abusing his power and bringing the Senate into dishonor and disrepute. Following the vote of censure, McCarthy was completely ignored by his fellow senators; his rantings about Communist influences in the United States were now being treated as expressions of a sick mind.

Interestingly, although Robeson spoke of a change in the political climate, he kept to the American side of the park, venturing no further than the international boundary marker, a four-sided tapered stone plinth, which he grasped with one arm while waving to the crowd with the other. As far as the US authorities were concerned, Robeson was at liberty to cross the line and, if he had wanted to, make his way to Vancouver or anywhere else in Canada. He did not know that on the morning before the day of his Peace Arch concert, a telegram arrived in Washington from the US consulate in Vancouver, informing the secretary of state that Robeson would be refused entry into Canada.

Not long after his Peace Arch concert, there was talk of Robeson doing a concert in Canada celebrating, in part, his release from American detention. There was no doubt in his mind that he was wholly obligated to Mine Mill for all they had done, and his first Canadian appearance would be for them. Preparatory plans were put in place. There was also some talk of extending this into a full-blown Canadian tour, but that idea was swiftly consigned to the back burner when Robeson got a call to appear in court in Washington.

Leonard Boudin had not been deterred by the earlier July meeting with State Department and Passport Office officials, which ended not with the hoped-for granting of Robeson's passport but only with the limited lifting of his ban on travel to Canada. Boudin gave the State Department time to return Robeson's passport, and when at the end of July there was no sign of the document, he took a more aggressive course. He pressed the United States Court of Appeals for the District of Columbia Circuit to attend to an action he had originally brought earlier in the year, on January 15, to obtain an injunction compelling the State Department to issue Robeson a passport. The hearing was scheduled for August 16.

The State Department took no chances that day. They retained the services of Leo Rover, a United States attorney for the District of Columbia. He had first come to prominence as a prosecutor in the famous Teapot Dome trials of 1926–30, a massive corruption scandal involving oil corporations and US government–held oil reserves in Wyoming. After that, Rover quickly rose through the ranks and was appointed a United States attorney in 1934, under President Coolidge—retaining the post through the Hoover and Roosevelt administrations. He was selected as "lawyer of the year" for 1952–53 by the Bar Association of the District of Columbia.

Most recently he had been chief prosecutor for the government in a perjury case against Owen Lattimore, a scholar and China expert at Johns Hopkins University whom Senators McCarthy and McCarran had both accused of being a Soviet spy. The only minor mark against Rover, from the State Department's point of view, was that he had been present, although not the chief government questioner, at the passport case brought by Otto Nathan, which, to the department's shame, they had lost earlier in the year. Boudin had represented Nathan in that case and his victory over Rover's side then might seem to give him the advantage in this hearing.

And there was even more good news for Boudin and Robeson. Judge Burnita Shelton Matthews, assigned to preside over the hearing, had also been previously involved in a passport case. She was the federal district judge who had ordered the State Department to give Clark Foreman a hearing, prompting them immediately and without an explanation to hand him his passport instead. According to an article on June 28,1955 by *New York Times* reporter Luther Huston, who took a special interest in the passport issue, Judge Matthews, in her decision to order Foreman's State Department hearing, was following the precedent by the Court of Appeals in the Nathan case.

Burnita Matthews had also spent many years working for the National Woman's Party, a militant suffrage organization, to give legal strength to their demand for voting rights. Her legal work in the Washington, D.C., area had come to the attention of many of her senior colleagues. In 1948, when Congress created more than two dozen new federal judgeships, Matthews threw her hat into the ring. In 1950 the Senate ratified her appointment as a judge in the United States District Court, the first woman to occupy such a post. She was seen as a liberal.

The circumstances, from where Boudin and Robeson were sitting, could not have been bettered. And so the hearing began. Rover, whom I. F. Stone unkindly referred to as a little bantam of a man, was, we can imagine, determined not to let the Nathan case go against him. Too many successful years on the District of Columbia circuit had puffed up his confidence. Rover got straight to the heart of the matter. Referring to the plaintiff not by name but as "this man," he began by telling the court that only a naive person could believe that Robeson's intention, as he had carefully described it in his many passport applications, was to go abroad "merely to sing and merely to act."

Why, Rover asked, didn't Robeson just do what he was asked to do: sign the affidavit. The stalemate, Rover suggested, was entirely Robeson's fault. "This man should be required to at least start the ball rolling by telling us whether he is or is not a Communist, and then we proceed from there," Rover declared. After all, he explained, despite what Robeson himself had said on many occasions, the State Department was not singling him out. On the contrary, whenever the department had information that an applicant was or had been a Communist, he (Rover used only the male pronoun) was asked the same question about his affiliation.

And the department had a lot of information indicating that Robeson was a Communist. The record that Rover referred to, which had been supplied to Frances Knight in the State Department's Passport Office by the FBI as soon as they heard that Boudin had filed a motion, began in 1947, when "he was active in Communist circles in Canada." What Rover meant by that is anyone's guess. Perhaps he was referring to Robeson's appearance in May 1947 in Toronto at an evening concert sponsored by the Canadian Tribune Publishing Company, owners of the

*Canadian Tribune*, the newspaper of the Canadian Communist Party. The Toronto Special Branch of the RCMP noted that prominent members of the Communist Party, including Tim Buck, its long-serving general secretary, were present. Robeson had arrived by air from New York that evening expressly for the concert and returned to New York next day on an early morning flight.

In cataloging the department's file on Robeson's politics, Rover pointed out that Robeson had addressed a meeting of the Jefferson School of Social Science, which was on the attorney general's list; had written articles published in the *Daily Worker*; and had sent a message to the recent (April) meeting of representatives of twenty-nine Asian, African, and Middle Eastern countries gathered in the Indonesian city of Bandung (the beginnings of the non-aligned movement). Robeson had been invited to attend himself, but without a passport all he could do was send greetings. Rover told the court that in the message Robeson had pointed "to the Soviet Union, Eastern Europe and China as examples of social progress."

That statement, Rover continued, "has an overtone that is definitely communistic . . ." Conveniently, Rover, who must have seen the full 1,000-word text (it had been printed in the April 1955 issue of *Freedom*), ignored Robeson's first and key statement: "The time has come when the colored peoples of the world will no longer allow the great natural wealth of their countries to be exploited by the Western world while they are beset by hunger, disease and poverty."

All of this "evidence" of Robeson's embracing of communism was, however, nothing when compared to that fateful speech in Paris in April 1949. This formed Rover's key accusation. "See if this sounds like a loyal American citizen," he told the court. Repeating that "this man" had stated in his Paris speech that African Americans would never fight against the Soviet Union, Rover tore into Robeson, accusing him of a "cruel, criminal libel against the members of his own race." Look at Arlington and war cemeteries abroad, he pleaded with the court in stirring, even overly emotional terms, where "under white crosses are boys of the colored race and boys of the white race sleeping the sleep of death side by side."

Everything the State Department had on Robeson stacked up to one accusation: he was a communist in sympathies and, as the informant Manning Johnson had asserted in 1949, a member of the Communist Party.

How much of this was news to the court we cannot say; most likely everyone there had heard it all before. After all, it was precisely what had been said about Robeson for the past half dozen years in the mainstream press.

Robeson had by now learned that it was the State Department's policy to silence him on the international stage, and that this was the reason he had no passport. To date, the department had revealed that they did not like his peacemongering or his support for the international struggle against colonialism, which they saw as political meddling. Now Rover added a third reason: "He repeatedly criticized the conditions of Negroes in the United States, and always with this [sic] making invidious comparisons between the treatment accorded them in this country and that accorded them and other minority groups . . . in the Soviet Union."

Rover concluded his defense of the State Department by asking "this man [to clear] this thing up . . . I say right now that if Robeson [according to the record this was only the second time Rover had mentioned him by his name] will sign this affidavit, unless he admits he is a Communist, he will certainly be given a hearing."

Boudin in his response did not counter any of Rover's accusations. Instead, he asserted that political considerations, as exemplified by the affidavit of Communist affiliation, were improper as grounds for denial of a passport; he also questioned how the security of the United States could be compromised by

Robeson's appearances abroad. But his main intent was to press Judge Matthews to act in the Robeson case as she had done in the Foreman case: to order the State Department to grant Robeson a "quasi-judicial hearing."

At what point did it begin to dawn on Boudin and Robeson that all of the optimism they had invested in their case had been misplaced?

Judge Matthews turned out to be a bitter disappointment, holding to the departmental line. Robeson had not followed through on its administrative procedures, she argued. In other words, he had not signed the affidavit. Robeson needed to go away and do that and then, if he found that the State Department was, in his opinion, acting arbitrarily or was guilty of an "abuse of discretion," he could return. But for now, as Judge Matthews put it, "the court feels that it must deny the plaintiff's motion for an injunction . . . and the plaintiff's motion for a summary judgment."

A photograph shows Robeson outside of the court building after the judgment. Dressed in a light-colored suit, and tipping his hat to photographers, he looks as if he is trying his best to smile, but there is disappointment on his face. When asked by a reporter about the hearing, Robeson referred to the affidavit: "Of course I won't sign it. I consider it an invasion of every constitutional liberty I have."

Interviewed many years later, Boudin claimed that the effect on Robeson was traumatic, that he felt deeply that he had indeed been singled out. But he certainly didn't show it. In a statement Robeson released following the hearing, he made it clear that he could not be cowed. With Rover in his sights, Robeson went on the attack: "Instead of persecuting me for criticizing the conditions of Negroes in America, the US attorney ought to be down in Mississippi prosecuting those who have unleashed against our people a reign of terror and bloodshed."

August 1955 was not a good month for Robeson. The passport still eluded him, and his magazine *Freedom*, which had regularly kept its readers informed about his fight with the State Department, published its final edition.

Yet despite the judicial setback, Boudin had not exhausted all his legal avenues. There was nothing to stop him from appealing Judge Matthews's decision. But, suddenly, everything legal was put on hold when Robeson noticed he was passing blood in his urine. His physician diagnosed degeneration of the prostate (cancer was suspected) and operated to correct the condition. The operation, which was carried out in October and which did not reveal any malignancy, went well, but Robeson's recovery was slow. It wasn't until the beginning of January 1956 that he was given the all clear to continue with his work.

By mid-January Robeson had agreed to fulfill his commitment to appear in Canada, first at a major concert in Toronto's Massey Hall, the main venue for the city's serious musical entertainments and the site of some very famous performances, including, less than two years before, a legendary Dizzy Gillespie–Charlie Parker concert; and then in Sudbury, about 300 miles north of Toronto, where Local 598 of Mine Mill was holding the union's Eighth Annual Canadian Convention.

The Toronto concert, Robeson's first outside the United States since August 1950, had originally been scheduled for October 22, 1955 but, because of Robeson's sudden illness, was rescheduled for February 11, 1956. That evening, Robeson was received with all the warmth and adulation that he had experienced and been moved by so often in the past.

Both major Toronto newspapers, though largely unsympathetic to his politics, nevertheless could not withhold in their descriptions of the sold-out evening the sheer magnetism of the man and the total devotion of the audience—"a hero-worshipping crowd of 2,600 persons." Both reviewers agreed that Robeson's voice was not in peak form and explained this by his recent illness.

Whether the audience, who had endured a snowstorm to get to the downtown venue, noticed this also is not known, but if they did, their reactions did not show it. "Mr. Robeson . . . was given a standing ovation as he stepped onto the stage, and applause punctuated the 21 listed songs on the program . . ." Among those in the audience was a police officer named Papworth, who beside offering his superiors an unemotional account of the evening's performance, also reported on all the phone calls Robeson made from his hotel room.

Whereas the Toronto performance was fully covered in the Canadian mainstream press, the Sudbury concert on February 29 presented to the Mine Mill convention scarcely made a ripple. Robeson's appearance in Sudbury had not been guaranteed like the concert in Toronto. When the application for renting the Sudbury Arena, where Robeson was scheduled to perform, came up for discussion in the Sudbury city council, Leo Landreville, a lawyer and the city's mayor, protested against it being rented for that purpose. His request for information about Robeson's political activities ended up at Special Branch, RCMP. The Sudbury Arena denied to him, Robeson performed instead at Mine Mill's union hall in the city.

The Sudbury denial was not an isolated event; it was more in keeping with the official Cold War political climate in Canada than the Massey Hall extravaganza. How much Robeson was aware of what was going on in the offices of the Department of Citizenship and Immigration in Ottawa when he was contemplating his return to the international stage is not known. Immigration officers were told to allow Robeson into the country upon arrival, on February 7, at Toronto's Malton Airport. When the department received a request that Robeson be allowed to extend his stay to perform in Sudbury, this, too, was granted. But for both appearances, Robeson had to abide by a provision, insisted on by Jack Pickersgill, the minister in charge, that he not make any "public addresses or appearances other than those authorized." And Robeson was given leave to remain in Canada only until March 4.

Being allowed out of the United States for the first time in more than five years must have given Robeson some taste of the freedom of movement he had once enjoyed and, no doubt, taken for granted. The idea of a Canada-wide tour, which had been floated in the previous year and which now seemed to be a logical extension of his Toronto and Sudbury appearances, began to take shape.

Now, however, the Department of Citizenship and Immigration were not as cooperative as they had been in February. Early in March they received an application from John Boyd, a managing director of the Montreal-based booking agency, Jerome Concert Management. On behalf of his company, Boyd was seeking assurances from the department that Robeson would be allowed into Canada to embark on a five-week, seventeen-city concert tour of the country, starting in Montreal and ending in Vancouver.

The department turned the application over to the RCMP, asking for their assistance and for information on all those concerned—Robeson, Boyd, and the booking agency. When at the end of the month the RCMP delivered their report, Pickersgill announced at a cabinet meeting that Robeson would not be welcome and that the tour was off.

When news of Pickersgill's decision reached the floor of the House of Commons in Ottawa, questions were asked. One of the principal questioners was James Coldwell, leader of the only socialist party in the Canadian parliament. When Coldwell asked why Canadian doors had suddenly been closed to Robeson, Pickersgill replied, "It did not seem to me to be reasonable to admit from some other country a person who is a known and, I believe, a professed Communist, who was coming here to perform under what were, according to the information I have, Communist auspices."

Without saying so explicitly, Pickersgill was referring to the RCMP report, which allegedly showed that all of the executive officers of the booking agency were members of the Communist

Party. No one seemed to remember that the same agency had booked Robeson for the Massey Hall concert.

Jerome Concert Management petitioned Pickersgill to reverse his decision, assuring him that Robeson would restrict his Canadian appearances to concerts only. Pickersgill stood fast. A lookout notice on Robeson was sent to all border immigration officers.

Robeson was again imprisoned in the United States. This time, he couldn't blame the State Department—not directly, at least.

# 15

# You Are the Un-Americans

In January 1955, Francis Walter, joint architect with Pat McCarran of the 1952 Immigration and Naturalization Act, took the reins as chairman of the House Un-American Activities Committee. Walter, who was now sixty-two, would stay in this position for ten years, longer than any other chairman in the Committee's almost twenty-five-year history.

Walter was determined, as he told a newspaperman from the *New York Times*, to step up the attack on Communists—not, as his predecessors had done, by targeting specific organizations, but by going after individuals. As he put it to the reporter, "If a few Communists are found to be machinists, why should a whole defense industry be put in question by labeling the inquiry? This goes for other areas of activity." Walter was determined to use HUAC in tandem with the McCarran-Walter Act, which helped define undesirables both coming into and leaving the country, to root out and expose Communists wherever they were in the United States.

And he got right down to business. By the end of February 1956, the Committee was investigating Communist activities in Fort Wayne, Indiana, a major Midwestern manufacturing center with strong links to the defense industry, an area of special interest to the committee. Between February and May, other parts of the country came within HUAC's brief—witnesses appeared and were questioned about Communist activities in New York, Seattle, Los Angeles, Milwaukee, St. Louis areas, and the Rocky

Mountain states—and Communist infiltration of government was made the focus of more than ten separate hearings.

And then, as one historian of HUAC has eloquently put it, "the committee turned to a subject close to the chairman's troubled heart": passports. Before the deliberations leading to the final passage of the McCarran-Walter Act, Walter had been recognized as the leading speaker on immigration matters in the House of Representatives.

He was not pleased that the courts were cutting in on State Department decisions and overturning them. The issuing of passports, he believed, should be subject to departmental regulations backed up by statute. When Otto Nathan was finally given a passport, to enable him to attend to Einstein's estate in Switzerland, Walter was incensed. He didn't believe a word that Nathan had said. Walter told a *Washington Post* reporter, "Einstein never had any estate. [Nathan] spent all his time in Geneva in conference with the Communist chemists [sic] and then he came back to the United States and sang hymns of hate all over New York."

In another case, the presiding judge ruled that applicants who were refused a passport on the grounds that information held by the State Department showed them to be a security risk had the right to confront their accusers and see the information. Walter could not accept this. He maintained that "Communists and people under Communist discipline" would in the future use the ruling to their advantage. "After denial," he explained, "they take their cases to the courts in order to break the doors to the secret files. There they want to find names of those who keep an eye on their activities . . . To abide by those court decisions would mean a fast and complete destruction of our entire security organization." He blamed the judges, whom he described as belonging to Americans for Democratic Action, a liberal anti-Communist group.

Walter had decided to take things in his own hands, and in the previous Congress he had introduced a bill that would give the

State Department wide-ranging yet precise powers when it came to Communists. Specifically, it would counteract recent court decisions that insisted on due process. Instead, the State Department would not issue passports to Communists, broadly defined to include anyone who supported Communist ideas, and in the event of a hearing (what the bill termed a formal administrative review), it would retain its right not to disclose confidential files. Any federal employee who issued a passport to someone defined as a Communist could face two years in prison and a $5,000 fine.

Walter's bill was currently in the committee stage. The *Washington Post* viewed the bill with enormous suspicion and cautioned its readers about Walter's intransigent views. "[He] has long since made it plain," an editorial on May 14, 1956, explained, "that he regards as a 'substantial supporter of the Communist movement' anyone who dares to criticize him or his committee or his immigration law or anything else which he chooses to consider sacrosanct."

It was against this background that Walter prepared his committee for a series of hearings, beginning in late May, titled "The Unauthorized Use of United States Passports."

Robeson was on Walter's list of witnesses. The subpoena to appear was served by a US Marshal on May 22. He was due in Washington a week later, but his doctors advised him not to travel, and his attorney, Milton Friedman, [not the economist by the same name] enclosed two letters from doctors attesting to Robeson's ongoing recovery from his surgery at the end of the previous year. The committee accepted that Robeson needed to be confined to his home and rescheduled his appearance for June 12.

At the same time, they didn't wholly trust him. Donald Appel, an investigator for HUAC, contacted the FBI for help in tracking Robeson's movements between May 29, the date of his originally scheduled appearance, and June 12. If, during their surveillance of his address, the FBI had discovered that Robeson had left his home, then the committee would have begun proceedings against him on the grounds of contempt. (Not everyone at the FBI was happy with this request. Someone—the handwriting is strikingly similar to J. Edgar Hoover's—scribbled a note at the bottom of the memo: "I don't think we should be making investigations for the House Committee." Someone else added, "I agree.")

Chairman Walter had already told the press what his committee would be doing. It had evidence, he asserted, that there had been a "skillfully organized Communist passport conspiracy by which party members and fellow travelers are enabled to travel abroad in the service of Soviet propaganda and subversion." International Communist agents, including spies, Walter maintained, had fraudulently obtained American passports and were using these to spread their evil. The recent court rulings played straight into the hands of international Communism. And so, as Walter opened the first morning's hearing in the caucus room of the Old House Office Building, he reminded those present of the purpose of the investigation: "To ascertain the procedures by which the Communist Party has been able to obtain passports and make possible illegal travel for Communist Party members and sympathizers." As if anyone might be in doubt that this was a Francis Walter production, he added that the Committee's brief included determining "if the situation can be remedied by legislation now being considered by the Congress." His bill, in other words.

Robeson hadn't done any acting since 1945. His last screen role had been in *Tales of Manhattan*, in which he had appeared opposite Ethel Waters. That film was released in the autumn of 1942. He had last appeared on stage—in the role of Othello—in the summer of 1945, following the highly successful Broadway opening of the production in the previous year and the countrywide tour thereafter.

As June 12 approached, Robeson would have learned that the committee's hearings were pure theater. The Caucus Room, which had high ceilings and ornate moldings, was set up to facilitate close confrontation. Raised above the floor area and arranged around three sides was a continuous bench, in the center of which sat the members of the committee. To the right of them were banks of cameras and lights glaring down at the large table below, at which sat the witnesses and their counsel. Also around the table were the clerks and other employees of the committee, and behind them sat members of the public.

Robeson came to Washington with some experience to draw on; this was not his first appearance before a committee investigating un-American activities. On October 7, 1946, he had gone to Los Angeles to appear as a witness in what was cumbersomely called the Joint Fact-Finding Committee on Un-American Activities in California—the Tenney Committee, nicknamed for its chairman, state senator Jack Tenney, who had guided its activities from 1941 to 1949. Tenney had earned a reputation as a determined anti-Communist. In 1941, for example, years ahead of the federal legislation, he had introduced a bill with the self-explanatory name "Subversive Organizations Registration Act," which became California law.

The Tenney Committee's interview with Robeson, as it appears in the transcript, covered philosophical issues in Marxism and interpretations of recent European history. Only once was Robeson asked the question, and it came from Tenney himself, "Are you a member of the Communist Party?" To which Robeson replied that he had been asked this question many times before, and added, "Only you might ask me if I am a member of the Republican or Democratic Party. As far as I know, the Communist Party is a very legal one in the United States." Robeson never answered Tenney's question exactly, merely saying that he was not a Communist. Tenney did not return to the issue.

Robeson would have known, if he had read the House Un-American Activities Committee's reports over the intervening years, that his ride in Washington was likely to be far rockier than the one in Los Angeles. Whether or not he had read these reports, Friedman would have briefed him about the kinds of questions he should expect.

The committee members were experienced and knew their script. Robeson, however, had many years of experience on stage and screen behind him, and more acting talent than all of the committee members combined. It was certain to be a titanic confrontation.

At 10 a.m. on June 12, 1956, the room was prepared for Paul Robeson's appearance. The committee had been in recess for more than two weeks. Previously, it had heard from eleven witnesses, including Frances Knight of the Passport Office, who had carefully set out the State Department's policies and practices.

Alongside Francis Walter that morning were three committee members—congressmen Clyde Doyle of California, Bernard Kearney of New York, and Gordon Scherer of Ohio. Staff members included Richard Arens, the staff director, and Donald Appel, the investigator.

Arens started the questioning. Within a minute or so it was quite clear that this was not going to be any ordinary hearing. Who would dominate the proceedings was established immediately as a major issue. Arens asked Robeson to identify himself and give his address and occupation. Robeson complied. Arens then asked him to confirm whether he was appearing today because of the subpoena that had been served. Robeson replied to that too, but not as Arens expected. "Just a minute," Robeson said, "Do I have the privilege of asking whom I am addressing and who is addressing me?" Thus Robeson reversed the position of questioner and respondent. Arens, who in fact had not been introduced to the witness, then said he was Richard Arens. And, Robeson continued, "What is your position?" "I am director of staff," Arens replied. No previous witness had turned the tables in this way.

Arens soon regained his composure and resumed his role. The subpoena required Robeson to bring all his former passports to the hearing. Did Robeson have them? No, he said. He had looked everywhere for them, enlisted his wife in the search but found nothing. He told Arens that he would have produced them if he had had them. Arens dropped the subject and then asked Robeson if he had filed a passport application on July 2, 1954. "I have filed about twenty-five in the last few months," replied Robeson.

And then, for several minutes, Chairman Walter, who until now had remained silent, was engaged in a side tussle by Fried-man over the right of the committee to question Robeson about his passport applications, since the matter was sub judice. Walter backed off talking about passports and handed the questioning back to Arens, who returned to the July 1954 passport application. "Were you requested to submit a non-Communist affidavit?" Arens asked. Robeson's answer, in which he took the opportunity to introduce members of the hearing to Leonard Boudin, who was in the room, was the longest he had given so far, but its point was absolutely unequivocal: "Under no conditions would I think of signing any such affidavit . . . it is a complete contradiction of the rights of American citizens." And, no, to answer Arens' exact question, he had not complied and would not comply with the request.

We have no way of knowing what was going through Arens's mind; but it is reasonable to suppose that he was exasperated. At any rate this was the moment he chose to ask the big question: "Are you now a member of the Communist Party?" What did Arens expect Robeson to say? Yes? No? I don't know? Robeson said none of these. "Oh please, please, please," was all Arens managed to get out of him.

The gloves were off. Gordon Scherer, the Republican congressman from Ohio, who had been in the House only since the previous Congress, now weighed in, insisting that Robeson answer Arens's question. Instead, Robeson quizzed Scherer about what he meant by the Communist Party, asking him, in an echo of his Tenney Committee hearing nearly a decade before, whether he meant the legally constituted political party, a party no different in that respect from the Republican and Democratic parties.

Scherer had nothing more to say. Arens asked again, "Are you now a member of the Communist Party?" Yes? No? Neither. "Would you like to come to the ballot box when I vote and take out the ballot and see?" Robeson teasingly answered, reminding Arens, once again, that, first, Americans legally could and did vote for the Communist Party and, second, who you voted for was your own business; the ballot was secret.

If Arens had felt exasperated a few minutes earlier, he must now have felt helpless. He turned to Walter to make Robeson answer. "You are directed to answer the question," Walter ordered. One thing Robeson had learned in his long career on stage and screen was the importance of timing. And so, with almost thirty years of such experience to call on, Robeson paused and leaned over toward Friedman for advice. After some time, he was ready to answer.

"I stand upon the Fifth Amendment of the American Constitution."

Now everyone in the hearing that day, or in fact on any day, would have known what the Fifth Amendment was and what it meant to invoke it. In simple terms, the Fifth Amendment was designed to protect a witness from self-incrimination: for example by inadvertently supplying information during questioning in a place other than in a court, such as at a hearing or in a police station, that might lead to criminal prosecution.

Witnesses in the House Un-American Activities Committee hearings often invoked both the Fifth Amendment and the First, which protects freedom of speech, in an attempt to stonewall the proceedings. But the ploy had its downside. Those who chose to stand behind the Fifth Amendment often found themselves blacklisted after they left the Caucus Room, and their lives quickly fell apart. How you answered the question about membership in the Communist Party had huge implications.

For many, yes, but not for Robeson. The State Department had already done everything it could to make his professional life as difficult as possible. He had already effectively been blacklisted during the same time that the State Department kept him imprisoned in his own country. He had nothing to fear from taking the Fifth.

Time and time again Arens and Walter tried to brush aside Robeson's right to remain silent, but Robeson stood his ground, reminding his inquisitors that laying wreaths on the graves of Communists who were among the first to die fighting Fascism in Europe, which Robeson had done, was not a crime.

Arens changed tack. "Have you ever been known under the name of John Thomas?" he asked. Was this question, based on a feed from the FBI suggesting, but not confirming, that Robeson's Communist Party name was John Thomas, meant to trap Robeson in some way? "Oh, please," Robeson said, "'John Thomas!' My name is Paul Robeson." "I ask that you direct the witness to answer the question. He is making a speech," Congressman Scherer ordered Friedman. This Robeson's legal counsel answered by complaining that the photographers' equipment was making "nerve-racking" noises and they should desist. Walter ordered them to go on as they were. At which point Robeson interjected the fact that he was used to it, having been in motion pictures. And then, sensing that a farce was brewing, Robeson turned to the cameras and asked, "Do you want me to pose for it good? Do you want me to smile?" Arens tried to drag Robeson back to the main event. "I . . . ask you to confirm or deny that your Communist Party name was 'John Thomas'?" Robeson invoked the Fifth and added, "This is really ridiculous."

Arens then threw him another name, and Robeson responded with the thing they hated most. He burst out laughing. "This is not a laughing matter," Congressman Scherer snapped in the direction of Walter. "It is a laughing matter to me; this is really complete nonsense," was Robeson's reply.

Now, the Committee took itself very seriously and could not bear it when a witness was anything but submissive. Robeson had already shown an unwillingness to submit, but laughing aloud was tantamount to demonstrating, as one commentator has recently argued, the very subversiveness of which he was accused—the reason why they had subpoenaed him in the first place.

The laughter had to be stopped, and Arens repeated his question. "I invoke the Fifth," Robeson shot back. Scherer complained that he couldn't hear Robeson, to which Robeson remarked, one imagines in a booming voice, "I can talk plenty loud, yes. I am noted for my diction in the theater."

Then names of alleged Soviet espionage agents and others were thrown at Robeson. Did he know Louise Bransten? "The Fifth." What about Mr. and Mrs. Vladimir P. Mikheev? "Not the slightest idea." And Gregory Kheifets?

Now it was Robeson's turn to remind the bench above him why he had been called: "Oh, gentlemen, I thought I was here about some passports." Arens wasn't ready to go down that road just yet. More names. John Victor Murra? Leon Josephson? Well then, what about Manning Johnson? A short pause as Arens read out Johnson's testimony at the committee's hearing on July 14, 1949, when he affirmed under oath that Robeson was a member of the Communist Party. Robeson told the hearing that Manning Johnson should be cross-examined.

More banter followed. The pattern was set. Did you say this? Do you know so-and-so? Were you at that meeting? "I invoke the Fifth Amendment." "Tell us whether or not you are the Paul Robeson alluded to in this document [a flier for the Council on African Affairs sponsored homecoming after his 1949 European tour]." "I would be the Paul Robeson."

And then Robeson, the showman, pulled an amazing stunt. He managed to get Chairman Francis Walter eating out of his hand, acting almost as if he were hypnotized. Walter began berating Robeson for not respecting what he termed the committee's "distasteful task." At which point Robeson, having had his own identity questioned repeatedly, asked Walter who *he* was? Without realizing that the tables were being turned, Walter, in what must have been a self-congratulatory tone, declared that he was the chairman of the committee. And then Robeson, witness turned inquisitor, took over the questioning. "Mr. Walter?" he asked; "Yes," answered Walter attentively. "The Pennsylvania Walter?" "That is right."

Having established who Walter was, Robeson began to lead his witness and, surprisingly, Walter followed. "You are the author of all of the bills that are going to keep all kinds of decent people out of the country?" "No," answered Walter, "only your kind." Now Robeson had him, and he moved into position for the kill; "Colored people like myself . . . ?" Walter was on the brink of tying himself in knots. "We are trying to make it easier to get rid of your kind, too," he asserted. "Your kind?" Robeson, in the manner of his inquisitors, repeated the question: "You do not want any colored people to come in?"

As if he had just woken up from a trance, Walter turned to Arens and demanded, "Proceed."

The Fifth Amendment. Laughter. Witness turned inquisitor. Robeson had a bag of tricks with him that morning and there was more to come.

Robeson had prepared a statement. When he first tried to read it, Arens told him that he could do so only if he told the committee the names of Communists at the core of the Council on African Affairs. Robeson replied to that by invoking the Fifth Amendment and then began to talk. It turned out to be the longest unbroken speech that anyone gave that morning, and in it, Robeson managed to incorporate most of the points he had intended to read from his statement.

Unlike his inquisitors, he dwelled on the reason for his being summoned to appear. It was not to find out whether he was or was not a Communist, as the questioning so far in the hearing suggested. No, it was because he was not being allowed to travel. The State Department wanted him silenced because he spoke against colonialism and criticized the American government for the injustices against his people. Robeson referred to the proceedings not as a hearing but as a trial. "I am being tried," he exclaimed, "for fighting for the rights of my people who are still second-class citizens in this country . . . I stand here struggling for the rights of my people . . . You want to shut up every Negro who has the courage to stand up and fight for the rights of his people . . . And that is why I am here today."

At this point Walter, who must have been under some sort of spell during Robeson's speech, called out, "Now just a minute," a show of authority that Robeson diffused by repeating, "All of this is nonsense."

The comedy continued and clearly the committee was growing increasingly frustrated with Robeson's alternating between invoking the Fifth Amendment and attempting to read his own statement, while not quite obstructing the proceedings in a legally culpable way.

Before too long, and not surprisingly, Arens, who had a pile of documents in front of him, began to ask Robeson about the Paris speech. The questions were no different than they had been in 1949 and had continued to be right up to this day. Robeson had had enough and launched in with a detailed statement that approximated what he had actually said, rather than what he was reported to have said, in Paris. "Four hundred million in India and millions everywhere have told you precisely that the colored people are not going to die for anybody and they are going to die for their independence. We are dealing not with fifteen million colored people [the widely quoted estimate of the African-American population]. We are dealing with hundreds of millions."

Robeson stopped the show. Bernard Kearney, congressman from New York, was satisfied that he had answered Arens's questions and that the Paris speech had been dealt with.

But 1949 was not yet fully covered: Arens kept after Robeson, asking him about what he had said in Prague that year, and in Moscow. In particular he wanted Robeson to admit that he had said in an article published in Moscow after his arrival there that "now after many years I am here again in Moscow, in the country I love more than any other." Robeson explained to the hearing that he had said that in Russia "I felt for the first time like a full human being," which was not how he felt in the United States. He repeated it: "It was the first time I felt like a human being, where I did not feel the pressure of colored [sic] as I feel in this committee today."

Congressman Scherer, who had joined in the questioning about Robeson's feelings toward the Soviet Union, then asked what seemed an innocuous question, but it gave Robeson a remarkable moment to claim his rights as an American. "Why," Scherer asked, "do you not stay in Russia?" In Scherer's face a quick, sharp history lesson: "Because my father was a slave, and my people died to build this country, and I am going to stay here and have a part of it just like you."

Arens was not through yet. He had his own bag of tricks, and now, for the first time in the morning's hearings, he got as close as anyone did to ruffling Robeson. The topic: Robeson's admiration for the Soviet Union. Had the hearing happened a few months earlier, or even a few weeks earlier, as planned, Robeson would not have had a problem.

Since the middle of March, newspapers around the world had been buzzing with reports that Nikita Khrushchev, who had been first secretary of the Communist Party of the Soviet Union since September 1953, had made a damning speech in late February in a closed meeting at the Twentieth Congress of the Communist Party, about Stalin, his predecessor, who had died in March 1953. Khrushchev had bitterly attacked Stalin and accused him of appalling crimes against his own people, including massacres and torture, over more than thirty years of rule. The speech itself had remained hidden from public view until exactly one week before this hearing, when first the *New York Times* and then other leading newspapers across the country and in other parts of the world printed what was claimed to be a true version of Khrushchev's speech of February 24, 1956, "On the Cult of the Personality and Its Consequences." Now anyone in the West (the speech was not published in Soviet newspapers until 1989) could read about the full horrors of Stalin's iron rule.

These sensational revelations were still fresh in people's minds and Arens took advantage of them in his battle with Robeson. Arens was also aware that Robeson had been awarded the Stalin Peace Prize in 1952 but had not been able to travel to accept the prize. For the first time that morning Robeson looked vulnerable. Arens kept asking Robeson about his feelings toward Stalin. Robeson would not be drawn, but his answers lacked the defiance and playfulness of the day's earlier encounters.

> MR. ARENS: While you were in Moscow [in 1949], did you make a speech lauding Stalin?
> MR. ROBESON: I do not know.
> MR. ARENS: Did you say in effect that Stalin was a great man and Stalin had done much for the Russian people, for all the nations of the world, for all working people of the earth?
> MR. ROBESON: I cannot remember.
> MR. ARENS: Do you have a recollection of praising Stalin?
> MR. ROBESON: I can certainly know that I said a lot about Soviet people, fighting for the peoples of the earth.
> MR. ARENS: Did you praise Stalin?
> MR. ROBESON: I do not remember.

But just as it looked as though Arens had him pinned in a corner, Robeson slipped through and regained his poise. He wasn't here to talk about Stalin, he told Arens. That was a matter for the Soviet people. Instead, Robeson turned the discussion back to conditions in the United States. "I would not argue with a representative of the people," he chided the committee, "who in building America wasted 60 to 100 million lives of my people, black people drawn from Africa on the plantations. You are responsible, and your forebears, for 60 to 100 million black people dying in the slave ships and on the plantations, and don't you ask me about anybody, please."

Arens and Scherer kept trying to get Robeson on Stalin, but now that he was out of the corner he would have none of it. Did you say this? Did you say that? Once again, "Did you, while you were in Moscow, make this statement?" Arens read the statement. Robeson had had enough. Up until then he had politely called his inquisitors "Gentlemen" and "Mister." Suddenly he switched to a form of address that had many layers of meaning: "Now you are making it up, brother. I would have to get my own copy of the speech."

Arens, joined by Walter, kept reading excerpts from the statement and from an article published in the *Daily Worker*. Robeson sternly and succinctly rebuked each of their questions. Then Arens, still reading from the article, asked Robeson to comment on its report that Robeson had begun to study Marxism in Moscow. No, Robeson told the committee, he had studied it in England, "so you cannot blame that on the Russians. You will have to blame that on the English Labour Party."

Robeson had said all he was going to about his political education. He remarked that 140,000 Yorkshire miners wanted him to sing for them. It was time for him to remind the committee why he was here. "Do you think you could let me go?" he asked politely. "We have nothing to do with that," Walter replied.

On that point he was certainly right. "Could you not make a suggestion to the State Department that I be allowed to go?" Robeson asked cheekily. No, Walter said, the courts had ruled that it was in the best interests of the country that he should stay put. "They have not done that," Robeson shot back. "They have ruled on a very technical problem, Mr. Walter, as to whether I sign an affidavit. That is all," he added. On this point, Robeson was, of course, right.

Arens could not let go of 1949. He tried Robeson on another alleged statement, this one made at a meeting, Arens insisted, when Robeson had lost his temper with the press. Arens was in for a shock. It was not at a meeting but at his son's wedding, and, yes, he had wanted to smash one of their cameras. The temperature in the room shot up—Arens had blundered into very personal space and Robeson was now close to losing his temper again. "I do not care what [the report] says," Robeson shouted.

Arens tried to change the subject by asking about Ben Davis, who Robeson agreed was one of his closest friends. Davis, along with ten others, had gone on trial in New York in 1949, accused of violating the Smith Act. Found guilty, Davis had spent more than three years in a federal jail. Then Arens committed another faux pas, treading once more in Robeson's personal space: "Did I understand you to laud his patriotism?" Arens had pushed him too far.

"I say that he is as patriotic an American as there can be."

Robeson could have left it at that but now the floodgates were opened; he turned on his inquisitors fiercely, angrily attacking them. "You gentlemen," he exclaimed, "belong with the Alien and Sedition Acts, and you are the nonpatriots, and you are the un-Americans and you ought to be ashamed of yourselves." No one had ever spoken like that to the Committee. Walter reacted immediately.

THE CHAIRMAN: Just a minute, the hearing is now adjourned.

MR. ROBESON: I should think it would be.

THE CHAIRMAN: I have endured all of this that I can.

MR. ROBESON: Can I read my statement?

THE CHAIRMAN: No, you cannot read it. The meeting is adjourned.

MR. ROBESON: [GETTING IN THE LAST WORD] I think it should be and you should adjourn this forever, that is what I would say.

The adjournment was carried. It was only 11 a.m.

# PART V

# LET ROBESON GO

# 16

# Kent v. Dulles

Robeson had given the committee a set of very valuable history lessons. He had revealed to them his talents as a lawyer and a performer; affirmed his dedication as an activist committed to world peace, colonial independence, and the struggle of African Americans; and reassured them that he was indebted to British socialists in the 1930s, not Russian communists in the 1940s, for his political education.

For this superb command performance his audience was anything but grateful. The committee wanted to punish Robeson. Blacklisting was useless, as was any other form of public disgrace. But they did have a powerful legal weapon at their disposal, which if deployed successfully could do real damage: a charge of contempt.

Contempt of Congress was a serious matter. Anyone found guilty of it could face a substantial fine and time in a federal prison. HUAC resorted to this form of punishment more often than did any of the other fourteen congressional committees. During its Cold War heyday, between 1945 and 1957, the House Un-American Activities Committee accounted for more than 60 percent of all the witnesses cited for contempt of Congress.

No sooner had Robeson left the Caucus Room than Walter, Scherer, and Kearney, who formally constituted a subcommittee, met and unanimously agreed to recommend that Robeson be cited for contempt. The next day, when all seven members of the committee met again, they voted unanimously to recommend congressional proceedings against Robeson.

When he was asked about his decision to cite Robeson, Walter said that there were three aspects of "the baritone's bellowing, bombastic testimony" that warranted action: first, his "entire conduct"; second, "his assault on the committee"; and third, a personal attack on Senator James Eastland. This final reference is interesting, because Robeson mentioned Eastland's name only once, when he stated that African Americans would never take up arms "in the name of an Eastland."

Senator Eastland, a Democrat from Mississippi who had served in the Senate since 1943, was one of the most outspoken anti–civil rights and anti-Communist legislators. He had already made his segregationist views known in 1954, when the Supreme Court handed down its verdict in *Brown v. Board of Education*, stating that having separate public schools for blacks and whites was unconstitutional. Eastland said then, "On May 17, 1954, the Constitution of the United States was destroyed because of the Supreme Court's decision." His anti-Communist credentials were just as strong. He took the reins of the Senate's Internal Security Subcommittee when the Democrats gained the majority in the November 1954 midterm elections, and in 1956 he extended his power by becoming chairman of the Senate Judiciary Committee, which between 1949 and 1953 had been headed by Senator Pat McCarran.

That Robeson even mentioned Eastland's name, in what many Americans would have thought a reasonable manner, was enough to provoke the committee to throw the book at him. What Walter would have done had he heard the statement he hadn't allowed Robeson to read is anyone's guess, but there is little doubt that he would have been even more enraged. It is worth recalling, for the record, what Robeson would have said about Eastland had he been given the chance:

Why does Walter not investigate the truly "un-American" activities of Eastland and his gang, to whom the Constitution is a scrap of paper when invoked by the Negro people and to whom defiance of the Supreme Court is a racial duty? And how can Eastland pretend concern over the internal security of our country while he supports the most brutal assaults on fifteen million Americans by the white citizens' councils and the Ku Klux Klan?

Robeson was the first to feel the committee's ire in this set of hearings, but not the last. Clark Foreman, director of the Emergency Civil Liberties Committee, faced the same charges of contempt. Arthur Miller was also cited, and Otto Nathan was threatened with such action. All of these witnesses were, in the committee's parlance, unfriendly.

Unlike Miller, whose name went forward to Congress, where an overwhelming majority of votes were cast in favor of the contempt resolution, Robeson's citing never made it to the floor of the House. Though Walter may have been incensed, strictly speaking there wasn't much of a case against Robeson. He had answered the questions put to him and thus was not in contempt. How much of this mattered to Congress in their decision not to take the matter further? It may be that the members realized that giving Robeson yet another platform on which to perform was not in their best interest.

Sitting in the Caucus Room that June morning with Robeson, facing his three examiners, it might have been difficult to see what their questioning had to do directly with HUAC's stated concerns. Obviously Francis Walter would have argued that in order to establish that American passports were being misused by the international Communist conspiracy, it was necessary to show that the witness was part of that conspiracy. Robeson's hearing did not in fact produce any legal evidence that he was part of that conspiracy. Judging by their proceedings, the committee members thought it did.

In any case, Robeson obviously thought it was all a bit of a sideshow. His main issue was not with the committee—he said as

much when he asked Francis Walter to help him get his passport—but with the State Department.

On that front Robeson was no further advanced than he had
been since the State Department allowed him to travel to Canada
in the previous year. As for travel overseas, he and Leonard
Boudin had tried repeatedly to get support from the courts and
failed. Their last such attempt had been on March 7, 1956, when
all eight judges of the Court of Appeals for the District of
Columbia sat to consider Robeson's case against the State
Department.

Three months later, the judges agreed that Robeson had still
not "exhausted his administrative remedies." He had refused to
sign the affidavit concerning past or present membership in the
Communist Party, and that was required in order to complete the
passport application. This civil action, in the court's opinion, was
premature. When Boudin appealed to the Supreme Court to issue
an order for the Court of Appeals to review its decision, this, too,
was denied.

After hearing the disappointing news of the Supreme Court's
decision, at the beginning of November, Boudin tried to get
Robeson to consider what to do next. It is clear from the letters
exchanged between them that Robeson was getting tired of the
legal battle, which was racking up expenses that he was now finding it hard to meet. Robeson had already turned down Boudin's
suggestion, after the Court of Appeals case fell apart, of taking
the case to the Supreme Court, arguing that it would be impossi-
bly costly.

So Boudin was left with no choice but to follow the Court of
Appeals' ruling and confront the State Department. But getting
the department to answer a letter, let alone agree to a hearing,
proved to be a long process; begun in January 1957, it dragged on
for four months, marked by long intervals of silence from the
department. While he waited for an answer, Boudin urged
Robeson to apply again for a passport to take him only to the
United Kingdom and Czechoslovakia for six months, just enough

time to fulfill the engagements he had been offered, playing Othello and appearing at the Prague Festival on the same program as the Cleveland Symphony Orchestra—the only other American musicians invited there.

Robeson filed for a passport on March 21, still without signing the affidavit about Communist activities. Almost two months later, on May 14, Boudin was told that the State Department would grant Robeson an informal hearing on May 29. Then on May 27 Robeson and Boudin learned that the passport application had been denied because he had not signed the affidavit. Boudin protested that they had been told of the fate of the application such a short time before they were due to appear at the hearing in Washington.

The hearing was held at 9:30 a.m. in one of the State Department Annex buildings. Leonard Boudin and Eslanda Robeson accompanied Robeson into the room. William Duggan, who had been with the Passport Office's legal department for more than twenty years, took the chair; his legal department colleague, Robert Johnson, represented the office's case against Robeson.

The meeting began well. There was nothing confrontational, nothing of the atmosphere of the House Un-American Activities Committee hearing of the previous year. Once formalities were dealt with, Johnson began talking to Robeson. He asked Robeson how, if a passport were issued to him, he would spend his time abroad. Would he, for instance, visit the Soviet Union? Yes, said Robeson, he would like to visit again, though he hadn't been invited. Would he try to go to Hungary (the State Department prohibited Americans from traveling there)? Certainly not, replied Robeson in a submissive tone. Then Johnson, after hearing Robeson describe how important it was for him to continue practicing his art, singing and acting, stepped outside of his official role and paid him a compliment. "I can say this," he remarked, "even listening to you talk, you have a musical voice, just listening to your narrative here."

Robeson replied, "It happens that my speaking voice is part of my singing voice. One of the great beauties of *Othello* is the beauty of the poetry . . ."

If at this point, Boudin, Eslanda, and Paul felt cheered by the progress of the hearing, they would have had every reason. But the spell was soon to be broken, when Johnson returned, as every one of Robeson's inquisitors had, to 1949, beginning with Manning Johnson's HUAC testimony. Boudin protested, as he had done on previous occasions, that Johnson had been shown to be an unreliable witness—a perjurer, in fact—and that the United States Government had stopped employing him as a professional witness. Duggan responded by adjourning the meeting until noon.

When the hearing resumed, Manning Johnson's testimony continued to be the subject, but Boudin stood with Robeson in refusing to answer any questions about it. Then out came the names, names of Communist Party officials. Did Robeson know these people? Boudin repeated that Robeson refused to answer. And more names. Objection. And then it was the turn of organizations, such as the Council on African Affairs. Did Robeson, in his position as chairman, receive "any instructions, policy directives, and the like, from the Communist Party or from any executive in the Communist Party?" "Same objection," Boudin called out. And then Johnson swung back to 1949 again, to the Scandinavian part of Robeson's European tour, asking Robeson to comment on statements he made at the time that were reported in State Department dispatches and that led it to conclude that he was a Communist. "Objection."

When 1949 was exhausted as a subject, Johnson asked the same questions about every year up to the present one. And then he popped the big question: "Mr. Robeson, are you now a member of the Communist Party? . . . Mr. Robeson, have you ever been a member of the Communist Party?" and asked it over and over again specifically about the Communist Party of each country Robeson had visited and lived in since 1928.

Boudin had had enough. He repeated that it didn't matter which Communist parties—Irish, British, Australian, or American—or any other political parties Robeson had or hadn't joined: "We do not believe that that has any relevance to the right of a man to travel." Johnson then reminded Robeson and Boudin that "refusal to make a full disclosure of present membership in the Communist Party . . . will halt the administrative processing of your application." In particular, Robeson's 1949 European tour was viewed within the State Department as a Communist-inspired event, and such past political activities rendered Robeson "ineligible for travel." Once the State Department had admitted this, Boudin asked the obvious question:

We are now in the year 1957, and Mr. Robeson has been prevented from traveling even in the Western Hemisphere now for many years . . . When does this end? When does he have the right to travel? . . . Is there, in the view of the department, a point—a point of time, whether it is six months from now or a year or two years—when the department will say, "We will not consider any more activities of '49, or a message of 1955, or a speech in 1953, as a ground for denying passport facilities," or are these always to remain a bar to travel in the absence of our yielding and giving you statements with respect to political association?

The State Department did not answer. At 3:05 p.m., the meeting was adjourned. Boudin was up against the wall. He had tried everything but a judicial proceeding against the State Department in the Supreme Court, a course that Robeson financially couldn't afford.

In an internal memo written promptly after the meeting was adjourned, Johnson referred to the hearing as a washout, meaning that Robeson had steadfastly refused to admit any Communist connections. The State Department would continue to refuse Robeson a passport, on the grounds stated in the letter they had sent to him on May 27.

At the hearing, Boudin had pointed out that the State Department was restricting Robeson's travel in two distinct ways: first by not granting him a passport; and second—which was less frequently mentioned—by blocking him from visiting countries that a United States citizen did not need a passport to enter. As recently as February 1957, the Immigration and Naturalization Service had alerted all airline and steamship companies to prevent Robeson's departure from the United States for any country except Canada. "Unlawful transportation of such a person," the letter went on to say, was punishable by federal law.

Although trying to get a passport for Robeson out of the State Department was futile, during the hearing Johnson had agreed to look into the restriction on Robeson's travel to countries where a passport was not required. A couple of days after the hearing, Boudin wrote to Frances Knight reminding her of Johnson's commitment and pointing out that, to the best of his knowledge, Robeson was the *only* [my emphasis] American citizen whose travel was restricted in this way.

Some time passed while the issue was discussed by various State Department officials, all of whom agreed that Robeson was unique in having this restriction placed on him and that he could not legally be singled out in this way. On August 9, Knight wrote to Robeson telling him that his application for a passport was stalled because he refused to answer questions about his Communist affiliations—nothing new there—but that the restriction on travel to countries not requiring a passport would be lifted. As of now, Robeson was told, he could travel anywhere in the western hemisphere not requiring a passport. That included American possessions, such as Alaska, Hawaii, and American Samoa, many parts of the Caribbean, Bermuda, and Mexico.

A victory of sorts. Unfortunately, in practical terms, none of this made much difference to Robeson as an artist, as he had no planned engagements in any of these places.

Boudin did not want Robeson to give up now, even though his case seemed hopeless. He wanted to start another lawsuit immediately; if they delayed, he said, "the argument . . . will be made and will have a psychological, if not a legal, effect, that we have been dilatory in pursuing our objectives."

At almost the same moment that Boudin wrote this to his client, Robeson received a wonderful offer from Glen Shaw, director of the Shakespeare Memorial Theatre in Stratford-upon-Avon, to play the part of Gower in a production of *Pericles, Prince of Tyre* directed by Tony Richardson, scheduled for the 1958 season.

Such a high-profile offer, Boudin felt, might give him more leverage with the State Department than he had had on previous occasions. On December 10, 1957, he wrote to Frances Knight requesting immediate consideration of his suggestion that Robeson should be granted a highly restricted passport allowing him only to go to England and only for the duration of this very prestigious engagement.

On January 17, 1958, Knight wrote back to say that the Passport Office's position would not change and they would not be issuing Robeson a restricted passport. Boudin responded by firing off a letter to Loy Henderson, deputy undersecretary for administration and Knight's boss, telling him in direct clear language that if he didn't give Robeson the passport he needed to play in *Pericles*, Boudin would start legal proceedings against the State Department.

Henderson would not budge. Boudin began drafting a complaint to present to the district court for the District of Columbia. A final draft was ready for submission in March. Several administrative procedures delayed the hearing, which by early June had still not begun.

While they waited for a chance to make their case in the district court, nearby, in another, more important, judicial building, a surprising and momentous decision was about to be made that would change the entire political landscape.

Leonard Boudin had been representing two other American citizens who, like Robeson, had been denied passports. Walter Briehl was a Los Angeles–based psychiatrist. In April 1955 he had applied for a passport to attend an international psychoanalytic congress in Geneva and a meeting of the World Mental Health Organization in Istanbul. Briehl had attended international meetings of this kind before and expected to be able to go. Instead, he received a letter from the Passport Office requesting that he sign the Communist affiliation affidavit. Boudin advised him not to submit the document, setting off a series of hearings, passport applications, demands, and refusals, between Briehl and Boudin on one side and the Passport Office on the other, that paralleled Robeson's experiences.

Briehl's lawsuit against the State Department in the Court of Appeals for the District of Columbia was argued on January 29, 1957. Later on the same day, Boudin presented a lawsuit for another of his clients, Rockwell Kent, a well-known artist who had been denied a passport in 1950 and had applied again in 1955 in order to visit a number of European countries for work and pleasure. On this second attempt, Kent had received the exact same treatment as Briehl and Robeson.

Just under five months later, the circuit judges presented their decision in the Kent case: On a vote of 5–3, the Court of Appeals had ruled in favor of the government. David Bazelon, one of the dissenting judges, and his two colleagues who shared his opinion, came as close as any judges had yet to arguing that political considerations could not be part of the passport application process. As Bazelon put it, "The word 'Communist' is not an incantation subverting at a stroke our Constitution and all our cherished liberties."

Boudin filed a petition for a writ of certiorari, hoping that the Supreme Court might take a different point of view from the majority on the Court of Appeals. This time it worked. The writ was granted on November 25, 1957. Because Briehl's case was materially identical to Kent's it, too, went to the Supreme Court.

In the following year, on April 10, 1958, Boudin argued that the Supreme Court should overturn the lower court's decision in both cases. On June 16, the Supreme Court came to the conclusion that the lower court's decision had to be reversed. The margin of that vote, five to four, could not have been narrower.

When word came out of the Supreme Court's conclusion and the details of the argument had been absorbed, it became clear that the majority's decision, for which Justice William O. Douglas delivered the opinion, was much more momentous than it seemed. In effect, the justices were saying that the State Department had no right to make the granting of a passport contingent on political beliefs. None of the secretary of state's actions since the passage of the Walter-McCarran Act of 1952, in denying passports to "petitioners because of their alleged Communistic beliefs and associations and their refusal to file affidavits concerning present or past membership in the Communist Party," could be authorized. The right to travel, the court concluded, "is a part of the 'liberty' of which a citizen cannot be deprived without due process of law under the Fifth Amendment."

The floodgates were opened, or so they should have been. In fact, the State Department did not rush to get the passports out. Rockwell Kent had to wait until July 5 for his.

Robeson was luckier. On June 25, Frances Knight wrote to Boudin, enclosing Robeson's passport, almost eight years after it had been declared null and void by the State Department. Richard Morford, executive director of the National Council of American-Soviet Friendship (cited as a subversive organization on the attorney general's list), was one of the first to congratulate Robeson on reclaiming his passport, thanking him for fighting relentlessly not just for himself but, as he put it, "for the rest of us, for all Americans."

Two days later, the *New York Times* published an article announcing that Robeson had been given a passport. An accompanying photograph showed Robeson in Boudin's office, beaming and holding the open document in both hands. "I wish to thank Mr. Boudin and, of course, the Supreme Court for what has happened, and also the thousands of people of all races and creeds who have been my well-wishers all these years in the struggle for a passport."

He was, he told the reporter, David Anderson, on his way to London.

# 17

# Telling America's Story

So Robeson had his passport back and was free to travel again. It wasn't because the State Department had relented but because it had been overruled by the Supreme Court. Although Robeson's own case never came before the justices, their verdict in the Kent and Briehl cases covered his circumstances precisely. The grounds on which he had ostensibly been denied a passport, his alleged Communist associations, had been declared unconstitutional; his right to refuse to sign the affidavit had been upheld by the highest court in the land. The State Department had lost the war.

What had kept them fighting one individual for so long?

At the summit of its power during the Cold War, the Passport Office had a staff exceeding 200 people and processed hundreds of thousands of applications for passports. How many American citizens had a passport application rejected for political reasons is unknown. Apparently, until 1954, no systematic records of refusals were kept. After that date, the State Department refused to publish the information, on the grounds that it was confidential. But at the beginning of 1958, Roderic O'Connor, head of the Bureau of Security and Consular Affairs at the State Department, revealed in an interview that in the previous year, the Passport Office had processed half a million applications, among whom only 450 had been denied on substantive grounds—aside from that, he provided no details. And no further details have come to light since, despite requests in recent years for information on that period from the State Department.

We know that many of those who applied for a passport and were rejected tried only once. Few were as persistent in applying as Robeson; certainly few received as many rejections. Very few indeed were so resolutely denied a passport for so long a time.

The determination of the State Department to keep Robeson in the United States, denying him an international stage on which to express his views, came out, as we have seen, through the hearings and court cases brought by Robeson. In public statements, the department never said anything more than that allowing Robeson to travel would not be in the country's best interest.

In the hearings, however, it emerged that the State Department considered Robeson a "political meddler" and did not want him to travel the world reminding people of United States–style segregation, lynching, Jim Crow laws, poverty, and social injustice. Race was the most sensitive issue for America's foreign policy and Robeson's stance was deeply embarrassing. He was an African American known all over the world whose views were respected by white and nonwhite alike. The State Department was right in this respect: People did listen to him and they believed him.

Whether he knew it or not, Robeson was caught in a substantial propaganda machine, part of a systematic attempt by the United States government to manage its image abroad and to influence countries throughout the world to embrace the American rather than the Soviet model.

To achieve this, the government enlisted the help of three principal organizations. One of these was the Central Intelligence Agency, established in 1947 through that year's National Security Act. In 1950, as part of its campaign to counter Soviet influence, the CIA began to fund Radio Free Europe and in the same year established the Congress for Cultural Freedom, a European-based coalition of anti-Communist intellectuals who produced magazines and sponsored cultural events. The second agency was the United States Information Agency, founded in 1953, whose activities were varied but included producing pamphlets, stocking libraries in foreign countries, and making films for distribution throughout the world.

But it was the State Department itself that had the greatest impact in managing the image of the United States abroad. One of the key elements in their strategy was travel. Both the Truman and Eisenhower administrations promoted travel as one way by which the world would learn about America, and under them, tourism mushroomed. Between 1953 and 1959 the number of Americans who went abroad increased sevenfold. Outside the Americas and the Caribbean, Europe was the main attraction for the seven million US citizens who ventured beyond their own borders in that six-year period.

This wave of tourism was swelled by huge increases in American disposable income and also by the expansion in air travel. As American tourism increased, so did the production of American travel writing, featuring authors like James Michener, specialist travel magazines such as *Holiday*, and regular travel features in the *Saturday Review* and *Reader's Digest*, two of the country's leading magazines.

The government not only encouraged the flow of American tourism but also saw it as an integral part of United States trade and foreign policy. Americans going abroad was a simple but very effective way of getting dollars to those parts of the world where American currency was in short supply but the demand for American goods was high. In short, for every dollar that an American spent abroad, the government was convinced—had evidence to show—that at least a good part of it would return to the country's industrial economy. How Americans spent that money was of interest to foreign-policy makers, too. In 1954, the State Department inserted a pamphlet in each passport it issued. The insert advised American citizens of what their government considered proper behavior for them as ambassadors of their country's new role in the world: They should not act arrogantly nor should they violate the "common bonds of decency." Several years later, the State Department took a further step along the road of directing "politically useful travelers" when it inserted in each passport a letter from President Eisenhower stressing that in those parts of the world where the United States was "less well understood," the presence and actions of US citizens should sustain the reputation of their country.

Only the right kind of Americans were allowed to travel. As a *Reader's Digest* article of October 1951 informed its audience in an article about Ruth Shipley, then still head of the Passport Office, "No American can go abroad without her authorization. She decides whether the applicant is entitled to a passport and also whether he would be a hazard to Uncle Sam's security or create prejudice against the United States by unbecoming conduct." Shipley and Knight, her successor, treated access to travel as an issue in foreign policy, insisting that American Communists should not be allowed to join their compatriots in seeing other parts of the world.

The Passport Office, then, controlled the outward flow of American citizens on political grounds. Citizens of other countries who wished to visit the United States and those persons living in the United States who were not American citizens were also strictly controlled based on their political beliefs. The legislative mechanisms were defined in the Subversive Activities Control Act of 1950 (the McCarran Act or the Internal Security Act) and the Immigration and Nationality Act of 1952 (the McCarran-Walter Act).

The result was that many foreign visitors were either turned back at US ports or were never granted a visa in the first place, because of their political beliefs. At the same time, high-profile individuals living but not born in the United States, such as Cedric Belfrage, editor of the *National Guardian*; C.L.R. James, the Trinidadian writer and political analyst; John Williamson, who had become one of the top officials in the American Communist Party (and was found guilty under the Smith Act); and the New York–based journalist and activist Claudia Jones, all fell victim to the deportation clauses of the McCarran-Walter Act, and there were other less well-known "aliens," Communists, labor leaders, journalists, writers and other artists who found that their political activities were defining them as undesirables. In 1953 alone, some 300 individuals were arrested for deportation. Ellis Island, which for so many immigrants in the late nineteenth and early twentieth centuries had been a portal into a new world, became in the 1940s and 1950s the exit point for what one writer called the "deportation nation."

Managing travel in its broadest sense was, therefore, one way in which the State Department managed America's image abroad and sustained its foreign policy. But there were other ways that the State Department also used to control information about the United States. Together, these came to be known as public or cultural diplomacy: a carefully planned propaganda campaign to win the "hearts and minds" of a large proportion of the world; a machine designed with the express purpose of "telling America's story to the world." Much of that machinery, designed for a cultural assault on the Soviet Union by showing off the best that America had, was put in place and rolled out by the State Department precisely during the eight years of Robeson's confinement and especially during the darkest days of Cold War repression.

In 1954 President Eisenhower got the ball rolling when he wrote to the House Committee on Appropriations asking for funds to finance a new American export drive. It was essential, he wrote, that the United States "take immediate and vigorous action to demonstrate the superiority of the products and cultural values of our system of free enterprise." The committee and Congress backed the president. Later that year, the Cultural Presentations Program was launched under the auspices of the Emergency Fund for International Affairs, a $2.25 million injection into the State Department to support American dance, music, theater and sports presentations in foreign countries.

Between that year and 1959, almost 150 groups of American performing artists and athletes visited more than ninety countries, advertising American cultural values. Amongst these were some of the most famous names in their fields: Dizzy Gillespie and Benny Goodman, with their racially integrated bands; the dance companies of José Limón and Martha Graham, the former traveling through Latin America while the latter visited countries in Asia; the Boston Symphony Orchestra and the New York Philharmonic; the African-American singers Marian Anderson and William Warfield, the baritone who played Joe in the 1951 MGM color film of *Showboat*; the University of San Francisco Dons, a highly successful integrated basketball team; and the Harlem Globetrotters.

All of them were intended to display a racially harmonious United States.

Given the amount of cultural propaganda being promoted by so many government agencies, aimed at showing how well integrated the United States was, no wonder Robeson had such difficulty in getting the State Department to change its stance. When they referred to him as a political meddler, they no doubt had in mind his outspokenness on racial issues as well as his opposition to colonialism and his promoting of peace and workers' unity. When Leonard Boudin asked Robert Johnson at the 1957 hearing if he could give a date when Robeson might receive his passport, Johnson's refusal to respond reflected the fact that the State Department had no intention of ever letting Robeson travel. As far as the department was concerned, the time would never be right for Robeson to give voice to his dissenting views abroad.

# 18

# Free At Last?

The State Department had less control over Robeson's movements and political utterances within the United States, but did whatever it could to restrict them. The Attorney General, the House Un-American Activities Committee and the Subversive Activities Control Board between them made it as difficult as possible for Robeson to find platforms from which to expound his political views.

What they could not suppress, however hard they tried, was Robeson's popularity. Although he had trouble getting bookings, it may be that Robeson's passport ordeal backfired. For just when it seemed that the government had him silenced, Robeson came back fighting.

Robeson got a first taste of victory in October 1957 when *Ebony*, the country's premier African-American magazine, published its first-ever interview with Robeson. On the front page of "Has Paul Robeson Betrayed the Negro?" was a photograph showing Robeson sitting on a sofa, his head tilted slightly to the right, mouth open and eyes full and bright, his hands stretched out, caught in a moment of making a point to Carl Rowan, the interviewer, who can be seen sitting in profile, intently writing notes in his pad.

Rowan was one of America's foremost black journalists. In 1955, as a staff writer for the Minneapolis *Tribune*, he had made a name for himself as the only African-American reporter to cover the Montgomery, Alabama, bus boycott that followed Rosa

Parks's refusal to give up her bus seat to a white passenger. While
reporting on the boycott he met its leader, the twenty-six-year-
old Reverend Martin Luther King, Jr.

*Ebony*, now in its twelfth year, had been styled after the mainstream magazine *Life* and although it did not shy away from
sensitive issues such as civil rights, it nevertheless focused its
coverage on stories about successful African Americans. It had a
huge following and not just among black readers; its circulation
was about a half million copies per month.

As Rowan remembered it, one day he received a call from
*Ebony*'s managing editor telling him that John Johnson, the
magazine's owner, had decided to run a piece on Robeson and
thought Rowan was the best person to do it. Johnson had said,
"Paul Robeson is getting a raw deal in the media and everyplace
else . . . You're the only journalist in America who can write the
truth and not get destroyed by the McCarthyites." Rowan didn't
hesitate; he headed straight for Oakland, where Robeson could
be contacted during a two-week concert tour of California.

The combination of Robeson and Rowan was sure to pack a
punch. Not since the days of *Freedom* had Robeson been given
such a platform. Moreover, *Ebony* readers were more diverse and
influential geographically, socially, and politically than *Freedom*'s
had been.

Rowan began his piece by recounting what he described as
Robeson's tragic decline over a period of three decades, from the
days when he had been "the world's most famous Negro [and]
one of its really great personalities" to now: "Paul Robeson's
voice is silent today . . . [his] name is anathema." Why, Rowan
asked, had this happened? Why had he spent the past seven years
in obscurity? Was it because the State Department considered
him a Moscow stooge and clamped him for it? Or was it because—
as Rowan said many African Americans thought—"the big white
boss" had had enough of Robeson's attacks on Jim Crow?

Robeson gave his version of events. He agreed that he had
insulted white America, but he was certain that American foreign

and domestic policy came "straight from the South"—that it was people like Senator James Eastland from Mississippi who ran the country. These people, Robeson argued, feared him because they saw in him "a symbol around which the Negro masses might rally to join hands with the 'black power that now is flexing its muscles in Asia and Africa.'"

Robeson was quick to display his internationalist politics, linking the African-American struggle for freedom in the United States with anticolonial movements in Africa and Asia. The key to success for both, he pointed out, lay in unity. "We don't have to go begging to these people," Robeson argued. "All we have to do is face this nation with a unified voice." But who should lead? Certainly not the current leadership, whom Robeson blamed for standing by and letting the State Department confine him without protest.

Rowan reminded his readers of the State Department's case: that Robeson was not granted a passport because the department had cause to believe that he was a Communist and had current law behind them. So, Rowan asked Robeson, was he "working for the black masses or the Red comrades?" Robeson answered, "I am not a part of any international conspiracy. All I ever said or did was in the interest of freeing my people." He noted that in 1946 at the Tenney Committee hearing he had testified under oath that he was not a Communist.

Rowan then allowed him the opportunity to expound on his political philosophy. Robeson pointed out the absurdity of men such as Senator Eastland, who themselves oppressed African Americans, telling their victims to fight the Russians, when without the presence of the Soviet Union and its military might there would have been no progress toward self-determination for former colonies in Africa and Asia. Without the Communist threat, white supremacists would have effectively crushed the movements for civil rights in those countries as they had done in the United States.

Rowan's account of the interview made it clear to readers that up to this point Robeson had engaged with the questions. But when Rowan asked Robeson to comment on Khrushchev's condemnation of Stalin, Robeson was evasive and uncomfortable, preferring to return to earlier themes. After trying several times to get him to talk about Khrushchev, without much success, Rowan gave up and changed the subject to what Robeson saw for the future. Robeson was optimistic and insisted that "the Negro should solve his problems within the American framework," with solidarity and backing from "all the colored people of the world."

As Rowan remarked to his readers, Robeson had engaged again. He began to hum snippets of material from what he hoped would be new concerts in a comeback: "I am singing at the top of my voice for my people's freedom," he exclaimed.

In the end, it was Robeson's belief in black power that caught Rowan's attention. Robeson, he concluded for his readers, was what he called a "black nationalist," longing, "for the day when the power of the world's black men will overwhelm the whites whom he sees as the blind purveyors of shame and misery for 'his people.'"

The power of numbers and the power granted by history would pave the way to freedom for the African Americans. Robeson stood tall as the symbol of that power: "Jim Crow, that stubborn old bird whose wings form the cloak of martyrdom that Paul Robeson wears—and now waves high for the colored world to see." Rowan ended his piece on an optimistic note—quoting Robeson, he remarked, "He is sure that the day will come when American Negroes will find that 'black power' holds the key to their freedom."

The issue of *Ebony* carrying Rowan's interview with Robeson hit the newsstands around the middle of September 1957. Included in the interview was Rowan's question about the State Department's reasons for keeping him silent, and Robeson's scornful response: "They can keep me from going overseas, but they can't keep news of Emmett Till and Autherine Lucy from going over."

Till, a fourteen-year-old from Chicago, had been brutally murdered two years earlier in Mississippi while on a family visit—a killing described as a lynching in the black press. Autherine Lucy had not been murdered, but her case nevertheless starkly showed Americans and those abroad the lawlessness of the South. In 1956, Lucy became the first African-American student to enroll at the University of Alabama. Just days after she begun her studies, mobs gathered to prevent her from attending classes; she was then expelled on the grounds that her presence was detrimental to the university. The story made it into every major American newspaper and soon appeared in newspapers throughout the world.

To these cases, Robeson could now add a third highly publicized instance of ugly race relations in the Southern states. At the beginning of September 1957, nine African-American students in Little Rock, Arkansas, were registered to attend previously all-white Little Rock Central High. Since 1954, when the Supreme Court ruled in the case of *Brown v. Board of Education*, that segregated schools were unconstitutional, schools throughout the country had had to make plans to integrate. The Little Rock School Board had agreed to do just that, but on September 4, when the nine students showed up to enroll, Governor Orval Faubus called in the Arkansas National Guard to stop them and make sure that the school would remain segregated.

Despite the school board condemning him and a personal plea from President Eisenhower that he abide by the Supreme Court's ruling, Faubus remained adamant. Louis Armstrong, who had been chosen by the State Department to lead one of their sponsored tours to the Soviet Union, upon hearing of what had happened in Little Rock, changed his mind. "The way they are treating my people in the South, the government can go to hell," he told a reporter in Grand Forks, North Dakota, where he was touring with his band. Armstrong referred to Eisenhower as having "no guts," and as for Faubus, he was nothing more than an "uneducated plow-boy." "It's getting almost so bad a colored man hasn't got any country . . . The people over there ask me what's wrong with my country; what am I supposed to say?" Armstrong added.

No one reading Rowan's interview in this context would fail to see how prescient and poignant Robeson's remarks had been.

Early in October, Rowan appeared on a nationally broadcast radio program. When asked about the Robeson interview, he said, "When he's talking about what's happening to Negroes or when he's crying out for freedom of Negroes or when he's talking about a constitutional issue like the freedom to travel, I find it very difficult to disagree with him." More than three decades later, Rowan published a memoir of his own full and controversial life. Recalling the interview, he said, "I felt proud that I had given the marvelous man a fair hearing, a decent break . . . journalistic peril does not lie merely in covering Saigon or Beirut; it lurks among the character assassins inside America who want to destroy those whose political and social views they detest."

In spite of Robeson's continuing problems with the State Department, in terms of his popular exposure his fortunes continued to ascend. Summer and autumn 1957 saw him on an extensive concert tour of the West Coast, where in all of the major cities Robeson pulled in crowds of stalwart left-wing unionists, religious leaders, intellectuals, and ordinary people.

And there was more to come. In the wake of the *Ebony* piece, in early 1958, Robeson self-published *Here I Stand*, a book part political statement and part autobiography. Written in conjunction with his friend Lloyd Brown, a labor activist and author, *Here I Stand* pulled no punches. It was a deeply assertive book. "I am a Negro" are its first words. Later Robeson adds, "I am an American," and then, to make clear what he had always claimed— the words that had been so distorted, so mangled by white and black politicians, commentators and journalists—"I speak as an American Negro whose life is dedicated, first and foremost, to winning full freedom, and nothing less than full freedom, for my people in America . . ."

As he explained further into the book, the struggle to win this freedom had to be a black affair, but from the beginning he wanted his black readers to know that he had had enough of the white leaders of America:

> I care nothing—less than nothing—about what the lords of the land, the Big White Folks, think of me and my ideas. For more than ten years they have persecuted me in every way they could—by slander and mob violence, by denying me the right to practice my profession as an artist, by withholding my right to travel abroad. To these, the real Un-Americans, I merely say: "All right—I don't like you either!"

The book's rhetoric placed Robeson firmly within the African-American freedom movement inspired by like-minded black trade unionists and black religious leaders—not the Communist Party. He resented and mistrusted a gradualist approach to civil rights, putting his trust instead in mass action and unity. In the book's more than one hundred pages, Robeson elaborated on many of the themes he had mentioned in his interview with Carl Rowan several months earlier.

Wholly ignored by the white mainstream papers, *Here I Stand* was noticed by the African-American press. The *Afro-American*, one of the most widely read black newspapers, serialized the book in installments that spring. The FBI, always on the alert, picked up through an informant at the end of January that the book was going to be published on the first Monday in February. J. Edgar Hoover wrote to the special agent in charge in New York to get details and to make sure that a copy was sent back to Washington. For the next few days, memos were passed around giving details of publication and a synopsis of the book's main argument; checks were made as to where the book could be purchased, what other literature was available at those stores, and who frequented them; and finally the name and political affiliation of the printing company and its owners was noted and filed. Typical FBI routine. The book did well. The 10,000-copy first run sold out within six weeks of publication and the book looked set to continue this success.

Robeson's career was definitely picking up. In late January 1958 he landed the first contract with a commercial recording company he had been offered since his passport problems immobilized him. Vanguard Records, set up in 1950 as a predominantly classical label, had made the bold venture into folk music in 1955 when it recorded the Christmas Eve Carnegie Hall concert by the Weavers.

Pete Seeger's group, which had been founded in 1948, after early success had been hounded during the Red Scare, like Robeson, and like Robeson they found their recording and performing opportunities disappearing rapidly. In 1953, Decca Records, which had signed them several years earlier, abruptly terminated their contract and deleted their back catalog. Vanguard stepped in to put them back on the recording road.

Besides their experiences together in Peekskill, Robeson and Seeger had many individual experiences in common. Seeger had appeared before a House Un-American Activities Committee hearing in August 1955; he was cited for contempt of Congress two years later. Now both musicians were being pulled out of recording silence by the same label. Robeson's first recording with Vanguard was made in February and March, and the following month *The Essential Paul Robeson* was released. He was back in the commercial record market.

Late March saw Robeson performing in Portland, Oregon, where he hadn't been for more than a decade, and early April saw him traveling to Chicago where he had been invited to share his sixtieth birthday (April 9, 1958) with the Chicago Council for American-Soviet Friendship. The *National Guardian*, one of the only newspapers to have covered Robeson's activities over the years, reported that birthday celebrations for the singer were going on simultaneously across the world in twenty-seven countries.

To the annoyance of the State Department, India, with over 400 million people, the world's largest democracy, was planning the most extensive celebrations, in many of its major cities.

Prime Minister Jawaharlal Nehru had given the planning his personal approval, referring to Robeson as a great humanist. The celebrations, Nehru argued, were as much a tribute to what Robeson stood for and had suffered as they were homage to a great individual.

Through Ellsworth Bunker, the American ambassador, the State Department tried to convince Nehru that Americans, among them "negroes prominent in all walks of American life . . . would certainly interpret the celebration as Communist-inspired and even anti-American and that many would regard celebration as evidence that India was going Communist." There was no justification, the ambassador continued, to single out Robeson "for such unusual honor." The celebrations went ahead anyway. American embassy officials were under strict instructions not to attend any of the events.

Robeson was back in demand as a concert artist. Offers were coming in from cities across the country and in Canada. In March, Paul Endicott, a concert manager based in Michigan, in a city close to Detroit, told Robeson that he had lined up a very well-paid ten-city tour for October. Near the end of April, the FBI learned from a source in Newark, New Jersey, that Robeson was scheduled to return to Carnegie Hall in New York on May 9. His last concert there had been in 1929, and he hadn't performed in New York City at all since 1947. Art D'Lugoff, an impresario who would later in the year open one of New York's most famous jazz clubs, the Village Gate, in Greenwich Village, made the engagement. The FBI checked its files on D'Lugoff and reported they had nothing on him; they concluded that he was just doing his job as an impresario.

The Carnegie Hall concert was sold out by early April. Twenty police officers, according to a reporter from the *New York Times*, were on hand to keep the peace, but they disbanded soon after it became apparent that there would be no disturbances. Robeson was greeted by a lengthy standing ovation. His program of folk music, sung in half a dozen languages, thrilled the audience. He sang, he lectured, and he recited from *Othello*. He was back on form. He gave three encores, the reporter noted, "among them 'Joe Hill' at which the audience started to applaud before he got into the music." Two weeks later, just as he had done in 1929 Robeson returned to Carnegie Hall for a second concert, which was also sold out. This audience, many of whom had obtained tickets from Harlem outlets, even outdid the first, joining Robeson in singing his encores.

At the beginning of June, Robeson took a recital directly to his people when he performed at the Mother A.M.E. (African Methodist Episcopal) Zion Church, the first black church in New York, where Robeson's brother, Ben, was the pastor. The church was filled to overflowing. Larry Brown accompanied Robeson for this historic moment. Robeson told the audience "A lot of the hard struggle is over . . . I've been waiting for this afternoon to come back and give my thanks . . ."

He didn't know then that this would be his last concert in the United States, or that the Supreme Court was about to make its momentous decision on the constitutional right to travel.

Within a day of hearing the Supreme Court's ruling, Robeson told Endicott that the Canadian tour was off. "We are literally packing our bags," Eslanda wrote to Endicott, "and will be off the moment we get the passport."

And so it was. On July 10, 1958, at 5:30 p.m., Paul and Eslanda Robeson settled into their seats for the transatlantic flight to London.

# The Final Tour

"Robeson Here Today" proclaimed the bold headline of the early edition of the *Daily Worker* of July 11, 1958. He was due at London Airport (now Heathrow) at 10:30 a.m. A host of famous names from the world of music and theater, including Sybil Thorndike, Bernard Miles, and Johnny Dankworth, whose photographs were lined up under the headline, had sent greetings to welcome him back.

Robeson was adored in Britain. No other country in the world did so much to keep Robeson in the public eye during his long containment in the United States; and no other country did as much to protest his treatment.

When the Provisional Committee to Restore Paul Robeson's Passport launched its campaign to put pressure on the State Department, in New York at the end of May 1954, sending letters to individuals and organizations throughout the world asking to them to write to their American embassy or directly to the State Department in Washington, the country that answered the call most vociferously was Britain.

Robeson's longtime friend William Patterson, a champion of civil rights who was closely involved in the legal battle to restore the passport, added his weight to that of the Provisional Committee in 1955, when he wrote an open letter to Robeson supporters throughout the world asking them for petitions, for invitations and for statements of support. Patterson reminded his friends that the world had changed, that the Spirit of Geneva was in the ascendant.

Peaceful coexistence, which Robeson had long advocated as the only way forward, had now been accepted by world leaders. President Eisenhower himself had proclaimed that "war could be the extinction of man's deepest hopes . . . atomic war could be race suicide," adding, "the spirit of Geneva, if it is to provide a healthy atmosphere for the pursuit of peace, if it is to be genuine and not spurious, must inspire all to a correction of injustices, an observance of human rights . . . Geneva spells for America . . . opportunity—opportunity for our own people and for people everywhere to realize their aspirations."

Patterson urged Robeson's supporters everywhere to capitalize on these words in Eisenhower's declaration. To put even more pressure on the State Department, in November Patterson circulated an open letter he had drafted to Secretary of State John Foster Dulles, and a petition to Eisenhower, both of which he urged friends to sign and send on.

Desmond Buckle, who had spent so much time with Robeson when he last toured Britain in 1949, was one of those who responded to the appeal. He wrote to Robeson, that until the call for action came, little information had filtered to Britain about his passport problems. This campaign, he assured him, would bring an end to the silence. Rose Grant, a member of the National Assembly of Women, was a typical responder in the sense that although she'd never met Robeson, she was outraged at the State Department's actions. She urged him to draw comfort from the support of the British people: "Be strengthened," she wrote to him, "in the knowledge that you have the love, esteem and strength and support of millions of British men and women among whom we are proud to be."

Another supporter was John Williamson, whom Robeson had first met when Williamson was one of the defendants in the Smith Act trials. Born in Glasgow in 1903, Williamson had emigrated to the United States with his family and as a young man devoted himself to the trade union movement and to the American Communist Party, becoming, in 1940, its national organizing secretary. In 1948, along with eleven other national leaders of the Party, he was arrested under the Smith Act and sent for trial. He was convicted and sent to Lewisburg Federal Penitentiary for almost five years, then transferred to Danbury Prison for another two and a half months before finally being deported from the United States, on May 4, 1955.

Robeson had done much to publicize the Smith Act trials (also known as the Foley Square trials) while he was in Britain in 1949, and when he and William Patterson were reunited in the United States in the same year, they had made public appearances in support of the twelve defendants. Williamson had never forgotten Robeson's generosity, and now, living in London and ranking high in the British Communist Party, he was able to return the favor.

Williamson soon began preparing a British campaign to restore Robeson's passport. His principal aim, apart from interesting as many people associated with the Communist Party as he could, was to get a conference of Scottish trade unionists, who were meeting in Glasgow on October 23, 1955, on the theme of "Democratic Rights in America," to put Robeson's case on the agenda.

Williamson told the delegates that they needed to act: "Robeson's outstanding popularity as a singer, his self-sacrificing qualities as a fighter for civil liberties and Negro rights—and the fact that he learned his militancy and politics here in Britain—all demand that we should help in the restoration of his freedom."

Williamson's work paid off. The conference, attended by nearly 200 delegates, passed a resolution in support of Robeson's passport fight and launched a nationwide petition to President Eisenhower, which it planned to deliver to the American ambassador in London on February 12 of the following year, the 146th anniversary of the birth of Abraham Lincoln. Robeson, no doubt at Williamson's instigation, sent the conference a message of greetings.

The Glasgow resolution built upon a previous resolution passed at the Trades Union Congress convention in September, when 250 delegates, including five members of Parliament and five members of the congress's general council, signed a telegram to President Eisenhower urging him, in the spirit of Geneva, to intervene on Robeson's behalf in securing his passport. "The British workers and people," the telegram read, "are anxious again to hear this great son of America." Robeson, through Williamson, thanked the delegates for their support in a personal letter to Roland Casasola, head of the Amalgamated Union of Foundry Workers.

The Glasgow conference also agreed that delegates should return to their local organizations and use their resources to agitate on Robeson's behalf. Whether it was through this initiative or some other route, one person who responded was Frank Loesser (Franz Loeser), a refugee from Hitler's Germany who was studying and living in Manchester. He, too, had suffered at the hands of American Cold War repression. Originally part of the Kindertransport, an emergency relief mission in 1938 that brought 10,000 children to Britain from Germany, Loesser, who was fourteen years old when he arrived, remained in Britain during the war years but then, when peace broke out, he emigrated to the United States, where he settled in Minneapolis, studying at the University of Minnesota and working as a laboratory assistant in the field of nuclear medicine.

Loesser had heard of Robeson when he was in the United States; as it happened, he had been present at the Peekskill concert of September 4, 1949, as a delegate of the Socialist Student Association of the University of Minnesota. The experience made a deep impression on him. In 1951, Loesser fell victim to the purge of left-wingers on American university campuses and associated workplaces and was expelled from the United States. He returned to Britain and settled in Salford, now part of the Greater

Manchester area, and continued his studies at the University of Manchester. By the end of 1955 he and his wife had begun a local campaign called the "Let Paul Robeson Sing Committee," working out of their home to bring together like-minded people in the Manchester area to agitate on Robeson's behalf.

Loesser, although not a member of the British Communist Party, was known as a particularly good organizer and largely sympathetic to the movement. His organizational skills were put to good use and the campaign went from strength to strength and grew from a local to a national force.

The campaign's first highlight was a public meeting held at the Free Trade Hall in Manchester on March 11, 1956, which drew sponsors from across the cultural and political field, including Sir Adrian Boult, six members of Parliament, and Len Johnson, the boxer, who had invited Robeson to the city in May 1949. Speakers included Will Griffiths, the Labour MP, Roland Casasola, the sponsor of the Trades Union Congress's telegram; and Cedric Belfrage, the founder and editor of the New York–based *National Guardian*, now deported back to Britain, where he carried on his newspaper job as "editor-in-exile." The climax of the evening was a taped address and recital by Robeson; the musical portion included Beethoven's "Ode to Joy," now given new lyrics as "The Song of Peace" and delivered over the hall's speaker system.

Some 500 people attended this public meeting. Partly because of the popularity of the evening and partly because of the representation of individuals and organizations from across Britain, the campaigners decided to make their Manchester organization a national one.

A little over two months later, delegates met in Manchester and agreed to establish a National Paul Robeson Committee with a provisional working committee consisting of Cedric Belfrage as chairman and Loesser as secretary. In a letter to Robeson, Belfrage complimented Loesser's unusual organizing talents, referring to him as "the spark-plug of the whole thing over here."

Over the coming months other planning meetings were held in

Manchester, culminating on December 2, 1956, with a national conference in the city's Free Trade Hall. The all-day affair resulted in the permanent creation of the National Paul Robeson Committee, with Will Griffiths, the Manchester MP, as president and Cedric Belfrage as one of two vice-chairs. The sponsoring council included many well-known British personalities, including, on the political side, Aneurin Bevan, Barbara Castle, and Anthony Wedgwood Benn, and on the cultural side, Benjamin Britten, Professor Max Gluckman and Professor Kathleen Lonsdale, the Canon of St. Paul's Cathedral and the Reverend Donald Soper. It was an impressive roll call.

The idea was to have Robeson sing down a transatlantic telephone line from New York to Manchester, accompanied by the National Union of Miners of South Wales's Imperial Glee Singers. This didn't happen, for technical reasons. Instead, the concert took place with Robeson singing on a tape that had been sent from New York as a backup.

As Belfrage reported it to Robeson, the campaign was beginning to snowball. But not before a setback halted its momentum. Frank Loesser, who had guided the now national campaign from its inception in his home in Salford, fell victim to the British government's own version of Cold War politics. Although he had now been living in Britain for some five years, the Home Office refused to grant him naturalization. Once his visa ran out, he would have to leave the country. On December 29, 1956, Loesser left London for East Berlin, where he would remain for more than two decades.

Probably because of this, the center of gravity of the campaign began to shift toward the capital. A London branch of the National Committee was already in place by early September 1956. By 1958, the National Paul Robeson Committee had its headquarters in London.

Whoever thought of it—and Cedric Belfrage and Jean Jenkins,

the St. Pancras Borough councilor who acted as secretary of the London committee, have each been credited with the idea—having Robeson sing down a transatlantic telephone line was certain to draw the crowds. The attempt in Manchester had failed, but new preparations made with the General Post Office (responsible for telephone as well as postal communications in Britain) looked promising.

The occasion was a concert planned for the evening of May 26, 1957, to be held in London's St. Pancras Town Hall. During the day there was to be a conference on Robeson's right to have a passport. Local organizations throughout the country were celebrating what they called National Paul Robeson Day.

That evening in the St. Pancras auditorium, the stage was emptied and a huge photograph of a beaming Robeson was unfurled from the ceiling. A reporter for the *Baltimore Sun*, one of the only newspapers in the United States to mention the concert, was in the audience that evening and caught the moment when Robeson's voice filled the hall:

> Then, suddenly a piano could be heard, and a great rich bass voice boomed out a song about Daniel in the lion's den. The quality of the sound, having passed through the new high-fidelity cable, was excellent. Almost 60 years of age, Robeson was in good voice.

From a recording studio in New York, Robeson's voice was broadcast over an amplified sound system and backed in the St. Pancras hall by the Dare Singers, a choir from Wales. According to the GPO technicians, this was the first time in their experience that the transatlantic line had been used to give a concert hall performance. The new cable enabling transatlantic telephone calls to be made had only become operational in the previous year. Though Robeson's phone call was scheduled to last fifteen minutes, already paid for, the audience would not let him go and demanded more of his time, for which they were willing to pay themselves. In the end he was on the line for twenty-three minutes.

The *Manchester Guardian*, one of many British newspapers covering the concert, put into words what many must have felt: "American Telephone and Telegraph in New York, and the General Post Office, in London, last night between them helped Paul Robeson to make the United States Department of State look rather silly." Desmond Buckle, who was at the concert, wrote immediately to Robeson telling him of the evening's technical and emotional success. "The audience was very moved," he wrote. Cedric Belfrage was also there and wrote a dazzling piece for the *National Guardian*, with the headline—"American Tel & Tel Breaks the Curtain to London." Belfrage added his voice to the *Manchester Guardian*'s when he wrote, "After the Cadillac curtain has been telephonically penetrated . . . we might even find the American press seeing a story in this history-making, dramatic, but essentially ludicrous procedure."

Just over four months later, Robeson's voice was once again carried across the Atlantic. A deputation of miners from South Wales who had attended the St. Pancras Town Hall concert had been so impressed by the evening that upon their return to South Wales, they convinced their union officials that they should invite Robeson to sing down a telephone line at their forthcoming Eisteddfod, scheduled for early October in Porthcawl. Some five thousand people crowded into the festival pavilion on the evening of October 5, 1957, and at 6:30 p.m. Robeson greeted his listeners and gave them a concert of songs. The Treorchy Male Voice Choir responded, and Robeson ended his part of the evening by singing a verse of the Welsh national anthem. In return, the entire Porthcawl audience joined the choir for a rendition of "We'll Keep a Welcome on the Hillside"—more than 5,000 voices booming down the cable to New York, promising Robeson a warm reception in Wales when he was free.

It was against this background of popular support across Britain that Robeson decided to fly to London as soon as he had a passport. He showed his commitment to his British followers and to his art by agreeing to play Othello in Stratford during the 1959 summer season, which meant that he would be away from the United States for a minimum of two years.

When the plane carrying Paul and Eslanda Robeson arrived at London Airport late morning on July 11, 1958, they were welcomed by more than 200 devoted fans, in addition to many close friends from the Let Paul Robeson Sing Campaign, including Cedric Belfrage, Peggy Middleton and John Williamson, and Claudia Jones, who was a close friend of both Robesons and who had also been deported from the United States, in December 1955, for her radical beliefs.

The British government, on the other hand, was not so welcoming, though Robeson didn't know this. To them, Robeson was a tricky commodity. The Home Office was unhappy with the prospect of his presence in the country but felt that excluding him would be embarrassing and provide fodder for propaganda to the British Communist Party. Their preferred modus operandi was to watch his movements as he went in and out of the country while ensuring that he was there "on a temporary footing"— never giving him leave to remain for too long a time and forcing him to reapply frequently for the labor permits that allowed him to be paid for his engagements.

However, although the government imposed a tedious routine, it was not Robeson, but his booking agent and British manager, Harold Davison, who handled the paperwork. This left Robeson free to enjoy all the wonderful offers, invitations, and engagements arranged for him.

After years of spending more time in hearings and meetings in Washington, D.C., than on the concert stage anywhere, Robeson now started his performance schedule at a furious pace that afterward hardly relented. He began almost immediately with a package of three television programs on Britain's first commercial network, ATV, which had only been in existence since late 1955. On August 3, Robeson was in Ebbw Vale in Wales for the National Eisteddfod, where 9,000 people packed into the pavilion to hear Aneurin Bevan, the MP for the local constituency, introduce Robeson in the flesh. A week later Robeson sang to a sell-out crowd at the Royal Albert Hall—Larry Brown, now his colleague for more than thirty years, flew over especially to accompany him on the piano.

The next stop was Moscow, where Robeson made a television broadcast and sang to 18,000 people in the Lenin Sports Stadium. This was followed by a short break spent in Georgia and Yalta, where he met and had dinner with Premier Khrushchev. Then back to Moscow for a couple of recitals before returning to London on October 12.

Robeson's next engagement was at St. Paul's Cathedral where he became the first black person to give a recital at the Evening Service: 4,000 worshippers attended the service—instead of the customary 400 or so.

The taste of freedom must have been exhilarating, but there was a price to be paid for his relentless pace.

The Robesons had intended to visit India after Moscow. They were keen to see the democratic postcolonial India and to renew their friendship with Nehru, who had resisted pressure from the United States to cancel the celebrations for Robeson's sixtieth birthday. Balked in their previous efforts to prevent Robeson being honored, the State Department planned to distribute counter-information—"discreet but widespread placement with Indian newspapermen," as they had done before. William Turner, the American consul general in Bombay, alerted Washington that they should expect "anti-American propaganda along color lines." As for himself, he thought he would be invited to participate in events to welcome Robeson, but he intended, as he put it, "to plead ill" and send a junior officer in his place, "to prevent charge that American officials are attempting persecute [sic] by boycotting eminent American citizen."

But soon, and to their great relief, American officials in India learned from their counterparts in Moscow that the trip had had to be canceled. Both Eslanda and Paul were in hospital in Moscow: Eslanda with serious bleeding and Paul with unexplained dizziness. He appeared exhausted, and the trip to India was put off while he remained in hospital to rest. His punishing schedule had taken its toll.

Robeson remained in the Soviet Union until March 9, 1959, when, after a very short stay in London he hurried up to Stratford, where rehearsals for the long-planned-for staging of *Othello*, with Robeson in the lead role, were beginning. From April 7 until November 26 he played the Noble Moor for the Shakespeare Memorial Theatre's 100th season—sometimes, as at the beginning of the run, four times a week, but toward the end, twice a week. This left him plenty of free time and he used it to the full. When not in Stratford, Robeson was everywhere else: London, on many occasions, and also Prague, Vienna, and Budapest.

The following year, 1960, saw no letup in Robeson's activities. If anything his schedule became even more hectic and extremely exhausting. It began with a three-week stay in Moscow, where both Eslanda and Paul underwent medical checkups, followed by a string of public engagements and radio and television interviews.

February saw Robeson back in London preparing for a taxing thirty-two-city tour of the United Kingdom, which lasted through the middle of May. Then, in June, he went to East Berlin, followed by Madrid, Brussels, Paris, Budapest, and, finally, during the first week of October, back to East Berlin.

No sooner had he returned to London than he and Eslanda packed their bags and got on a plane heading for Sydney and the beginning of a two-month visit to Australia and New Zealand.

The Robesons' plans for 1961 were equally frenetic, ranging from Moscow to Edinburgh and Cardiff to East Berlin, Romania, Hungary, and Bulgaria and back to the Soviet Union, and finally, as the highlight, a trip that Robeson had wanted to take for a long time, to Ghana, at the invitation of its new president, Kwame Nkrumah. Nkrumah, an old acquaintance from London in the 1930s, just a few years earlier had steered his country into independence. But none of these dreams, apart from the visit to Moscow, which did take place in March, were fulfilled.

Instead, Robeson's health and spirit failed. For nearly three months, from late June through mid-September 1961, Robeson sought medical help at an exclusive sanatorium on Moscow's outskirts. But no sooner had he returned to London with the approval of his Russian doctors than he lapsed into a severe depression. Immediately, Eslanda arranged for Paul to be admitted to the Priory, a private psychiatric hospital in Roehampton, southwest London.

And that was where he stayed through the rest of 1961, all of 1962, and more than half of 1963. During his time there he had as many as fifty-four ECT (electroconvulsive therapy) treatments and was also given powerful psychiatric drugs. Yet Robeson grew steadily worse, until finally a friend who had been trained as a psychiatric nurse was so shocked by the ferocity of the treatment that she advised Eslanda to remove him from the clinic—to "get him out of there."

And that's precisely what Eslanda did. She took her husband out of the Priory and the couple flew to Berlin, where he entered the Buch Clinic. There, all drug treatments were stopped, there were no more ECTs, and over the nearly four months that he stayed there, his health improved. His doctors told him he could leave and on December 17, 1963, Eslanda and Paul flew back to London. Five days later, they were once more at London Airport. They had decided in Berlin that they were going home for good.

The Robesons' extended visit to Europe hadn't turned out entirely as they'd hoped: In the end Paul spent as much time in clinics as he had on the road. He did not get to visit Africa or China, nor Cuba, as he had also intended.

During this time of illness, depression, and disappointment, the State Department decided to make his life even more difficult. In May 1962, while Paul was still being treated at the Priory but spending weekends in his London home, the Robesons applied to renew their passports, so they would be able to extend their British residency permit. They had renewed their passports without a problem in 1960, but now in 1962 it was not so simple. Six weeks after making their passport applications in person at the American embassy in London, as required, they were informed that the State Department had once more invoked Section 6 of the Internal Security Act of 1950, which denied the right of any member of a Communist organization to apply for a passport. The Robesons were told they must sign affidavits that they were not members of the Communist Party of the United States currently or at any time during the preceding twelve months. Eslanda signed, but for Paul it was a problem. He had always refused to sign any such affidavit, seeing it as an abridgement of his constitutional rights. He had not changed his mind about that but was eventually persuaded to sign—perhaps an indication of his failing strength.

The consular official at the American Embassy had described Robeson to the State Department as a "very frail and subdued old man." Even the FBI reported, "Since there is no evidence of present or recent CP membership on the part of the subjects in view of the Department's interpretation of the passport sanction violation, it is not believed that a possible violation of the passport sanction exists on the part of the subjects."

Since the FBI had always fed the State Department information about Robeson, the State Department knew perfectly well that they had no case. Nevertheless they insisted on their pound of flesh. Signing such an affidavit was no longer part of the normal passport application procedure. Once again Robeson had been singled out for special and punitive treatment by the department, now under new management: Dean Rusk, secretary of state for the Kennedy administration.

There had been many changes in the United States during

Robeson's five-year absence. A Democratic president had been elected and there had been high hopes for a new, improved America under Kennedy. The civil rights March on Washington had taken place on August 28, when as many as 300,000 people heard Reverend Martin Luther King, Jr., deliver his "I Have a Dream" speech in front of the Lincoln Memorial. Then, on November 22, 1963, only a month before Robeson's return, Kennedy had been assassinated, and in December the nation was still mourning and in shock.

For the Robesons, personally, the next few years brought little comfort. Ben, Paul's brother, pastor of the Mother A.M.E. Zion Church in Harlem, had died just four days before Robeson's plane touched down in New York; Claudia Jones in London and Lorraine Hansberry in New York died within weeks of each other, at the end of December 1964 and early January 1965, respectively. And then came the biggest blow. A year later, on December 13, 1965, Eslanda died.

After a short period spent in New York following Eslanda's death, Robeson moved to Philadelphia, in late 1966, and remained there, under the care of his sister Marian. He never performed in public again. He died on January 23, 1976.

# Epilogue

# Freedomways

On April 22, 1965, just a few weeks after celebrating his sixty-seventh birthday, Robeson attended a ticket-only tribute given for him at the Hotel Americana, in New York City's Times Square. This was only the third time that he had appeared publicly during that year: the first had been at the funeral of Lorraine Hansberry, where he delivered the eulogy; and the second at a memorial for W.E.B. Du Bois, where he spoke about the meaning of his friend's life and sang "Jacob's Ladder."

More than 2,500 friends and admirers were packed into the Hotel Americana's Imperial Ballroom to salute their hero. The evening's program consisted of a number of speeches by prominent writers, activists, and community leaders—James Baldwin, Hope Stevens, the prominent Harlem attorney, and John Lewis, chairman of the Student Nonviolent Coordinating Committee and one of the organizers of the March on Washington. Dizzy Gillespie, the pianist Billy Taylor, Earl Robinson, who had composed "Ballad for Americans," and Pete Seeger, among others, provided the music. The list of sponsors' names, more than 170 in total, was as impressive as the lineup. They came from all walks of life: John Coltrane's name was there, as was the comedian Dick Gregory's; also on the list were the songwriter "Yip" Harburg and Linus Pauling, two-time winner of the Nobel Prize.

The magazine *Freedomways* hosted the tribute. Building upon the political philosophies of Robeson and Du Bois, "the two giants of the century," and continuing the tradition of their jointly founded newspaper, *Freedom*, *Freedomways* had been launched in April 1961 at Manhattan's Hotel Martinique before an enthusiastic audience of five hundred people.

The first issue signaled the magazine's clear mission. It would provide a public forum to debate the problems facing African Americans; it would set these within a context of the experience of people of African descent throughout the world; it would inform readers about the struggle for national liberation in Africa and "new forms of economic, political and social systems now existing or emerging in the world." The editors invited writers of whatever background or discipline to submit their work in this exciting new venture.

"Lift every voice and sing—of Freedom," the editors proclaimed. The contributions to the first issue mirrored the mission statement precisely: There was an article by Du Bois on "The Negro People and the United States"; one by Shirley Graham on "Minority Peoples in China"; an address to the United Nations by Kwame Nkrumah; and an essay by the celebrated sculptor Elizabeth Catlett titled, "The Negro People and American Art." Robeson's influence could be seen on every page. No wonder *Freedomways* felt they owed him a tribute.

The audience at the Hotel Americana included "old-timers," those who "had stood with the man they called Paul at the Battle of Peekskill" and "young people from the Southern battlefront and northern campus movements," new "freedom fighters" who had never seen Robeson before. Also in the crowd were ordinary people from New York's black communities, from Harlem and Bedford-Stuyvesant, who attended because "our freedom movement has now caught up with many of the things Paul Robeson fought for all these years; it's time we openly acknowledged his contribution."

Ossie Davis, one of the evening's masters of ceremonies, began the program by announcing to the audience, "Our guest of honor has arrived in the hall and has been seated, so will the real Paul

Robeson please stand." The place went wild when the spotlight crossed over to the family group and caught "the great towering figure of Paul Robeson, with that affable smile, still, at the age of 67, the very embodiment of the dignity of man."

Then the speeches and cultural program began, all together lasting three hours. In the audience that evening, listening attentively to the proceedings, was Charles Howard, the Iowa attorney and publisher, a friend and supporter of Robeson's since the days of the Wallace presidential campaign of 1948, and now the UN correspondent for the *National Negro Press*. Let him take up the story of what happened next:

> There was an unusual quality about the audience. No one expected him to speak to the group. They seemed satisfied to just look at him. So that when Robeson moved to take the platform, bedlam broke loose. There he stood with that broad smile turning every way to face his cheerers, he too, clapping his hands in honor of the occasion. It was obvious that only his voice could stop the bedlam.

And Robeson began to speak. He had never had a reception like this before, he said and thanked everyone associated with the tribute to him. And then for twenty-five minutes he reminded his audience of his beliefs, none of which had altered over the years. He spoke about the African-American struggle for democratic rights—the abolition of "the system of Negro second-class citizenship." He spoke of peaceful coexistence with socialism and communism, asking for the people to decide in which system they wished to live. He spoke about peace as well, but most importantly he spoke of a common humanity reflected in art. Despite differences in language and in political systems, people understood each other through art, especially music. Songs, Robeson explained, carried the message of all oppressed people while inspiring, uniting, and sustaining them in their struggles. "How wonderful to hear these songs tonight . . . the beautiful old songs" and those "newly composed in the heat of the day . . . 'We Shall Not Be Moved' and 'Ain't Gon' Study War No More.'"

On previous occasions when he had finished speaking, Robeson had begun singing. Tonight, however, he didn't. Though he had performed "Zog Nit Keynmo," a Yiddish resistance song from the Warsaw ghetto, many times, tonight he chose to close the program by reciting one verse from it in English instead. Nothing better summed up his own life and struggles.

> Never say that you have reached the very end,
> When leaden skies a bitter future may portend:
> For surely the hour for which we yearn will yet arrive
> And our marching steps will thunder "We survive!"

# Acknowledgements

Over the more than four years that I have been researching and writing this book I have been fortunate in having many people generously give of their time to assist me. I thank them all. They are: Hakim Adi, Carol Anderson, Joellen El Bashir, Inger Beaty-Pownall, the late Peter Blackman, Stephen Bourne, Carolyn Brown, Lauren Brown, Ann Curthoys, Sean Creighton, Michael David-Fox, Todd Decker, Martin Duberman, the late Andre Elizee, Alex Goodall, Nick Grant, Jeff Green, Leslie James, Sergei Kapterev, Joseph Keith, Mark Kristmanson, Craig Lloyd, Daniel Lucks, Tony McElligott, Sam Markham, Ruth Martin, Hannah Middleton, Ani Mukherji, John Munro, Monique Patenaude, Susan Pennybacker, Barbara Ransby, Tom Riis, Ian Rocksborough-Smith, Benedetta Rossi, Marika Sherwood, Steve Smith, Sterling Stuckey, Kira Thurman, Dan Whittall, and Clive Wilson.

In particular I would like to thank Leah Weinryb Grohsgal, whose research skills in Atlanta were invaluable, and Veronika Soul, who acted as my research amanuensis in New York when I could not be there myself.

Research for this book took me to many parts of the world, where the staff of archives and libraries were always welcoming and helpful. I met them at the following places and I would like to thank them all. Archives of American Art, Washington, D.C.; Akademie der Künste, Berlin; Associated Press Archives, New York; California State Archives; Charles H. Wright Museum of

African American History, Detroit; Columbia University Libraries Manuscript Collection; Emory University Manuscript, Archives and Rare Book Library; Franklin D. Roosevelt Library and Archives; Field Library, Peekskill, New York; George Mason University, Special Collections and Archives; Hoover Institution Archives, Stanford University; Harry S. Truman Library and Museum; Howard University, Moorland-Spingarn Research Center; Hull History Centre; International Social History Institute, Amsterdam; Library and Archives Canada; Library of Congress; Marx Memorial Library, London; National Archives of Australia; National Archives and Records Administration, College Park, Maryland; New York State Archives; People's History Museum Archive and Study Centre, Manchester; Rare Book, Manuscript, and Special Collections Library, Duke University; Rutgers University Libraries Special Collections and University Archives; Robert W. Woodruff Library Archives and Special Collections, Atlanta University Center; Schomburg Center for Research in Black Culture, New York Public Library; Seeley G. Mudd Manuscript Library, Princeton University; Schlesinger Library, Radcliffe College; Smith College; Southern California Library; Tamiment Library and Robert F. Wagner Labor Archives, New York University; The National Archives, Kew, London; UCLA, Special Collections; University of British Columbia Manuscripts Collection; University of Kent, Special Collections and Archives; University of Minnesota Archives; University of Rochester, Special Collections; University of Sussex, Special Collections; University of Warwick Modern Records Centre; Wichita State University Special Collections and University Archives; Wisconsin Historical Society; Working Class Movement Library, Salford; York University Clara Thomas Archives and Special Collections.

I would also like to thank the staff at University College London Library's Interlending and Document Supply Department for cheerfully providing me with material from here, there, and everywhere.

At Verso, I would like to thank Tom Penn, who first commissioned this work, and Leo Hollis, my present editor, who has done so much to improve the final product. Mark Martin and Jane Halsey did a terrific job in getting the book into production and improving it even further along the way.

Will Francis, my agent, has been unflinching in his belief in and support of this project. His kind words have been great comfort to me.

The Society of Authors generously financed a number of important research trips to the eastern United States.

My sons, Danny and Ben, have always understood what book writing means to me, and I thank them for that understanding; and I thank my sister Pearl, who was there that day when the seed for this book was first sown.

I leave to the end the greatest thanks of all: to Dallas, whose love, patience and insight has made this book a joy to do as much as she is a joy to me. She has helped me with this book at every stage. I couldn't have done it without her.

# Notes

I have adopted the following scheme for citing the sources I have used in writing this book. For manuscript sources, I have abbreviated the name of the archive or library (see below) and then continued the citation using that repository's own cataloging method. For published works, I cite the author's surname followed by a shortened title of the item—no more than the first few words. The full citations can be found in the bibliography.

*Abbreviations*

| | |
|---|---|
| AAA | Archives of American Art |
| AK | Akademie der Künste, Berlin |
| APA | Associated Press Archives |
| CHWMAAH | Charles H. Wright Museum of African American History |
| CSA | California State Archives |
| CULMC | Columbia University Libraries Manuscript Collection |
| FL | Field Library, Peekskill, New York |
| FOIPA | Freedom of Information and Privacy Act |
| HA | Hakim Adi Private Collection |
| HIASU | Hoover Institution Archives, Stanford University |
| HSTLM | Harry S. Truman Library and Museum |
| HU | Howard University, Moorland-Spingarn Research Center |
| LAC | Library and Archives Canada |

| | |
|---|---|
| MML | Marx Memorial Library, London |
| NAA | National Archives of Australia |
| NARA | National Archives and Records Administration, College Park, Maryland |
| NYSA | New York State Archives |
| PHMASC | People's History Museum Archive and Study Centre, Manchester |
| PNAACP | Papers of the NAACP, held on microfilm |
| SSC | Sophia Smith Collection, Smith College |
| RBMSCLDU | Rare Book, Manuscript, and Special Collections Library, Duke University |
| RULSCUA | Rutgers University Libraries Special Collections and University Archives |
| RWWLASC | Robert W. Woodruff Library Archives and Special Collections, Atlanta University Center |
| SCHRBC | Schomburg Center for Research in Black Culture, New York Public Library |
| SGMML | Seeley G. Mudd Manuscript Library, Princeton University |
| SLRC | Schlesinger Library, Radcliffe College |
| TLRWLA | Tamiment Library and Robert F. Wagner Labor Archives, New York University |
| TNA | The National Archives, Kew, London |
| UBCMSSC | University of British Columbia Manuscripts Collection |
| URSC | University of Rochester, Special Collections |
| US | University of Sussex, Special Collections |
| UWMRC | University of Warwick Modern Records Centre |
| WCML | Working Class Movement Library, Salford |
| WHS | Wisconsin Historical Society |
| WSUSCUA | Wichita State University Special Collections and University Archives |
| YUCTASP | York University Clara Thomas Archives and Special Collections |

PREFACE: IN THE PRESENCE OF GREATNESS

There has been and continues to be a major reevaluation of the civil rights movement in the United States. It began with a groundbreaking article published in 1988, Korstad and Lichtenstein's "Opportunities." It then progressed through a major statement of revision published in 2005, Hall, "The Long," in which the author made a powerful and influential case for broadening, in the sense both of time and place, our understanding of the civil rights movement, away from the familiar story based around Martin Luther King and the politics of Southern activism and toward one that embraced the work of the radical Communist activists, particularly in the Northern states—Robeson and people like him. Since Hall's publication, many historians have entered the debate. Recent additions include Cha-Jua and Lang, "The 'Long'"; Lieberman and Lang, *Anticommunism*; Lewis, Nash, and Leab, *Red*, and, a short while ago, a symposium focusing on the work of Eric Arnesen and published in *American Communist History*, vol. 11, 2012.

INTRODUCTION: BEING PAUL ROBESON, BECOMING RADICAL

I have relied on all modern biographies of Robeson to tell the story of his early years: these are Duberman, *Paul Robeson*; Brown, *The Young*; Robeson, *The Undiscovered: An Artist's*, and Boyle and Bunie, *Paul Robeson*. As an account of Robeson's life from his birth to 1939, and for its attention to detail, its use of secondary and primary sources and its insights, there is, in my opinion, nothing better than Boyle and Bunie's book. It is a shame it is not better known and an even greater shame that the promised second volume never appeared—Andrew Bunie died on February 12, 2012.

The quotes about Princeton come from Brown, *The Young*, pp. 19 and 22 respectively. The quote attributed to Einstein also comes from this source, pp. 133–4. Further information about the African-American Princeton community can be found in Washington, *The Long*. Greene, "A History" documents African-American experiences in New Jersey from the colonial period. The story about Robeson's experience of racism on the football field is recounted in Brown, *The Young*, pp. 60–64. Robeson's own recollections of his days before Rutgers are in Robeson, *Here*.

John Payne's London home was open to African Americans. He had come to London from the United States in 1919 with the all-black Southern Syncopated Orchestra. His house was open to visitors, such as Robeson, from 1921. I would like to thank Sean Creighton and Jeff Green for information about Payne. See his entry in the *Oxford Dictionary of National Biography* (by Stephen Bourne) and the following articles: Rye, "The Southern," and Rye, "Southern," for more on the Southern Syncopated Orchestra. For the black music scene in London, see Green, "The Negro," and Parsonage, *The Evolution*. When they first met in London in the summer of 1922, Brown was accompanying Roland Hayes on his European tour, which had begun in 1920; the circumstances of Robeson meeting Brown are recounted in Seton, *Paul Robeson*.

There are many excellent accounts of the Harlem Renaissance. One of the latest is Ogbar, *The Harlem*, which contains references to much of the preceding literature. Among single narratives, one of the best treatments is still Lewis, *When Harlem*, though it should be supplemented by Corbould, *Becoming*. Stewart, in "Paul Robeson," places his subject in the context of this dynamic cultural period.

On Oscar Micheaux's career, see McGilligan, *Oscar*, and for a detailed study of the film *Body and Soul*, see Musser, "To Redeem."

Though the Greenwich Village Theatre recitals are generally considered Robeson's debut as a concert singer, he had made several concert appearances before that date. Compared with the Greenwich Village recitals, however, they were small affairs. For this see Schlosser, "Paul Robeson."

Du Bois's congratulatory letter is dated May 4, 1925, and is in the W.E.B. Du Bois Papers, MS 312, Special Collections and University Archives, University of Massachusetts Amherst Libraries. For a study of the enduring friendship and mutual respect between Du Bois and Robeson, see Balaji, *The Professor*.

Robeson's appreciation of Hayes appeared in the *Chicago Defender*, November 22, 1924. Hayes sang spirituals but never built a whole program around them, interspersing them within sets of songs from the classical repertoire. A succinct biographical study of Roland Hayes can be found in Campbell, "'Deep River.'" Hildebrand, "'Two Souls,'" and Green, "Roland Hayes" have much more on Hayes's career, the latter particularly on his time in London. Northern American and European audiences were first introduced to the Negro-spiritual canon when the Fisk Jubilee Singers, an a cappella ensemble of students from Fisk University, began touring the northern United States and Europe in the 1870s. This history is covered in Anderson, *Deep River*. Seroff, "The Fisk," tells the story of the singers' early visit to Britain. They were in London giving recitals in 1924 and 1925.

Sandburg's comparison of Robeson and Hayes appears in Duberman, *Paul Robeson*, p. 81.

*Black Boy*'s tour is discussed in detail in Boyle and Bunie, *Paul Robeson*, pp. 175–9. Kern's recollection of seeing Robeson in the play can be found in Decker, "Black/White," p. 64.

For the history of *Show Boat*, both as a novel and as a musical, I am indebted to recent cutting-edge scholarship from Todd Decker and Katharine Leigh Axtell. Their dissertations—Decker, "Black/White," and Axtell, "Maiden"—have significantly and convincingly altered the received wisdom on how *Show Boat*, the musical, took on its form. Decker's dissertation has now been published, with even more research, in book form as Decker, *Show Boat*. Other sources that I have used include McMillin, "Paul Robeson," and Decker, "Do You" and "Who Should." I would like here to thank Todd Decker for allowing me to see the draft of the latter piece.

For a discussion of why Robeson turned down *Show Boat*, see Decker, *Show Boat*. In his biography of his father, Paul Robeson Jr. argues that

Robeson objected to the use of the word *nigger* in the show and that was why he turned down the part (Robeson, *The Undiscovered: An Artist's*, p. 143). This seems an unlikely explanation, as Robeson had no trouble saying the word in *Black Boy*, in which he had starred the year before—Boyle and Bunie, *Paul Robeson*, p. 175.

An excellent introduction to the African-American and African presence in interwar Paris can be found in Boittin, *Colonial Metropolis*; Stovall, *Paris*; Gillett, "Crossing," and Edwards, *The Practice*. See also Eburne and Braddock, "Introduction."

That it was Ziegfeld who approached Robeson is borne out in a letter written by Essie to Larry Brown, reproduced in Decker, *Show Boat*, p. 132. The Drury Lane production, as well as all the other productions of *Show Boat* in which Robeson performed, are covered in Decker, *Show Boat*. For the recordings of "Ol' Man River," I have relied on Decker, "'Who Should.'" Decker, *Show Boat*, provides a detailed description of the 1936 film.

Robeson's Othello in 1930 is the subject of Morrison, "Paul Robeson's" and Swindall, *The Politics*. Over the years Robeson's films have attracted a lot of scholarly attention. The most recent contribution to the field is Nollen, *Paul Robeson*, but see also Musser, "Paul Robeson"; Petty, "'Doubtful Glory'" and Bourne, *Black*.

The radical anticolonial politics of interwar London has been the subject of much recent work. Four PhD dissertations, which draw on substantial new material, have provided a new understanding of this vital part of British imperial history: James, "'What We Put'"; Matera, "Black Internationalism"; Prais, "Imperial," and Whittall, "Creolising." Makalani, *In the Cause*, takes up many similar issues. For an excellent overview of the political context, see Pennybacker, *From Scottsboro* and Rush, *Imperialism*. Other useful sources, some of which are discussed in the material above, are Matera, "Black Intellectuals"; Schwarz, *West Indian*, and "Black Metropolis"; Adi, *West Africans*; Robinson, "Black," and Rush, "Reshaping." On communism and British imperial politics, see James, "'What We Put'"; Smith, "'Class'";

Sherwood, "The Comintern," and Adi, "The Comintern" and "The Negro." On the Italian invasion of Ethiopia and its role in promoting radical pan-Africanism, see Bush, *Imperialism*; Meriwether, *Proudly*; Putnam, "Ethiopia," and Harris, *African-American*.

On C.L.R. James, see Høgsbjerg, "C.L.R. James," and Bogues, "C.L.R. James." On James's play *Toussaint Louverture*, see Høgsbjerg, *Toussaint*. For the Unity Theatre, the best source is Chambers, *The Story*.

Andre Van Gyseghem's quote is from Boyle and Bunie, *Paul Robeson*, pp. 329–30. On the founding of the International Committee on African Affairs, see Lynch, *Black*, and Von Eschen, *Race*. In 1942 the ICAA changed its name to the Council on African Affairs, and in the following year the council published its first issue of *New Africa*, a journal specializing in African issues. On the coverage of African affairs in the African-American press see Von Eschen, *Race*, pp. 14–17; on the London black press, see Macdonald, "'The Wisers.'" Newspapers published in the West Indies and in West Africa also circulated in London, as their francophone equivalents did in Paris. George Padmore was one of the journalists working out of London who frequently reported on African affairs. See James, "'What We Put.'"

The quote from Robeson's speech at the rally for the Basque children refugees is taken from Duberman, *Paul Robeson*, p. 212. The change in lyrics in "Ol' Man River" is discussed in Duberman, *Paul Robeson*, p. 214. For more on Robeson's political immersion and emergence, and its relationship to his art, see Creighton, "Paul Robeson's"; Dawson, "The Rise"; Spohrer, "Becoming"; Reid, "Race," and Stephens, "'I'm the Everybody.'"

On the Spanish trip in early 1938, see Ransby, *Eslanda*, especially pp. 125-31, and Adamson, *Charlotte Haldane*. For the Abraham Lincoln Brigade in general, see Carroll, *The Odyssey*, and for the African-American volunteers assigned to it, see Kelley, *Race*, pp. 123-58. At this time, and for more than a decade after, the United States military was segregated. The quote from a British volunteer comes from

Duberman, *Paul Robeson*, p. 218. On the British volunteers in the International Brigades, see Baxell, *British* and *Unlikely*.

For the section on Robeson and Wales, I have relied heavily on the excellent dissertation by Exton, "Paul Robeson." Part of Tommy Adlam's quote comes from this source, p. 45, and part from a transcript of an interview with Adlam in the author's possession. For further information on Horner and the South Wales Miners, see Fishman, *Arthur Horner*.

On the importance of Moscow to the articulation of a Black International, see the following works: Leslie, "'What We Put'"; Adi, "The Negro"; Baldwin, *Beyond*, and Mukherji, "The Anticolonial." See also Carew, *Blacks*; Stern, *Western*, and David-Fox, "The Fellow." On race in the Soviet Union in the 1930s, see Matusevich, "An Exotic" and "Black." For Robeson's stay in the Soviet Union in the 1930s, see Baldwin, *Beyond*; Lewis, "Paul Robeson" and McConnell, "Understanding." Robeson's meeting in Moscow with fellow African Americans is described in Duberman, *Paul Robeson*, p. 189, and his comment about the racial discrimination he experienced growing up appears in Duberman, *Paul Robeson*, p. 207.

Robeson's FBI file is online at the agency's website. I received the Council on African Affairs file through a FOIPA request. Robeson's RCMP file is in LAC, Canadian Security Intelligence Service Fonds, R929-0-4E, vol. 4272, and his MI5 file can be found in TNA, KV2/1829 and 1830.

Robeson's activities between 1939 and 1949 are well discussed in Duberman, *Paul Robeson*, and Robeson, *The Undiscovered: Quest*. For the meaning and impact of "Ballad for Americans," see Barg, "Paul Robeson's," and Stephens, "'I'm the Everybody.'" Robeson's growing interest in the political situation in China is covered in Robinson, "Internationalism." For changes in the American labor movement during the period, see Devinatz, "Filling In"; Korstad and Lichtenstein, "Opportunities"; Cherney, Issel, and Taylor, *American Labor*, and Stromquist, *Labor's*. For Robeson's role in the labor struggle, see

Wright, *Robeson*. A clear sense of Robeson's widening political engagement can be gauged from the speeches he made between 1939 and 1949, reprinted in Foner, *Paul Robeson*. Robeson's final American appearance in *Othello* is discussed in Swindall, *The Politics*.

CHAPTER ONE: POSTWAR BRITAIN

For the situation in postwar Britain, Kynaston, *Austerity*, is very helpful. A good overview of decolonization after the Second World War can be found in Thomas, Moore, and Butler, *Crises*. Bayly and Harper, *Forgotten Wars*, focuses on Southeast Asia and, in particular, the Malayan Revolution.

The bulk of the information used in this chapter was collected from security service files in the United Kingdom and United States and from the *Daily Worker*, which unlike the more centrist and right-wing British newspapers was assiduous in reporting on Robeson's tour and political appearances (further information about the relationship between the *Daily Worker* and the British Communist Party can be found in Morgan, "The Communist Party"). Robeson's MI5 file, open for several years now, is in TNA, KV 2/1829 and 1830. His FBI file, also available to the public, is online at the FBI's FOIA website. For information on Peter Blackman I have relied on his MI5 file in TNA, KV 2/1838 and 1839; Sherwood, "Peter Blackman," and Macdonald, "'The Wisers.'" For Desmond Buckle, Adi, "Forgotten Comrade?" proved invaluable, as did Duberman, *Paul Robeson*. The photograph of Robeson being greeted by Blackman and Buckle was probably taken by Julius Lazarus, a well-known photographer who was particularly interested in documenting people and events associated with the American radical left. Lazarus accompanied Robeson on the *Queen Mary* and during his European tour. The photograph in question is in AK Paul Robeson Archiv. Corroborating evidence that the two men are indeed Blackman and Buckle was found on the website for the Associated Press image archive; in MML, Photographic Archive and in *Deuxième Congrès*. The connection between Buckle and Patterson emerges from a letter the latter wrote to the former, which is in the Civil Rights Congress Papers, microfilm edition, Part II, reel 3, frame 607; and a letter in the reverse direction, from Buckle to Patterson, cited in Duberman, *Paul Robeson*, p. 685, n. 7. For information about the London meeting of the preparatory committee, I am indebted to the Hull History Centre, Hull, England, who kindly supplied me with important information. For a short overview of Patterson's career, see Horne, "William Patterson."

For those aspects of Robeson's British tour not covered in the sources above I have relied on Robeson, *The Undiscovered: Quest*. The interview Robeson gave to the *National Guardian* was reprinted in *Reynolds News* on January 1, 1949, from which I have taken the quotes attributed to him. For the background to Robeson's American contractual difficulties, I have used a number of works. These are: Horne, *The Final Victim*; Gladchuk, *Hollywood*; Everitt, *A Shadow*; Doherty, *Cold War*, and Schrecker, *Many*. On the trial of the Communist leadership, important sources are Horne, *Communist*; Belknap, *Cold War*, and Martelle, *The Fear*. Desmond Buckle's quote regarding Robeson's concert tour is taken from Buckle, "Paul Robeson."

CHAPTER TWO: PEACE TALKS IN THE SALLE PLEYEL

The Salle Pleyel, named after the Pleyel Piano Manufacturing Company, opened its doors to the classical music public in October 1927 with a gala concert dedicated to the music of Europe's foremost composers. Igor Stravinsky and Maurice Ravel shared conducting duties. Providing classical performances was the Salle Pleyel's main function, but in early June 1933, the hall played host to a meeting of the European Congress Against Fascism and War and gave its name to a short-lived but highly significant pacifist movement, the Amsterdam-Pleyel movement, normally associated with the French writer and Nobel laureate Romain Rolland (see Fisher, *Romain Rolland*, and Santamaria, "Un prototype"). The Paris Peace Congress can be seen as upholding this relatively new tradition.

By April 17, 1949, Robeson had decided to attend the Paris Peace Congress. This is stated in a letter he wrote to Alphaeus Hunton, now in HU, Paul and Eslanda Robeson Collection.

For the Wrocław meeting I drew mostly on *Congrès mondial des intellectuels* and Wittner, *One World*. For background on the participation of the Women's International Democratic Federation, I relied upon material in SSC, Women's International Democratic Federation Collection and *Second Women's*. Weigand, *Red Feminism*, provides an excellent account of the American women's movement and its relationship to international issues.

On the Truman Doctrine I found Merrill, "The Truman" and Frazier, "Kennan," very useful, and for the Marshall Plan I consulted Di Biagio, "The Cominform"; Narinskii, "The Soviet Union," and Roberts, "Moscow." The sources for the founding of Cominform and its relation to political developments in the West are scattered. Judt, *Postwar*, provides the broadest context for all of the postwar developments, including Cominform. Claudín, *The Communist*, summarizes many of the main issues about Cominform, but it needs to be supplemented by the following work, all of which I found useful: Di Biagio, "The Cominform"; Roberts, "Moscow," and Swain, "The Cominform." Zhdanov's speech can be found in several places, including on the Internet. I have used the version found in Procacci, *The Cominform*, pp. 217–51.

Information on the steps that were taken between Wrocław and the proposed meeting in Paris comes from a variety of sources: *Congrès mondial des partisans*; Pinault, "Le Conseil mondial," and *Frédéric Joliot-Curie*, pp. 437-42; and NARA, RG59, CDF 1945-49, 800.00B/6-749. Caffrey's comment on the likely effect of the Paris meeting is in NARA, RG59, CDF 1945-49, 851.00B/3-349 (March 4, 1949).

Several sources that I consulted cover aspects of the European and American peace movements during this period: Lieberman, *The Strangest*; Jenks, "Fight"; Nehring, "Resisting" and Ziemann, "Peace

Movements." Santamaria, *Le Parti*, is a comprehensive account of the relationship between the French Communist Party and the peace movement.

The thoughts of the Foreign Office on the "peace offensive" are contained in TNA, FO 982/16 and FO 1110/271. See also Ullrich, "Preventing Peace," and Deery, "The Dove." American reactions to the "peace offensive" in 1949 can be found in NARA, RG59, CDF 1945-49, 800.00B/6-749 and in *Foreign Relations of the United States*, vol. V, 1949, pp. 823-51. The House Un-American Activities Committee published its views of the Soviet peace offensive as displayed in the peace congresses, beginning with the one in Wrocław, in *Report*. For France, see Le Cour Grandmaison, "Le Mouvement"; Vaïsse, *Le Pacifisme*; Spina, "Yves Farge"; Rousseau, "Les Mouvements," and Santamaria, *Le Parti*.

The descriptions of and speeches given at the Paris Peace Congress come from *Congrès mondial des partisans*. Joliot-Curie's biographical details were taken from Pinault, *Frédéric Joliot-Curie* and "The Joliot-Curies."

For Bernal, I relied on the essays in Swann and Aprahamian, *J.D. Bernal*. Bernal's relationship with Joliot-Curie and the beginnings of the World Federation of Scientific Workers are covered briefly in Wittner, *One World*, and in more detail in Petitjean, "The Joint," and Pinault, "The Joliot-Curies"; on Farge and the French peace movement, I used Spina, "Yves Farge." A photograph showing Robeson with Helen Thierry sitting at the piano is in APA.

The quote describing Robeson at the podium is taken from *World Congress*. James Crowther's observations on Robeson and the comment on Zilliacus come from US, James G. Crowther Collection.

Information that it was Hunton who told Robeson about the adverse press coverage is in the May 7, 1949, issue of the newspaper *Afro-American*.

CHAPTER THREE: GARBLED WORDS

All of the information concerning Joseph Dynan's career, his wire from Paris and the front page of the *Florence Evening News*, comes from APA. Robeson's verbatim speech was printed in *Congrès mondial des partisans*, pp. 91–2. The *World Peace Congress Bulletin* appeared in the five official languages of the congress and reported on the previous day's activities. The scheduled speeches by delegates were normally printed in full. The shortened version of Robeson's speech was printed in Number 27, April 21, 1949, p. 7. The report on the peace congress prepared by the American embassy in Paris is in NARA, RG59, CDF 1945–49, 800.00B/6-749. Robeson's newspaper interview in Copenhagen is reproduced in Foner, *Paul Robeson*, pp. 197–8.

I have used two sources to set the debate over desegregation in the American military as a context for the African-American press's reaction to Robeson's speech: Dalfiume, *Desegregation*, and Slagle, "Mightier." On the FBI's investigation of the African-American press during the Second World War, I found Washburn, *A Question*, very useful. For a general history of the African-American press, I turned to Washburn, *The African*.

Walter White's and Mary McLeod Bethune's State Department statements can be found in PNAACP, Part 18, Series C, reel 29. White's postwar political views are examined in Janken, "From Colonial" and *White*. An analysis of Bethune's civil rights and human rights work and her relationship with the National Council of Negro Women can be found in Gallagher, "The National."

The quote about the unwritten law regarding how and where criticisms of the United States can be made is attributed to Bayard Rustin, a prominent civil rights leader who believed in the strategy of nonviolence, and reproduced in Duberman, *Paul Robeson*, p. 344.

Very perceptive discussions of the postwar split in the politics of the African-American community can be found in Von Eschen, *Race*;

Anderson, *Eyes*, and Arnesen, "No" (together with a number of contributions to the same journal issue) and "A. Philip Randolph."

Robeson's letter to Freda Diamond is quoted in Duberman, *Paul Robeson*, p. 349.

CHAPTER FOUR: LEGAL LYNCHING, JERSEY STYLE

The case of the Trenton Six is the subject of a new book, Knepper, *Jersey Justice*. Most of what I have to say about it comes from that publication, supplemented by Horne, *A Communist*. The quote from Robeson's speech at the February rally in Trenton comes from Knepper, *Jersey Justice*, pp. 96–7. Pennybacker, *From Scottsboro*, is my source for the case of the Scottsboro Boys. For William Patterson and the Civil Rights Congress, there is nothing to compare with Horne, *Communist*, for comprehensiveness. For background information on the International Labour Defense I mostly used Martin, "The International." A succinct coverage of the cases the Civil Rights Congress supported in the Southern states is provided in Martin, "The Civil Rights," and Deery, "'A Divided,'" provides good biographical information on O. John Rogge.

The story of Len Johnson is told in Herbert, *Never*, and Howard, *Len Johnson*. I have mostly relied on the former source.

Information about the New International Society can be found in Herbert, *Never*, but the main source is the unpublished file in WCML. Johnson described the work of the New International Society in the *Daily Worker* of October 12, 1949.

Johnson wrote about meeting Robeson in *Topical Times*, February 18, 1933, in part of a series of more than a dozen articles he wrote about boxing and about his own experiences. The meeting happened in Manchester, where Robeson was giving a concert. Johnson does not explain how he happened to meet Robeson that day.

Johnson's letter to Robeson inviting him to take part in a public meeting in Manchester on behalf of the Trenton Six is in HA. For background material on Hutchinson and the Meerut Conspiracy Trial, I have used Pennybacker, *From Scottsboro*. For Dadoo and Lim respectively I have used Raman, "Yusuf Dadoo" and Stockwell, "Leaders."

A description of Gordon Schaffer's friendship with Robeson and the beginnings of the press coverage of the Trenton Six can be found in Schaffer, *Baby*.

I used Sherwood, *Manchester* for background information on Manchester on the eve of the Pan-African Congress. For the congress itself, I relied on a number of works—Adi and Sherwood, *The 1945*; Kendhammer, "DuBois"; Esedebe, *Pan-Africanism*; Lemelle and Kelley, "Introduction"; Aptheker, *The Correspondence*; Adi, "George Padmore," and Makonnen, *Pan-Africanism*. Also useful is Munro, "The Anticolonial." The background to the meeting in Paris on October 3, 1945, when the World Federation of Trade Unions was formed, can be found in Kofas, "U.S. Foreign," and in Carew, "The Schism." Almost thirty years went by before the Sixth Pan-African Congress took place. On this see Williams, "From Anticolonialism."

Ras Makonnen's biography can be constructed from a number of sources, all of which I used. They include Makonnen, *Pan-Africanism* (Makonnen's own memoir); Sherwood and Adi, *Pan-African History*; Sherwood's entry on Makonnen in the *Oxford Dictionary of National Biography*, and McLeod, "A Night." On Nkrumah's relationship with Makonnen and Padmore I used Sherwood, "Kwame Nkrumah," and Lawson, "Kwame Nkrumah's Quest."

Robeson's appearance in Gateshead was the subject of a constabulary report that made its way into his MI5 file, where it can now be read.

Liverpool around the time of Robeson's visit is described in Murphy, *From the Empire*, and Brown, *Dropping Anchor*.

The letters exchanged between the Pan-African Federation, Peter Blackman and the Emergency Defense Committee for Coloured People are in HA. Peter Milliard's letter to Larry Brown is in SCHRBC, Lawrence Brown Papers, box 3/1.

Fryer, *Staying Power* details the immigration of West Indians to postwar Britain, beginning with the arrival of the *MV Empire Windrush*.

CHAPTER FIVE: STRIKE TWO

Max Yergan's life is covered in Anthony, *Max Yergan*. Further information about Yergan, Robeson, Hunton, and the early years of the International Committee on African Affairs and the Council on African Affairs can be found in Von Eschen, *Race* and Lynch, *Black*, both of which helped me in this section of the chapter. I also consulted Duberman, *Paul Robeson*. For the history of the National Negro Congress, see Gellman, *Death Blow*.

A few words are needed regarding the date when Robeson and Yergan first met. In short, no one has been able to pinpoint it. The two men certainly knew each other by 1936. Paul Robeson Jr. does not provide a date, but he says in the first volume of his biography that it was Walter White of the NAACP who introduced the two men, though he gives no further details (Robeson, *The Undiscovered: An Artist's*, p. 240). Neither White's most recent biographer (Janken, *White*) nor White in his autobiography (White, *A Man*) makes any mention of this. Some writers assert that Robeson and Yergan met in 1931 (Von Eschen, *Race*, p. 18, for example), but that is an error caused by a misreading of a passage in Anthony, *Max Yergan*, pp. 114–5, previously published in Anthony, "Max Yergan," pp. 39–40. Anthony states that Yergan was in London in 1931, adding "and it is possible if not probable that he may have encountered Robeson…at that time" (*Max Yergan*, p. 179).

Robeson's praise of Yergan's decision to resign from the YMCA can be found in Anthony, *Max Yergan*, p. 164. A copy of the letter Yergan wrote to Robeson on May 25, 1937, thanking him for his belief in the International Committee on African Affairs and for his substantial financial contribution to it is in HU, Paul and Eslanda Robeson Collection.

Yergan's political about-face is covered in Anthony, *Max Yergan*. My account is supplemented by Yergan's FBI file, number 100-210026. A copy of his file and documents furnished by other governmental agencies came to me through a FOIPA request to the Federal Bureau of Investigation.

Robeson was invited by Yergan to contribute a regular column to *People's Voice*, which he did on July 26, 1947. Robeson resigned from this job early in January 1948 because of Yergan's political turnaround. (This information comes from Robeson's FBI file and from Anthony, *Max Yergan*).

Copies of the various speeches given at Robeson's homecoming rally are in HU, Paul and Eslanda Robeson Collection. The description of the day's events is taken from items in the collection and from the report of the rally published in the New York *Daily Worker* on June 20, 1949.

There is a photograph of Robeson addressing the audience at his homecoming rally in Robeson, *The Whole*, p. 173. Robeson's Rockland Palace speech was printed with the title "For Freedom and Peace" and distributed nationwide as a Council on African Affairs pamphlet. I have taken the quotes from that publication. Press reactions to Robeson's speech can be found in Duberman, *Paul Robeson*, pp. 358–9.

Copies of letters and telegrams to President Truman are in HSTLM, Harry S. Truman Papers, Official File 1763. Hate mail to Robeson is in HU, Paul and Eslanda Robeson Collection.

CHAPTER SIX: LIKE A DUCK

On the history of HUAC, I found Goodman, *The Committee*, and Schrecker, *Many*, very helpful. The first few years of HUAC's existence, and particularly its exclusive interest in communism to the exclusion of other "un-American" ideologies—especially right-wing ones—are covered in Carr, *The House*. On the relationship between the FBI and HUAC, see Deery, "'A Blot.'" A comprehensive list of all the hearings of HUAC up to and including this one can be found in *Internal*. The story about the Black Belt Republic is mentioned briefly in Kelley, *Hammer*, and in more detail in Johnson, "'We Are.'"

All of the quotes and proceedings of the hearings held on minority groups and Communists are from Committee on Un-American Activities, *Hearings*. The telegram from the NAACP to Wood, and his response, can be found in PNAACP, Part 18, Series C, reel 19, frames 724–5.

Manning Johnson is mentioned in several sources, including Goodman, *The Committee*, and Schrecker, *Many*, but the most detail I have come across is in Sabin, *Red Scare*, pp. 130–6 and Navasky, *Naming*. There is also a little on Johnson in Woods, *Black*, in a section in which Woods discusses this particular hearing. Johnson's career as a professional witness was a long one. His slippery relationship with the truth was frequently exposed, but he continued to lie on the stand. He died with perjury charges pending against him—see Rader, *False Witness*, pp. 192–3 and Deery, "'Running,'" p. 489.

The FBI had concluded, though on what evidence is not known, that Robeson had joined the Communist Party under the assumed name "John Thomas" (Robeson FBI file); there is more about this in Chapter Fifteen. MI5 was convinced that he had joined the Party in the 1930s when he was in Moscow (TNA, KV 2/1838 and 1839).

Velde's favorite expression, as he called it, is quoted in Committee on Un-American Activities, *Hearings*, p. 468. Velde had spent several years during the Second World War working as a special agent for the FBI. He had won the Republican Party's congressional primary in 1948 with the slogan "Get the Reds Out of Washington and Washington Out of the Red." He became the chairman of HUAC in 1953, replacing John Wood, who chose not to seek reelection in the 1952, instead returning to his Georgia law practice (see Goodman, *The Committee*).

CHAPTER SEVEN: I AM A RADICAL

The story of how Jackie Robinson crossed the baseball color line has been told many times. Sources I found particularly useful include Early, *A Level*; Tygiel, *Baseball's*; Dorinson and Warmund, *Jackie Robinson*, and Elias, *The Empire*. Lester Rodney's little-remembered but critical battles with baseball segregation are covered in Silber, *Press*, though some of his conclusions and those of Rusinack, "Baseball," are disputed in Fetter, "The Party." For the African-American press and the issue of desegregation, see Weaver, "The Black Press," and for the Jackie Robinson story in the context of US foreign policy, see Thomas, "Playing." A good overview of the literature can be found in Lomax, "Baseball's" and "Introduction." Robeson's 1939 meeting with Landis is mentioned in Rampersad, *Jackie Robinson*, p. 121, and the 1943 meeting with club owners is described in Duberman, *Paul Robeson*, pp. 282–3. An overview of Robinson's civil rights involvement can be found in Lomax, "'I Never,'" and in Long, *First Class*.

Robinson's appearance in front of HUAC is mentioned in most of the sources above but is dealt with more extensively in Smith, "The Paul Robeson."

The description of the committee room comes from a report published in the *Cleveland Call and Post* on July 23, 1949, and from a photograph by the Associated Press.

The reaction to Robinson's speech from a member of the audience was reported in the *New York Times*, July 19, 1949, p. 1.

There is a little about Lem Graves reporting for the *Norfolk Journal and Guide* from Europe during the Second World War in Broussard and Hamilton, "Covering." The relationship between Alvin Stokes and Jackie Robinson is recounted in Falkner, *Great Time*, pp. 184–203. Information about the United Negro and Allied Veterans comes from Robinson's FBI file, available at the FBI's website. Both Stokes and Johnson in their testimony to HUAC mentioned that the attorney general had named the African-American veterans' organization as a Communist front.

The background to the writing of Robinson's speech can be found in Kahn, *The Era*, p. 203 and Falkner, *Great Time*, p. 199. Granger's article was printed on page 18 of the newspaper. The quote attributed to Rachel Robinson comes from Rampersad, *Jackie Robinson*, p. 213.

Lester Granger's letter to Jackie Robinson is printed in Long, *First Class*, pp. 6–7. The quote from one of Robinson's biographers appears in Tygiel, *Baseball's*, p. 334. Frankel, *Great Time*, on pp. 252-3 refers to the Spingarn Medal acceptance speech. Robinson's interview in *Look* appeared on January 22, 1957. The exchange between Malcolm X and Robinson can be found in Long, *First Class*, pp. 186-9. Robinson's thoughts on Robeson as he expressed them to Alfred Duckett in the early 1970s are printed in Robinson, *I Never*, p. 98. Besides helping Jackie Robinson with his autobiography, Duckett collaborated with the Reverend Martin Luther King, Jr., on a book and speeches, including the famous, indeed iconic, "I Have a Dream" speech for the 1963 March on Washington.

Robeson's statement, an account of the press conference at the Hotel Theresa and his declaration in Newark can all be found in Foner, *Paul Robeson*, pp. 218–21. The comment about the Klan as an American institution was actually uttered by John Rankin, a Democratic congressman from Mississippi and a member of HUAC, but there is little doubt that Wood thought similarly—see Wade, *The Fiery*, p. 274.

CHAPTER EIGHT: PEEKSKILL

The invitation extended to Robeson to sing to the residents of Mohegan Colony is referred to in the reminiscences of Walter Schwartz, who was there at the time. His memories were recorded in 1979 and are in TLRWLA, Barbara Kopple Peekskill Riots Collection, Transcripts, TAM, OH-02.4-9. Information about the Mohegan Colony and the summer residents in general in this part of New York State can be found in Shargel, "Leftist"; Mishler, *Raising*, and Walwik, *The Peekskill*, which also contains a short description of Robeson's 1946, 1947, and 1948 appearances in the area. Reminiscences of life in Mohegan Colony are contained in Avrich, *Anarchist*.

The incidents in Peoria, Albany, and Toronto are related in Duberman, *Paul Robeson*, pp. 317–19. I have also consulted issues of the *Peoria Star*, for April 15, 16, 18, and 19, 1947. The controversy in Albany is treated by the following sources: SGMML, American Civil Liberties Union Records, MC001.02.01, box 562, folder 5 and URSC, Thomas E. Dewey Papers, series 5:280:40.

The history of People's Songs and People's Artists is covered in several sources. Pete Seeger's own reminiscences can be found in Dunaway, *How*. Lieberman, *"My Song,"* is the most detailed history of People's Songs (other accounts have been published in Lieberman, "The Culture" and "People's Songs"); Reuss and Reuss, *American Folk*, does the same for People's Artists. The larger context of American politically inspired folk music and protest songs in general is the subject of Cohen, *Rainbow*, and Lynskey, *33 Revolutions*, especially Chapters 2 and 3.

Seeger's recollection of the lead-up to the August 27 Peekskill concert is taken from Dunaway, *How*, p. 14.

Unless otherwise stated, I have relied on the following secondary sources for telling the story of the Peekskill concerts and riots: Walwik, *The Peekskill* (the only book-length account); Castledine, "Wake Up"; Shapiro, *White*, Fast, *Peekskill*, and McKeon, "The Robeson." Curran, *Peekskill's*, features a discussion of the riots in the context of race relations in the town.

I consulted the relevant clippings from the August issues of the *Peekskill Evening Star* in FL, Local History Collection, where they have been assembled in the file "Robeson Riots."

The account of the August 27 event is told in Walwik, *The Peekskill*. Walwik relies on newspaper reports and police interviews, which are in URSC, Thomas E. Dewey Papers, series 5:222:36. I have used these sources and supplemented them with others: depositions made to the Civil Rights Congress, which have been microfilmed as *Papers of the Civil Rights Congress* and can be located on reel 15, Part I, Cases, frame 703–920; and TLRWLA, Barbara Kopple Peekskill Riots Collection, Transcripts, TAM, OH-02.4-9, where the interviews with Helen Rosen and Sidney Danis can be found. Rosen's and Danis's recollections pretty much support each other. The problem is trying to account for Robeson's movements once he left Danis's car. Danis recalled that he drove Robeson back to his house in the country and then dropped him off at the train station. According to Martin Duberman (who conducted his own interviews), Danis drove Robeson not to the station but to the home of Robert Rockmore, Robeson's friend and attorney, where he spent the night before being driven back to New York City the following morning (Duberman, *Paul Robeson*, p. 365). Paul Robeson, Jr., has an account very similar to Duberman's (Robeson, *The Undiscovered: Quest*, p. 168).

For the events leading up to the rescheduling of the concert for September 4, 1949, I relied on material in TLRWLA, Barbara Kopple Peekskill Riots Collection, TAM 307, boxes 1 and 4. Stokes's report to HUAC is in TLRWLA, Barbara Kopple Peekskill Riots Collection, TAM 307, box 1, and Sergeant Davis's report is in URSC, Thomas E. Dewey Papers, series 5:222:35—copies of the flier "Rally Against The Klan" and the flier from the Fur Workers Union are in the same collection. A copy of the flier "The Swastika Behind The Fiery Cross" is in FL, Local History Collection, Robeson Riots. Robeson's Golden Gate Ballroom speech is reported in the *New York Times*, August 13, 1949, and in Robeson, *The Undiscovered: Quest*, p. 170.

Heshie Marcus's, Leon Straus's, and Sol Silverman's recollections are in TLRWLA, Barbara Kopple Peekskill Riots Collection, Transcripts, TAM, OH-02.4-9.

David Fanshel's deposition is in *Papers of the Civil Rights Congress*, Part I, Cases, reel 15, frame 723.

The depositions by Archie Lipshitz and Marshall Marotta are in *Papers of the Civil Rights Congress*, Part I, Cases, reel 15. The transcript of Sid Marcus's interview can be found in TLRWLA, Barbara Kopple Peekskill Riots Collection, Transcripts, TAM, OH-02.4-9.

On-the-spot police reports can be found in a number of archives: TLRWLA, Barbara Kopple Peekskill Riots Collection, TAM 307;

URSC, Thomas E. Dewey Papers, series 5:222:35; NYSA, A0795, New York State Division of State Police, Special Services Unit, Non-Criminal Investigation Case Files, boxes 6 and 7; and WSUSCUA, Paul Robeson Concert Police Documents, MS 86–12. The Bureau of Criminal Investigation's reports following their enumeration of private cars at the August 27 and September 4 concerts are in NYSA, A0795, New York State Division of State Police, Special Services Unit, Non-Criminal Investigation Case Files, B7, f. 204. Letters to the editor of the *Peekskill Evening Star* are in TLRWLA, Barbara Kopple Peekskill Riots Collection, TAM 307, box 4, f. 18 and 19; letters to District Attorney George Fanelli are in TLRWLA, Barbara Kopple Peekskill Riots Collection, TAM 307, box 3, f. 48; letters to Governor Dewey are in URSC, Thomas E. Dewey Papers, series 5:223:1–44 and 5:224:1–36 and telegrams to President Truman are in HSTLM, Harry S. Truman Papers, Official File 1763.

A report on the press conference at the offices of the Council on African Affairs appears in the *New York Times* of September 6, 1949. Eugene Bullard's story of what happened before he was beaten at the concert is told in Lloyd, *Eugene Bullard*. Bullard left his Georgia home in 1912, when he was twelve years old, and did not return to the United States until 1940. For most of that time he lived in Paris. Bullard's own reminiscences of the years before his return to the United States are found in Carisella and Ryan, *The Black*.

I have relied on the appropriate editions of the *New York Times* to tell the story of the various investigations into the Peekskill riots. Dewey's biographer suggests that he had to walk a tightrope between his strongly held beliefs in the right of the American people to free speech and assembly and his hatred of Communism (Smith, *Thomas E. Dewey*, pp. 557–9). Fanelli's, Ruscoe's and Gaffney's reports to Governor Dewey are printed in Dewey, *Public Papers*, pp. 607–24. Copies of the reports by the ACLU and the Westchester Committee for a Fair Inquiry into the Peekskill Violence, and the grand jury's concluding statement are widely available, predominantly in major American university libraries and in specific archives, such as SGMML, American

Civil Liberties Union Records, MC #001, box 1888, f. 14 and box 750, f. 8; FL, Local History Collection, Robeson Riots. Ralph Gwinn's speech of September 22, 1949, is printed in *Congressional Record*, 81st Congress, First Session, vol. 95, part 16, pp. A5836–A5837.

The FBI memo, dated April 11, 1950, is in Paul Robeson's FBI file, section 4b, p. 47. The copies of the reports follow but both have blacked-out sections. Clean copies exist: "Inquiry on Racial Incitations Practiced by Communists" is in HIASU, Karl Baarslag Papers, box 4, and "Inquiry Concerning Quasi-Military Forces Organized by the Communists" is in HIASU, Elizabeth Churchill Brown Papers, box 20, f. 1; both are in RBMSCLDU, J.B. Matthews Papers, box 453, f. 4.

The history of *Firing Line* and its predecessor titles is told in De Rosa, "American Legion Firing Line." Karl Baarslag's unpublished autobiography is in HIASU, Karl Baarslag Papers, box 3. Its existence has been known of for some time, but as far as I am aware, no one before Jacqueline Castledine had referred to the two reports that Baarslag prepared for the grand jury. I thank her for allowing me to have a copy of her senior year thesis, "Wake-Up," in which she discusses these reports and concludes that Baarslag is the most likely author of the reports. Baarslag is mentioned in Schrecker, *Many*, and there is a little more about him in Bach, "Non So," (pp. 113–27), which has an excellent account of the American Legion's anti-Communism program. Baarslag deserves much more attention from historians than he has so far received. In addition to his papers in HIASU, there is also a small collection of Baarslag material, predating his time with the American Legion, at the Hoover Presidential Library.

CHAPTER NINE: STRIKE THREE

There have been several biographies of A. Philip Randolph, but Anderson, *A. Philip Randolph*, is the most comprehensive. The recent Bynum, *A. Philip Randolph*, focuses on the years from the *Messenger* to the March on Washington movement. I have used both of these works in preparing the background to Randolph's attack on Robeson. The history of the *Messenger* is covered in Kornweibel, *No Crystal*. On the Brotherhood of Sleeping Car Porters, two works are particularly important—Bates, *Pullman*, and Chateauvert, *Marching*. I have mostly relied on Arnesen, "A. Philip Randolph: Labor" and "A. Philip Randolph, Black." The quotes relating to Randolph as a spokesman for African Americans as well as his 1940 newspaper interview come from the latter source, respectively on p. 139 and p. 145. For the National Negro Congress, see Gellman, *Death Blow*.

Good sources for the March on Washington movement include Bynum, *A. Philip Randolph*; Anderson, *A. Philip Randolph*, and Pfeffer, *A. Philip Randolph*. The quote from the *Messenger*'s editorial in 1918 comes from Anderson, *A. Philip Randolph*, p. 104. Randolph's statement to President Truman appeared in the *New York Times*, March 23, 1948; and the proceedings of the Senate Armed Forces Committee were reported in the *Chicago Defender* on April 10, 1948. Randolph's quote stating that Communists would sacrifice America and more is in Arnesen, "A. Philip Randolph, Black."

Randolph's appearance in Los Angeles was reported in the *New York Times*, on November 7, 1949. The quotes referring to his nationwide tour are from Arnesen, "A. Philip Randolph, Black," p. 147 and the report concerning his address in Richmond, Virginia was published in the *Chicago Defender*, February 4, 1950, as well as in other African-American newspapers.

Du Bois's correspondence with President Jenkins appears in Aptheker, *The Correspondence*, vol. 3, pp. 257-9.

Aside from newspaper accounts, I have relied on a number of sources to tell the story of the cancellation of the NBC program on which Robeson was to appear: MacDonald, *Blacks*, and WHS, National Broadcasting Company, MSS 17AF, box 102, from which the details of the public reaction to the announcement of Robeson's appearance are taken. Baldwin's statement and the notice that he had telegraphed Elliott Roosevelt can be found in this file. The Progressive Party's statement is in *The Paul Robeson Collection*, microfilm, reel 8, frame

245. Eleanor Roosevelt's explanation of her use of the word *misunderstood* can be found in Black, *The Eleanor*, p. 317.

The sources I used to tell the story about Robeson's short trip to London were TNA, KV2/1829 and 1830; Robeson's FBI file on the FBI's website and TNA, FO 1110/346 and 347.

Robeson's speech in Madison Square Garden is reproduced in Foner, *Paul Robeson*. The quotation I have used is on p. 253.

The episode concerning the special agents of the Internal Security Division of the State Department is taken from an internal State Department report. The term *flat feet* used to describe the agents was in a telegram found in Robeson's FBI file. The FBI was at pains to point out to the newswire services Associated Press and United Press that it was agents of the State Department and not of the FBI who demanded that Robeson surrender his passport.

For the reaction of the African-American press to Robeson having had his passport nullified, see Beeching, "Paul Robeson."

CHAPTER TEN: BUT NOT OUT

There are several good sources on the background to the attorney general's list, but the most comprehensive is Goldstein, *American*. An earlier and shorter version of the book's main arguments was published in Goldstein, "Prelude." The quote about the list's circulation comes from that article, p. 22. Another good, but less comprehensive, source, is Caute, *The Great*.

All of the shenanigans leading up to the passage of the McCarran Act are revealed in Ybarra, *Washington*. For the formation of the Subversive Activities Control Board, I have relied on Schrecker, "Introduction." The quote attributed to Karl Mundt is from the latter publication, p. v. Further information about the McCarran Act can be found in Caute, *The Great* and Goldstein, *American*. A very good example of how the loyalty issue affected one person can be found in Friedman, "The Strange."

I have used the FBI's Council on African Affairs file, 1054645-000 (obtained through FOIPA) to discuss the process by which the Subversive Activities Control Board attempted to prepare the case against the council. There is a copy of Alphaeus Hunton's subpoena in *The Papers of W.E.B. Du Bois*, microfilm copy, reel 70, frames 549, 550. The story of W.E.B. Du Bois's arrest is told in Dougherty, "Left." The surviving papers of the Council of African Affairs are in SCHRBC, Alphaeus Hunton Papers, reels 1 and 2. Hunton's letter to Mr. Marks is on reel 1. For background material, I have relied on the following sources: Von Eschen, *Race*; Lynch, *Black*, and Brock, "The 1950s."

The history of *Freedom* and all of those individuals and organizations associated with it during the first half of the 1950s had been mostly forgotten until quite recently. We now know much more than we did, but most of the information is locked away in a number of excellent PhD dissertations. One of the first, and still influential, pieces to bring attention to the survival of a black radical movement in Harlem during the 1950s (a period when according to most of the literature it was long gone) is Washington, "Alice." Shortly after that article appeared, the first full-length study of *Freedom* appeared: Lamphere, "Paul Robeson, *Freedom* Newspaper, and the Black Press." A shortened and more focused piece by the same author appeared as "Paul Robeson, *Freedom* Newspaper and the Korean War." Soon scholars began to recover the voices of black women radical activists attracted to the ideas espoused by Robeson and Du Bois—voices that had previously gone unrecorded in the literature. In this vein are the following works: Welch, "Spokesman" and "Black"; Higadisha, "To"; Wilkins, 'Beyond'; Castledine, "'In'"; McDuffie, "A 'New'" and *Sojourning*; Lieberman, "'Measure'"; and Gore, *Radicalism*, "'The Law'" and "From"; Anderson, "Lorraine," and Davies, *Left*. Gore, *Want*, an edited work, contains several important essays on the role of radical women in the struggle for African-American freedom, including a piece on Shirley Graham Du Bois and one on Esther Jackson. On Esther and James Jackson, see the special issue of *American Communist History*, vol. 7, 2008, the contributions to which were published as a book, Lewis,

Nash, and Leab, *Red*. In addition to this material, without which I could not have written this section focusing on *Freedom*, I also benefited from Caldwell, "'It Will'"; Rocksborough-Smith, "'Filling'" and "Bearing," and Singh, *Climbin.'*

Information about Louis Burnham comes from Hughes, "We Demand" and from the obituary that appeared in the *National Guardian*, February 22, 1960. McDuffie, *Sojourning*, from which the quote is taken (p. 176), is the most comprehensive study of the Sojourners for Truth and Justice. Gore, *Radicalism*, is also useful.

A good representative selection of Robeson's regular contribution to *Freedom* has been published in Foner, *Paul Robeson*.

The FBI's assessment of Freedom Associates is in Lorraine Hansberry's FBI File obtained through a POIPA. The plan for a "Freedomobile" is outlined in *The Paul Robeson Collection*, microfilm, reel 8.

Lorraine Hansberry's recollections of the first three years of *Freedom's* operations are in SCHRBC, Lorraine Hansberry Papers, box 57, folder 16.

CHAPTER ELEVEN: LYNCHING, SOUTHERN STYLE

The lynching statistics published by the Tuskegee Institute are widely available on the Internet. They are being reexamined and reevaluated. See Cook, "Converging," and Eckberg, "Reported." The quote about uppity African Americans comes from Anderson, "Clutching," p. 91.

On the antilynching movements before World War II, I used Hill, *Men*; Little, "'Death'"; Francis, "The Battle," and Brown, "'Eradicating.'"

The Monroe, Georgia, lynching is the subject of a full-length book, Wexler, *Fire*. Also useful is Warren, "'The Best.'"

Einstein's friendship with Robeson has only recently surfaced. Robeson's name is never mentioned in the countless Einstein biographies, and Einstein's name barely gets a mention in books about Robeson, although the biography by Paul Robeson, Jr., has more references than the rest. For recovering the Einstein-Robeson connection, we have to thank Fred Jerome, who has brought the two men's relationship out of obscurity in a number of works, all of which I consulted to write this part of the chapter: Jerome, "Einstein" and *The Einstein*, and Jerome and Taylor, *Einstein*.

The quote referring to Einstein's view on racism is from an article he wrote, "The Negro Question," published in the January 1946 issue of the magazine *Pageant* and reprinted in Jerome and Taylor, *Einstein*, pp. 139–42.

Robeson's telegram to Du Bois is in *The Papers of Du Bois*, reel 59, frame 463; his telegram to Einstein is referred to in Jerome, *The Einstein*, p. 76. A list of sponsors of the American Crusade to End Lynching can be found in the RWWLASC, Southern Conference for Human Welfare Papers, box 11, folder 8.

What happened in the meeting with Truman was reported widely in the American press. I have used a number of these reports to tell the story: *Chicago Defender*, September 21 and 28, 1946; *New York Times*, September 23 and 24, 1946; *Chicago Daily Tribune*, September 24, 1946; *Philadelphia Tribune*, September 24, 1946, and *Washington Post*, September 24, 1946.

On the NAACP's reaction to Robeson's crusade and the exchange of views between White and Du Bois, I have relied on Duberman, *Paul Robeson*, pp. 306-7. Robeson had a complicated relationship with the NAACP. For a flavor of this, see Anderson, "Rethinking." The FBI's assessment of the American Crusade to End Lynching can be found in Albert Einstein's FBI file, available on the agency's website.

Material in RWWLASC, Southern Conference for Human Welfare Papers, box 11, folder 8, and SCHRBC, George Marshal Papers, MG541, box 25(36) were essential for the one-hundred-day campaign. The ending of the crusade in Washington is told in the *Chicago Defender*, January 4, 1947. The Lincoln Memorial, since its dedication on May 30, 1922, has been the scene of many African-American celebratory moments—on the symbolism of the site, see Sandage, "A Marble House."

A good overview of Truman's civil rights record can be found in Gardner, *Harry Truman* and Anderson, *Eyes* and "Clutching." For the President's Committee on Civil Rights, see Franklin, "A Half-Century."

My discussion of the two attempts to petition the United Nations on racial oppression in the United States relies on Anderson, "From Hope." All quotations in this section of the chapter are from that essay. Anderson has explored the many fissures that these petitions opened in *Eyes*.

Not much has been written about the Robeson-Patterson petition. The materials I used mostly include Patterson, *The Man*; Martin, "Internationalizing," from which most of the quotes originate; Shapiro, *White*; Horne, *Communist*, and Anderson, *Eyes*. I also used newspapers of the time. American senators continued to block ratification of the Convention on the Prevention and Punishment of the Crime of Genocide for almost forty years until finally, on February 19, 1986, it was actually enacted.

Robert Mallard, Amy Mallard's husband, was lynched in Toombs County, Georgia, on November 20, 1948. His killers were acquitted. Francis Grayson, Josephine Grayson's husband, was one of a group of African-American men, the Martinsville Seven, who were accused of raping a white woman while she was traveling through the black district of Martinsville, Virginia. Grayson was executed in the electric chair on February 5, 1951, the last of the seven to be killed. On the Martinsville Seven, see Rise, *The Martinsville*; Martin, "The Civil Rights," and Gore, "'The Law.'" I secured a copy of Patterson's FBI file through a FOIPA.

For Edith Sampson, see Laville and Lucas, "The American." Channing Tobias is the subject of Smith, "Channing."

The report that Patterson was subjected to a personal search appeared in the *Manchester Guardian*, January 24, 1952. Other information, such as Ralph Bunche having avoided Patterson in Paris, comes from HU, William Patterson Papers. The source for the details of the Convention on Genocide is the United Nations website.

CHAPTER TWELVE: THE LONGEST UNDEFENDED BORDER

I have used a number of sources to reconstruct the events leading up to and including the day that Robeson was stopped at the American-Canadian border in Blaine, Washington. On the American side, there are documents in Robeson's FBI file, available on the FBI's website. Robeson had a substantial file with the Royal Canadian Mounted Police (RCMP). This can be found in LAC, Canadian Security Intelligence Service Fonds, R929-0-4E, vol. 4272. Internal documents of the American Immigration and Naturalization Service relating to Robeson were collected by Dr. Charles Wright and are now in CHWMAAH, Charles H. Wright Papers. I have also used a number of Vancouver-based newspaper accounts, all of which had been posted to Robeson's RCMP file. Unless otherwise stated, my account of Robeson's Canadian experiences is based on material in these sources. For background information, I found Kristmanson, *Plateaus*, critical. Also of use was MacDowell, "Paul Robeson." For background on the British Columbia division of the International Union of Mine, Mill, and Smelter workers I relied on Isitt, *Militants*.

The State Department and FBI's interest in Robeson's presence in Canada in 1947 is the subject of a number of telegrams and memos, copies of which are in RULSCUA, Paul Robeson Collection, R–MC 011, box 14. Information about the Canadian Department of External Affairs' response to Robeson's visits to Canada in 1948 comes from LAC, Special Registry, R219-102-X-E.

Robeson's quote concerning his meeting with Officer Everett is from his March 1952 column in *Freedom*, reprinted in Foner, *Paul Robeson*, p. 312. King, *Red*, p. 116, reproduces the file memorandum that mentioned the phone call from the Canadian embassy in Washington.

Robeson's comments after his interview with Officer Strapp were reported in the *Vancouver News Herald*, February 2, 1952. Al King's recollection of Murphy inviting Robeson to return to the border is in King, *Red*, p. 115.

Jerry Tyler's letter to Eddie Tangen is in YUCTASP, Ray Stevenson Fonds, 2000-040/002.

I have relied on a number of sources to tell the story of the 1952 Peace Arch concert. They include local Vancouver newspapers, Robeson's RCMP file, Robeson's FBI file and UBCMSSC, International Union of Mine, Mill, and Smelter Workers (Canada), box 55. I have also used Kristmanson, *Plateaus*, and MacDowell, "Paul Robeson." The most recent contribution is Verzuh, "Mine Mill's," from which I took the point that it was Harvey Murphy's idea to hold a Peach Arch concert (pp. 75–6). Another source that confirms this is in UBCMSSC, Paul Robeson Memorial Concert Collection, box 1, where there is also a flier advertising the June 4, 1950 Youth Peace Rally held at Peace Arch Park.

Robeson's and Harvey Murphy's words are from a transcript of the Peace Arch Concert in UBCMSSC, International Union of Mine, Mill, and Smelter Workers (Canada), box 55. It is reprinted in MacDowell, "Paul Robeson," pp. 201–3.

Duberman, *Paul Robeson*, pp. 400-402 describes the Seattle incident.

There is a great deal of material on most of the Peace Arch concerts in *The Paul Robeson Collection* microfilm of the original in SCHRBC.

CHAPTER THIRTEEN: A POLITICAL MEDDLER

Information that Robeson was planning to go to Italy in August comes from Robeson's FBI file. The evidence that Robeson's attendance at peace meetings was of concern to the State Department in 1950 is in the State Department's argument in the case Robeson brought to the Court of Appeals in 1956. A copy of this is in TLRWLA, Rabinowitz and Boudin Legal Files, TAM 287, box 33.

Deery, "The Dove," and Ullrich, "Preventing," cover the story of the ups and downs of the Second World Peace Congress. A good factual account of the peace movement from Paris in 1949 to Warsaw in 1950 is in TNA, FO 1110/347, which I found very helpful. An excellent general discussion of the peace campaign using Russian archives is Johnston, "Peace." The Stockholm Peace Appeal is covered in Wittner, *One World*.

Correspondence between Nathan Witt and the State Department in 1950 can be found in SGMML, American Civil Liberties Union Records, MC#001, box 828, folder 23.

Decisions taken at the Second World Congress of Partisans of Peace, including the election of the members of the presidium, are covered in *Deuxième*.

Letters referred to between Nathan Witt and the State Department leading to the granting of a meeting are in SGMML, American Civil Liberties Union Records, MC#001, box 828, folder 23. The details of the meeting are in the news release from the Council on African Affairs, August 25, 1950. A copy of it was placed in Robeson's MI5 file, which is in TNA, KV2/1829 and 1830.

I have taken the details about Robeson's suit against Acheson from newspapers of the time as well as from the circular "The Facts of the Case," a copy of which is in HU, William Patterson Papers but can also be found in *The Paul Robeson Collection*, microfilm copy, reel 6.

Newspapers of the time cover Robeson's suit and its subsequent failure. I have supplemented these sources with information from "The Facts of the Case," referred to above.

A copy of the State Department's brief for the Court of Appeals is in SGMML, American Civil Liberties Union Records, MC#001, box 828, folder 37. A copy of Robeson's brief is in Special Collections at San Diego State University Library. I thank Jesica Brubaker for kindly providing me with a copy of the item. Robeson's speech at the 1953 Peace Arch Concert is reprinted in Foner, *Paul Robeson*, pp. 363–6.

Details of both the McCarran Act (1950) and the McCarran-Walter Act (1952) can be found on many websites. The background to both pieces of legislation can be found in Ybarra, *Washington*, and Caute, *The Great*. The quotation about the McCarran Act is from Kahn, "The Extraordinary." Robeson's comment about Francis Walter was made in a speech he gave at the National Convention of the Progressive Party in Chicago, on July 4, 1952. It is reprinted in Foner, *Paul Robeson*, p. 321.

Boudin, "The Constitutional," covers the relationship between the statement on national emergencies and previous legislation with respect to passports. Notice of the lifting of Truman's national emergency proclamation can be found in *Ernesto Espinoza-Castro v. Immigration and Naturalization Service*, no. 99-70588, 242 F.3d 1181, United States Court of Appeals for the Ninth Circuit, 2001, downloaded from the Internet. For a general discussion of presidential powers in national emergencies, see Relyea, "National."

The State Department's May 1952 description of passport policy appeared in *Department of State Bulletin* 26, 1952, pp. 919-20. The *New York Times* article of May 25, 1952, was fairly accurate in its reporting, apart from one glaring misreading, deliberate or otherwise: It stated that, according to the congressional findings concerning the McCarran Act of 1950, "Communist members, representatives, and agents travel *only* [my emphasis] to further Communist revolution and sabotage." But the act simply stated that travel was the means by which Communists spread their ideas. The August 28, 1952, regulations were printed in *Department of State Bulletin* 27, 1952, pp. 417-18. Leonard Boudin's reading of the September 2 regulations appears in Boudin, "The Constitutional," p. 62.

Robeson's attempts to get a passport in 1953 and 1954 are detailed in "The Facts of the Case." The State Department's responses are in TLRWLA, Rabinowitz and Boudin Legal Files, TAM 287, box 33. The list of Robeson's alleged Communist affiliations and sympathies appear in a letter from the director of the Passport Office to Paul

Robeson, May 27, 1957, in TLRWLA, Rabinowitz and Boudin Legal Files, TAM 287, box 33. Robeson's complaint on one occasion about the discretionary use of the oath was printed in a press release in 1955, a copy of which can be found in *The Paul Robeson Collection*, microfilm copy, reel 6.

Details of the Otto Nathan case are from *John Foster Dulles v. Otto Nathan*, United States Court of Appeals District of Columbia Circuit, no. 12727, 225 F.2d 29, 1955. Boudin's career as a lawyer is told in Braudy, *Family*.

I have relied on newspapers of the day, especially the *New York Times*, to tell the story of the Nathan and Shachtman cases. The full text of the court's decision on Shachtman's passport application can be found in the *New York Times*, June 24, 1955.

On Martin Kamen's case, see Anon., "Passport." The Foreman case is covered in the *New York Times*, June 28, 1955, and Clark's case appears in "The Facts of the Case." Boudin, "The Constitutional" covers the Nathan, Shachtman and Foreman cases from a judicial viewpoint. Martin, "Securing" provides an excellent discussion of the work of the Emergency Civil Liberties Committee in the field of passports.

Stone's comment on Joseph Clark appeared in *I. F. Stone's Weekly*, July 18, 1955, p. 4. For an assessment of Stone as a political commentator and more, see Guttenplan, *American*. What is presently known about the life and career of Ruth Shipley can be found in Kahn, "The Extraordinary," where the comments from Gressman and Acheson can be found. I. F. Stone referred to Shipley as the Czarina in *I. F. Stone's Weekly*, July 4, 1955, p. 2. State Department memoranda about the dangers of giving American Communists passports are in NARA, RG 59, CDF 1945-49, 800.00B/5-949.

Boudin's memorandum and the telegrams referred to are in TLRWLA, Rabinowitz and Boudin Legal Files, TAM 287, box 33.

CHAPTER FOURTEEN: A CRUEL, CRIMINAL LIBEL

Details about all of Robeson's appearances in the United States, including those that were planned but did not go forward, can be found in *The Paul Robeson Collection*, microfilm copy, reels 3, 4 and 5. Outside of Harlem, Chicago was a mainstay of Robeson's popularity, with a fiercely loyal following. For Robeson's Chicago appearances, see Powers and Rogovin, "Paul Robeson."

The material used for the fourth Peace Arch concert is in UBCMSSC, International Union of Mine, Mill, and Smelter Workers (Canada) box 55, supplemented by Verzuh, "Mine-Mill's." The telegram from Vancouver to the U.S. Secretary of State is in Robeson's FBI file.

A copy of the Peace Arch concert program is in UBCMSSC, International Union of Mine, Mill and Smelter Workers (Canada) box 55, as are the letters between New York and Vancouver regarding future Canadian concert dates.

The January 15, 1955 date for Boudin's action is mentioned in a letter from Boudin to Frances Knight in TLRWLA, Rabinowitz and Boudin Legal Files, TAM 287, box 33. Aspects of Leo Rover's early career, but especially his role in the Lattimore perjury case, are covered in Newman, *Owen Lattimore*.

Judge Burnita Shelton Matthews's biography has been sketched out in Greene, "Burnita."

I. F. Stone's comment on Rover appeared in *I. F. Stone's Weekly*, November 1, 1954, in his writing on the Lattimore case.

A partial record of what happened in Washington on August 16, 1955 is found in "Case of Paul Robeson—Why Some Americans Can't Get Passports," *U.S. News & World Report*, August 26, 1955, pp. 79–81. My discussion is mostly based on this account.

Correspondence between the FBI and the State Department leading to the release of the FBI's records on Robeson can be found in Robeson's FBI file. Robeson's 1947 Toronto concert is the subject of an early section of Robeson's RCMP file—see LAC, Canadian Security Intelligence Service Fonds, R929-0-4E, vol. 4272.

The full text of Robeson's Bandung message has been reprinted in Foner, *Paul Robeson*, pp. 398–400.

Boudin's recollection of the August 1955 court hearing comes from Duberman, *Paul Robeson*, p. 433, which also, on pp. 435–6, provides details of Robeson's illness. The statement in which Robeson berated Leo Rover is in *The Paul Robeson Collection*, microfilm copy, reel 6.

The details about Robeson's concerts in Toronto and Sudbury are from LAC, Canadian Security Intelligence Service Fonds, R929-0-4E, volume 4272. Newspaper reports are in the RCMP file. The New York *Daily Worker* also carried a report of the Toronto concert. The October 1955 arrangements for a Massey Hall concert are in a letter from Jerome Concert Management to Paul Robeson, September 21, 1955, and can be found in HU, Paul and Eslanda Robeson Collection. An annotated copy of his Sudbury speech is in UBCMSSC, International Union of Mine, Mill, and Smelter Workers (Canada), box 55. A photograph of Robeson with Mine Mill officials and Alan Booth, his accompanist for that concert and the one in Toronto, is reproduced in Solski and Smaller, *Mine Mill*, p. 118.

All of the official discussions leading to Pickersgill barring Robeson from Canada are in LAC, R. A. Bell Fonds, MG32 B1, vol. 113, file 8. The House of Commons questions are from newspaper reports reproduced in LAC, Canadian Security Intelligence Service Fonds, R929-0-4E, vol. 4272.

CHAPTER FIFTEEN: YOU ARE THE UN-AMERICANS

The best guide to the Francis Walter period of the House Un-American Activities Committee is Goodman, *The Committee*, which provided the quote (p. 389) concerning Walter's interest in passport issues. There is further useful information in Caute, *The Great*.

A letter from Dr. V. McKinley Wiles and another from Dr. Aaron O. Wells, attesting to the medical advice they gave against Robeson traveling, are in HU, Paul and Eslanda Robeson Collection. The memo referring to Donald Appel's request for the FBI's help in watching Robeson is in Robeson's FBI file. Martin Duberman, Robeson's biographer, also came to the conclusion that the hand-written note is Hoover's (Duberman, *Paul Robeson*, p. 439). An example of Hoover's handwriting can be found at http://handwritinguniversity.com/members/weekly-newsletters/john-edgar-hoovers-handwriting-analyzed.

Francis Walter's pronouncements on the committee's brief are taken from *Hearing* (Part 1), p. 4305. The transcript of Robeson's Tenney Committee hearing can be found in CSA, California Un-American Activities Committee, Hearing Transcripts, October 7, 8, 9, and 10, 1946, Ac 93-04-12. A selection of the hearing's questions and answers was published in *Third Report of Joint Fact-Finding Committee on Un-American Activities*, Sacramento, California, 1947. The full transcript appeared in the newspaper *Westwood Hills Press*, on October 18, 1946, a copy of which is in HU, Paul and Eslanda Robeson Collection. For background information on Tenney and his committee, I relied on Scobie, "Jack B. Tenney."

The theatricality of the House and Senate hearings in general is explored in Murphy, *Congressional*. Perucci, *Paul Robeson* and "The Red Mask" do the same for Robeson's HUAC appearance.

The transcript of Robeson's hearing, on which I based this chapter, was first printed in *Hearings* (Part 3), pp. 4491-4510. All of the direct quotes are from this source. The transcript is also reproduced, with some minor alterations to the text, in Bentley, *Thirty*. An excellent discussion of the use of the Fifth Amendment and its consequences can be found in Murphy, *Congressional*. For an overview of the origins of the Fifth Amendment privilege, see Hazlett, "The Nineteenth."

"John Thomas" was a well-known British slang term for penis. Whether some clever person was stringing the FBI along or whether the agency's informant really believed that a John Thomas a.k.a. Paul Robeson existed, we will probably never know.

On the committee's reaction to humor from its unfriendly witnesses, see the excellent discussion in Litvak, *The Un-Americans*, which points to Robeson's role as a black trickster. For the world of alleged and identified Soviet agents working in the United States during this period, see Haynes and Klehr, *Venona*, and Theoharis, *Chasing*.

For Khrushchev's speech and the events leading up to its disclosure and publication in the West, see the following: Rettie, "How Khrushchev" (written by the Reuters correspondent who first took the story out of the Soviet Union), Deery and Calkin, "'We All,'" and Pries, "Khrushchev's."

Robeson never got a chance to read his statement, nor did Walter allow it to be entered into the record. It was printed, with a few changes, in a pamphlet written by Eslanda Robeson under the title "Paul Robeson Goes to Washington," and published in Salford, England, by the National Paul Robeson Committee. It is reprinted in Bentley, *Thirty*.

Arthur Miller was HUAC's other star witness this year. His two greatest plays, *Death of a Salesman* and *The Crucible*, had already ensured his international fame. Miller was called on June 21. On the interesting and highly revealing differences between Robeson's and Miller's comportment during and attitude toward their inquisitors, see Bigsby, *Arthur Miller*.

CHAPTER SIXTEEN: *KENT V. DULLES*

The figures about the contempt of Congress citations are taken from Caute, *The Great*, pp. 96–7. Congressman Francis Walter's comments on the reason why Robeson was cited for contempt were reported in the *Chicago Defender*, June 14, 1956.

The decision of the District of Columbia Court of Appeals in *Robeson v. Dulles* is cited as No. 12983, 235 F.2d 819, along with the court's argument. Copies of the "Brief for Appellant," the "Amici Curiae" (testimony and argument from friends supportive of Robeson, the appellant), and the "Petition for a Writ of Certiorari" are in CULMC, National Emergency Civil Liberties Committee Papers, box 19. The "Petition for a Writ of Certiorari" has recently been published in *The Making of Modern Law: U.S. Supreme Court Records and Briefs, 1832-1978*, available from Gale Publishing, both online and in a print edition. A draft of the State Department's submission is in TLRWLA, Rabinowitz and Boudin Legal Files, TAM 287, box 33.

When Robeson brought the case against the State Department Warren Burger was the country's assistant attorney general. At the beginning of April 1956 he wrote to J. Edgar Hoover informing him that friends and supporters of Robeson's had got together to file a brief as amici curiae. Burger thought Hoover would be interested in the names of those individuals, which he listed in his memo. Burger also supplied Hoover with an extract from the brief in which the authors explained in no uncertain terms what Robeson stood for and why the State Department wanted to stop him from going abroad. The names Burger mentioned were quickly absorbed into the FBI's surveillance system and dispatched to the appropriate field offices for cross-checking. Not long after the case was heard in the District of Columbia Court of Appeals, Burger was appointed to the court as a judge. In 1969, Richard Nixon, then president of the United States, appointed Burger as the fifteenth chief justice of the Supreme Court. Burger's memo is in Robeson's FBI file, available on the agency's website.

Letters exchanged between Robeson and Boudin are in TLRWLA, Rabinowitz and Boudin Legal Files, TAM 287, box 33. The transcript for the May 1957 hearing can also be found in this source. Another copy is in Robeson's FBI file, but not in the file that is available publicly through the agency's website.

Correspondence between Boudin and the Passport Office is in TLRWLA, Rabinowitz and Boudin Legal Files, TAM 287, box 33. The stop notices from the Immigration and Naturalization Service and the internal State Department memo provide confirmation that Robeson was the only American citizen prevented from traveling to countries not requiring a passport. These documents are in the copy of Robeson's FBI file in the author's possession.

Boudin's correspondence with the State Department and with Robeson from late 1957 through early summer 1958 is in TLRWLA, Rabinowitz and Boudin Legal Files, TAM 287, box 33.

Walter Briehl's case in the District of Columbia Court of Appeals is referenced as 248 F.2d 561; Rockwell Kent's is 248 F.2d 600. All of the background information on both cases are in these documents, easily available online. Kent's fight with the State Department following the first refusal of his passport application in 1950 can be pieced together from his folder in TLRWLA, Rabinowitz and Boudin Legal Files, TAM 287, box 12b; there is more extensive material in AAA, Rockwell Kent Papers. See also Lawless, "Continental." The Supreme Court case is referenced as 357 U.S. 116. This contains Justice Douglas's majority opinion as well as Justice Tom Clark's dissenting opinion, representing the other three justices of the minority opinion. The full text was also published in the *New York Times* of June 17, 1958.

Francis Walter was incensed that the Passport Office was handing out passports before the Supreme Court's mandate was made "effective," that is, before twenty-five days had expired, during which time the government had leave to ask for a rehearing (the deadline for this was July 11). However, State Department officials had no plans to ask for a rehearing, and therefore the Passport Office considered it right to proceed. Walter also pointed out that several passport bills, one of which was his, were in the committee stages and might be passed before the Supreme Court's deadline. The State Department disputed Walter's optimism. All of this was reported in the *New York Times*, July 23, 1958.

For an overview of significant court cases that bore on the issue of the right to travel during the Cold War, see Rogers, "Passports." A scholarly analysis of the constitutionality of foreign travel can be found in Laursen, "Constitutional." A history of the Court of Appeals in Washington, D.C. is contained in Morris, *Calmly*.

Richard Morford's letter is in HU, Paul and Eslanda Robeson Collection.

CHAPTER SEVENTEEN: TELLING AMERICA'S STORY

The data for passport applications and Roderic O'Connor's remarks are in Kahn, "The Extraordinary."

"Telling America's Story to the World" was a phrase coined by the United States Information Agency (USIA) to capture the essence of its propaganda efforts. The history of this is told compellingly in Cull, *The Cold War*.

The history of the Congress for Cultural Freedom is told in Saunders, *Who*, and Scott-Smith, *The Politics*. Some of the Congress's cultural events are explored in Scott-Smith, "'The Masterpieces.'" The history of Radio Free Europe is covered in Johnson, *Radio*. On the USIA's film production and distribution, see Cull, "Film." One of USIA's most significant exhibitions was "The Family of Man," a collection of the photographs of Edward Steichen, which traveled to thirty-eight countries. See Cull, *The Cold War*, and Sandeen, *Picturing*. The opposite side of the film propaganda coin was the deliberate suppression of American films that displayed the actual nature of US race relations. One such film was *Salt of the Earth*, about a strike in the zinc mines of New Mexico, which should have been released in 1954. Made by blacklisted Hollywood artists, the film depicted the conditions endured by the mineworkers, most of whom were Mexican Americans—and used Mexican-American actors to portray them. Further information about the film and its suppression can be found in Lorence, *The Suppression*, Balthaser, "Cold War," Weinberg, "Salt," and McDonald, *Feminism*.

The elements of a politics of travel during the Cold War era are described in Klein, *Cold War*. I have benefited enormously from Klein's insights. Although she focuses on the relationship between the United States and Asia, her comments can be generalized. Interestingly, she uses Robeson's case as an example of how travel was politicized. Further information on what was called the People-to-People Program can be found in Osgood, *Total*.

On the use of the 1950 and 1952 acts to restrict entry to the United States and provide for grounds for deportation, I have relied on Caute, *The Great*. The phrase *deportation nation* is taken from the book of that title, by Kanstroom. The story of Belfrage's, James's, Williamson's, and Jones's deportations is told in Caute, *The Great*, but in somewhat more detail in Schrecker, "Immigration," Belfrage, *The Frightened*, Davies, "Deportable," Keith, "At the Formal," and Williamson, *Dangerous*.

There is a vast literature on American cultural diplomacy as it was organized through the State Department. Hixson, *Parting*, published in 1997, is an early example of work that recognized the importance of thinking culturally about the Cold War, and the field has grown substantially since then. More recent broad overviews are Belmonte, *Selling* (a shorter version of the main arguments can be found in Belmonte, "Exporting") and Caute, *The Dancer*. The 1954 Eisenhower initiative is explored in detail in Osgood, *Total*—Eisenhower's quote about the need to display America's cultural and industrial preeminence internationally is on p. 214.

Some of the best examples of the material available on various facets of this fascinating topic are: (jazz) Von Eschen, *Satchmo*, Cohen, *Duke*, which also covers the classical singers Marian Anderson and William Warfield, Davenport, *Jazz*, and Monson, *Freedom*, which has a very good section on jazz tours, Africa, and the civil rights movement in the United States; (general and classical music) Rosenberg, "Fighting," and the special issue of *Diplomatic History* vol. 36, January 2012, especially its articles Rosenberg, "America," Fosler-Lussier, "Music," and

Gienow-Hecht, "The World"; (dance) Prevots, *Dance*, Geduld, "Performing," Copel, "The State," Brown, "'Cultural,'" and Croft, "Funding," a dissertation that focuses on the tours from the early 1960s but also presents a very good introduction to the politics of dance diplomacy. On sports as a tool of cultural diplomacy, see Thomas, "Let the Games" and *Globetrotting*. On print propaganda during this period, a good source is Yarrow, "Selling."

Before embarking on its substantial program of sending touring companies and individuals abroad, the State Department sponsored the tour of *Porgy and Bess* to Vienna and Berlin in 1952. Some historians see the success of this production as a major factor in the department's decision to expand cultural diplomacy. There were, in fact, later tours of the opera under the State Department's program. See Monod, "Porgy," Monod, "Disguise," and Taylor, "Ambassadors."

CHAPTER EIGHTEEN: FREE AT LAST?

Carl Rowan's recollections of his coverage of the Montgomery bus boycott are in Rowan, *Breaking*. Rowan was still on the staff of the *Minneapolis Tribune* when he interviewed Robeson. His memories of that event and the quotes I have used are on pp. 156–8 of his book.

For the lynching of Emmett Till, see Whitfield, *A Death*, Metress, *The Lynching*, Pollack and Metress, *Emmett Till*, Thornton, "The Murder," Henderson, "Policing," and Till-Mobley, *Death*.

Louis Armstrong's newspaper interview appeared in several places, including the *New York Times*, September 19, 1957. For more on Armstrong and the State Department tours, see Von Eschen, *Satchmo*, and for the wider context of civil rights, see Dudziak, *Cold*.

An interesting interview between Lloyd Brown and Mary Helen Washington, professor of English at the University of Maryland provides useful information on Brown's career—see www.autodidact-project.org/other/lloydbrown.html.

For my account of Robeson's return to the regular concert stage in 1957 and 1958, I have relied on Duberman, *Paul Robeson*, and Robeson, *The Undiscovered: Quest*. The FBI material that I have referred to is in Robeson's file on the agency's website.

It is not clear who decided to sign Robeson to Vanguard Records. It may have been Vanguard's owners, brothers Maynard and Seymour Solomon, who shared some of Robeson's political views, or John Hammond, a highly successful jazz-record producer who made a great name for himself in the jazz community in the 1930s and 1940s. The Solomons hired him in 1954 to expand their catalog to include jazz. Hammond, too, shared Robeson's politics, and, more importantly, he was his good friend. On Hammond's career, see Prial, *The Producer*.

I used the State Department dispatches from India for my account of the disagreement between Nehru and the Americans. A copy of these can be found in RULSCUA, Paul Robeson Collection, R-MC 011. HU, Paul and Eslanda Robeson Collection, has a copy of the "All India Paul Robeson Celebration Committee" brochure.

Letters exchanged between Paul Endicott and Robeson are in HU, Paul and Eslanda Robeson Collection.

CHAPTER NINETEEN: THE FINAL TOUR

Copies of letters written to Robeson in response to the appeal from the Provisional Committee in New York can be found in *The Paul Robeson Collection*, on microfilm version of originals in the SCHRBC, reel 6. A copy of William Patterson's open letter asking for support is in PHMASC, CP/CENT/ORG/01/10. Eisenhower's words on the "Spirit of Geneva" formed part of an address he gave to the Annual Convention of the American Bar Association on August 24, 1955, which is available online at www.sageamericanhistory.net/coldwar/documents/IKESpiritGeneva. Patterson's November 17, 1955 open letter to Dulles and a copy of the petition are in *The Paul Robeson Collection*, microfilm version, reel 6.

John Williamson recounted his personal history in Williamson, *Dangerous*. The story of the Smith Act defendants and the Foley Square trial is told in Martelle, *The Fear*.

The details of the Glasgow Conference on Democratic Rights in America can be found in PHMASC, CP/CENT/ORG/01/10. A copy of Robeson's letter to Roland Casasola is in PHMASC, CP/CENT/ORG/01/11. In his biography of Robeson, Duberman acknowledges the primacy of Williamson in initiating a campaign, although he, too, fails to establish the connection between Williamson and Loesser—see Duberman, *Paul Robeson*, p. 424-5. Paul Robeson Jr.'s biography of his father sheds no light on this issue. The internal party document, probably written by John Williamson, dated December 23, 1957, is in the same folder.

For background information on Loesser (also still spelled Loeser in the United States), I have relied on his autobiography, Loeser, *Sag Nie*, his biographical entry in Müller-Enbergs, *Wer*, vol. 1, p. 810, an article in *Der Spiegel* from August 6, 1984, and information from the University of Minnesota Archives, via an online search using the name Loesser. The climate of repression on American university campuses is the subject of Schrecker, *No Ivory*.

In his autobiography, Loesser suggests that he made the decision, along with some friends, to do what he could to help Robeson. Loesser's memories of Peekskill are in Loeser, *Sag Nie*, pp. 109–14. The decision to make the campaign nationwide is referred to in a letter from Frank Loesser to a Mr. Brown, dated March 13, 1956, now in AKs, Paul Robeson Archiv, 74. A copy of the program for the "Let Paul Robeson Sing" public meeting of March 11, 1956 is in *The Paul Robeson Collection*, microfilm version, reel 6.

The letter from Belfrage to Robeson referring to Frank Loesser's role in the campaign is in HU, Paul and Eslanda Robeson Collection.

The national conference held on December 2, 1956 is covered in PHMASC, CP/CENT/ORG/01/11. The details of the taped concert can also be found in copies of correspondence from Cedric Belfrage and Frank Loesser to Robeson.

A copy of Frank Loesser's farewell letter to John Williamson, in which he tells Williamson that he is being forced to leave Britain, is in PHMASC, CP/CENT/ORG/01/11. Cedric Belfrage told Robeson of the successful conference and of Frank Loesser's imminent departure in a letter dated December 3, 1956, now in AK, Paul Robeson Archiv, 333.

Details of the planning leading up to the May 26, 1957 St. Pancras Town Hall conference and concert, and the related newspaper reports, can be found in UWMRC, Papers of Clive Jenkins, MSS.79/6/CJ/3/110. Other information about the London committee, including the minutes of the meetings before the concert, is in AKs Paul Robeson Archiv, in several files.

Desmond Buckle's letter to Robeson, dated May 26, 1957, is in HU, Paul and Eslanda Robeson Collection. The *National Guardian* report on the concert appeared in the issue of June 10, 1957.

For my account of the transatlantic Porthcawl concert, I have relied on the narrative in Exton, "Paul Robeson."

On Claudia Jones, see Davies, *Left*. The British government's early Cold War policies, especially as they related to events in the United States, are explored in Goodman, "The British." Robeson's Home Office file is in TNA, HO 382/6.

For details of Robeson's time away from United States until his return on 1963, I have relied on Duberman, *Paul Robeson*; Robeson, *The Undiscovered: Quest*, and Ransby, *Eslanda*.

The August Eisteddfod is covered in Exton, "Paul Robeson" and the relationship of Bevan and Robeson is explored in Williams, *Aneurin Bevan*. The State Department's dispatches from India and Moscow are in NARA, Central Decimal File, 1955-59, 032—Robeson, Paul Leroy. For more details on Robeson's season in Stratford, see Swindall, *The*

*Politics*. For information on Robeson's October visit to East Berlin, I would like to thank Kira Thurman for letting me see her unpublished paper, "Ol' Man River in the Promised Land: Paul Robeson in East Germany." It was during the Berlin visit that Robeson finally got to meet Frank Loesser, who acted as his guide and interpreter there. Loesser's recollections of this time are in Loeser, *Sag Nie*, pp. 169–74. The Australian part of the autumn 1960 tour is covered in Curthoys, "Paul Robeson's" and "'You Got.'" The State Department reports about Robeson's Berlin, Australia and New Zealand visits are in NARA, Central Decimal File, 1955–59, 032—Robeson, Paul Leroy. HU, Paul and Eslanda Robeson Collection, has a considerable amount of material—correspondence and newspaper clippings—from the Australia and New Zealand tour.

Information about Paul and Eslanda's passport renewal applications comes from Robeson's FBI file, available on the agency's website.

Aside from the main biographies—Duberman, Robeson, and Ransby—there is scattered correspondence describing the illnesses and treatment of both Paul and Eslanda, which can be found in TLRWLA, Cedric Belfrage Papers; MML, Marie Seton Papers; AK, Paul Robeson Archiv; and SLRC, Florence Hope Luscomb Papers.

EPILOGUE: FREEDOMWAYS

In an earlier issue, *Freedomways* announced that Robeson had returned home. The editors were quick to link Robeson's arrival with the continuing struggle for African-American rights. In particular, they addressed their message to younger African Americans, "who proudly inherit the traditions and dedication of which Paul Robeson is such a towering symbol and a legend in his own time." (*Freedomways*, vol. 4, 1964, p. 7).

On the lineup and names of sponsors for the *Freedomways* tribute, I drew on accounts in the *New York Amsterdam News*, April 17 and May 1, 1965 and the *Baltimore Afro-American*, June 12, 1965.

For the background to the launch of *Freedomways*, I relied on Rocksborough-Smith, "'Filling,'" and "Bearing"; Smethurst, "SNYC," and Nash, *"Freedomways."* Esther Jackson's recollections of the magazine are in Jackson, *Freedomways*. Her quote on "the two giants of the century" is taken from Rocksborough-Smith, "'Filling.'" The political work of Esther and James Jackson is the focus of volume 7, issue 2 of *American Communist History* (2008), which was published as Lewis, Nash, and Leab, *Red*.

*Freedomways* was the brainchild of Louis Burnham and his friend Edward Strong, both founding members of the influential Southern Negro Youth Congress. Burnham, also the editor of *Freedom*, died suddenly in early 1960. The group of close friends around him, the next generation of political activists, including his wife Dorothy, Strong's wife Augusta and Esther and James Jackson, together with support from a number of activists, artists and writers in the New York area, made the idea a reality. Du Bois provided advice; his wife, Shirley Graham, who had written a biography of Robeson in 1946, agreed to act as general editor; and Alphaeus Hunton, Robeson's right-hand man at the Council on African Affairs, became the associate editor. The history of the Southern Negro Youth Congress is covered in Matthews, "The Southern," and Richards, "The Southern."

The description of the audience at the tribute and Ossie Davis's introduction are taken from *Freedomways* 4, 1965, pp. 363–4. Howard's report appeared in the *Baltimore Afro-American*, June 12, 1965. Robeson's speech was published in *Freedomways* 4, 1965, pp. 373–77 and is reprinted in Foner, *Paul Robeson*.

# Bibliography

Adamson, Judith, *Charlotte Haldane: Woman Writer in a Man's World*, Basingstoke, 1998.

Adi, Hakim, "The Comintern and Black Workers in Britain and France 1919–37," *Immigrants & Minorities* 28, 2010, 224–45.

———, "Forgotten Comrade? Desmond Buckle: An African Communist in Britain," *Science & Society* 70, 2006, 22–45.

———, "George Padmore and the 1945 Manchester Pan-African Congress," in *George Padmore: Pan-African Revolutionary*, Fitzroy Baptiste and Rupert Lewis, Rupert, eds., Kingston, Jamaica, 2009, 66–96.

———, "The Negro Question: The Communist International and Black Liberation in the Interwar Years," 'in *From Toussaint to Tupac: The Black International Since the Age of Revolution*, Michael O. West, William G. Martin, and Fanon Che Wilkins, eds., Chapel Hill, NC, 2009, 155–75.

———, *West Africans in Britain, 1900–1960: Nationalism, Pan-Africanism, and Communism*, London, 1998.

Adi, Hakim and Sherwood, Marika, *The 1945 Manchester Pan-African Congress Revisited*, London, 1995.

Anderson, Carol, "Clutching at Civil Rights Straws: A Reappraisal of the Truman Years and the Struggle for African American Citizenship," in *Harry's Farewell: Interpreting and Teaching the Truman Presidency*, Richard S. Kirkendall, ed., Columbia, MO, 2004.

———, *Eyes Off the Prize: The United Nations and the African American Struggle for Human Rights, 1944–1955*, New York, 2003.

————, "From Hope to Disillusion: African Americans, the United Nations, and the Struggle for Human Rights, 1944–1947," *Diplomatic History* 20, 1996, 531–63.

————, "Rethinking Radicalism: African Americans and the Liberation Struggles in Somalia, Libya, and Eritrea, 1945–1949," *Journal of the Historical Society* 11, 2011, 385–423.

Anderson, Jervis, *A. Philip Randolph: A Biographical Portrait*, New York, 1972.

Anderson, Michael, "Lorraine Hansberry's Freedom Family," *American Communist History* 7, 2008, 259–69.

Anderson, Paul Allen, *Deep River: Music and Memory in Harlem Renaissance Thought*, Durham, NC, 2001.

Anon., "Passport Refusals for Political Reasons: Constitutional Issues and Judicial Review," *Yale Law Journal* 61, 1952, 171–203.

Anthony, David Henry III, "Max Yergan in South Africa: From Evangelical Pan-Africanist to Revolutionary Socialist," *African Studies Review* 34, 2001, 27–55.

————, *Max Yergan: Race Man, Internationalist, Cold Warrior*, New York, 2006.

Aptheker, Herbert, ed., *The Correspondence of W.E.B. Du Bois*, vols. 1, 2, and 3, Amherst, MA, 1976 and 1978.

Arnesen, Eric, "A. Philip Randolph, Black Anticommunism, and the Race Question," in *Rethinking U.S. Labor History: Essays on the Working-Class Experience, 1756–2009*, Donna T. Haverty-Stack, and Daniel J. Walkowitz, eds., New York, 2010, 137–67.

————, "A. Philip Randolph: Labor and the New Black Politics," in *The Human Tradition in American Labor History*, Eric Arnesen, ed., Wilmington, DE, 2004, 173–91.

————, "No 'Graver Danger': Black Anticommunism, the Communist Party, and the Race Question," *Labor: Studies in Working-Class History of the Americas* 3, 2006, 13–52.

Asukile, Thabiti, "J. A. Rogers' 'Jazz at Home': Afro-American Jazz in Paris During the Jazz Age," *The Black Scholar* 40, 2010, 22–35.

Avrich, Paul, *Anarchist Voices: An Oral History of Anarchism in America*, Princeton, NJ, 1995.

Axtell, Katherine Leigh, "Maiden Voyage: The Genesis and Reception of *Show Boat*, 1926–1932," unpublished PhD dissertation, University of Rochester, 2009.

Bach, Morten, "None So Consistently Right: The American Legion's Cold War, 1945–50," unpublished PhD dissertation, Ohio University, 2007.

Badger, Reid, *A Life in Ragtime: A Biography of James Reese Europe*, Oxford, 1995.

Balaji, Murali, *The Professor and the Pupil The Politics and Friendship of W.E.B Du Bois and Paul Robeson*, New York, 2007.

Baldwin, Kate A., *Beyond the Color Line and the Iron Curtain: Reading Encounters Between Black and Red, 1922–1963*, Durham, NC, 2002.

Balthaser, Benjamin, "Cold War Re-Visions: Representation and Resistance in the Unseen Salt of the Earth," *American Quarterly* 60, 2008, 347–71.

Barg, Lisa, "Paul Robeson's *Ballad for Americans*: Race and the Cultural Politics of 'People's Music,'" *Journal of the Society for American Music* 2, 2008, 27–70.

Bates, Beth Tompkins, *Pullman Porters and the Rise of Protest Politics in Black America, 1925–1945*, Chapel Hill, NC, 2001.

Baxell, Richard, *British Volunteers in the Spanish Civil War: The British Battalion in the International Brigades, 1936–1939*, London, 2004.

————, *Unlikely Warriors: The British in the Spanish Civil War and the Struggle Against Fascism*, London, 2012.

Bayly, Christopher and Harper, Tim, *Forgotten Wars: The End of Britain's Asian Empire*, London, 2007.

Beeching, Barbara J., "Paul Robeson and the Black Press: The 1950 Passport Controversy," *Journal of African American History* 87, 2002, 339–54.

Belfrage, Cedric, *The Frightened Giant: My Unfinished Affair With America*, London, 1957.

Belfrage, Cedric and Aronson, James, *Something to Guard: The Stormy Life of the "National Guardian,"* New York, 1978.

Belknap, Michal R., *Cold War Political Justice: The Smith Act, the Communist Party, and American Civil Liberties*, Westport, CN, 1977.

Belmonte, Laura A., "Exporting America: The U.S. Propaganda

Offensive, 1945–1959," in *The Arts of Democracy: Art, Public Culture, and the State*, Casey Nelson Blake, ed., Philadelphia, 2007, 123–50.

———, *Selling the American Way: U.S. Propaganda and the Cold War*, Philadelphia, 2008.

Bentley, Eric, ed., *Thirty Years of Treason: Excerpts From the Hearings Before the House Committee on Un-American Activities 1938–1968*, New York, 1971.

Bigsby, Christopher, *Arthur Miller 1915–1962*, London, 2008.

Black, Allida, ed., *The Eleanor Roosevelt Papers, Volume 2: The Human Rights Years, 1949–1952*, Charlottesville, VA, 2012.

Bogues, Anthony, "C.L.R. James, Pan-Africanism and the Black Radical Tradition," *Critical Arts* 25, 2011, 484–99.

Boittin, Jennifer Anne, *Colonial Metropolis: The Urban Grounds of Anti-Imperialism and Feminism in Interwar Paris*, Lincoln, NE, 2010.

Boudin, Leonard B., "The Constitutional Right to Travel," *Columbia Law Review* 56, 1956, 47–75.

Bourne, Stephen, *Black in the British Frame: The Black Experience in British Film and Television*, London, 2001.

Boyle, Sheila Tully and Bunie, Andrew, *Paul Robeson: The Years of Promise and Achievement*, Amherst, MA, 2001.

Braudy, Susan, *Family Circle: The Boudins and the Aristocracy of the Left*, New York, 2003.

Bricktop and Haskins, James, *Bricktop*, New York, 1983.

Brock, Lisa, "The 1950s: Africa Solidarity Rising," in *No Easy Victories: African Liberation and American Activists Over Half a Century, 1950–2000*, William Minter, Gail Hovey and Charles Cobb Jr., eds., Trenton, NJ, 2008, 59–81.

Broussard, Jinx Coleman and Hamilton, John Maxwell, "Covering a Two-Front War: Three African American Correspondents During World War II," *American Journalism* 22, 2005, 33–54.

Brown, Jacqueline Nassy, *Dropping Anchor, Setting Sail: Geographies of Race in Black Liverpool*, Princeton, NJ, 2005.

Brown, Lauren Erin, "'Cultural Czars': American Nationalism, Dance, and Cold War Arts Funding, 1945–1989," unpublished PhD dissertation, Harvard University, 2008.

Brown, Lloyd L., *The Young Paul Robeson: "On My Journey Now,"* Boulder, CO, 1997.

Brown, Mary Jane, "'Eradicating This Evil': Women in the American Anti-Lynching Movement, 1892–1940," unpublished PhD dissertation, Ohio State University, 1998.

Buckle, Desmond, "Paul Robeson in Britain," *New Africa* 8, 1949, issue 4.

Bynum, Cornelius L., *A. Philip Randolph and the Struggle for Civil Rights*, Urbana, IL, 2010.

Caldwell, Katrina Myers, "'It Will Be Social': Black Women Writers and the Postwar Era 1945–60," unpublished PhD dissertation, University of Illinois at Chicago, 2009.

Campbell, Gavin James, "'Deep River': The Life of Roland Hayes," *Southern Cultures* 3, 1997, 112–121.

Carby, Hazel, *Race Men*, Cambridge, MA, 1998.

Carew, Anthony, "The Schism Within the World Federation of Trade Unions: Government and Trade-Union Diplomacy," *International Review of Social History* 29, 1984, 297–335.

Carew, Joy Gleason, *Blacks, Reds, and Russians: Sojourners in Search of the Soviet Promise*, New Brunswick, NJ, 2008.

Carr, Robert K., *The House Committee on Un-American Activities 1945–1950*, Ithaca, NY, 1952.

Carroll, Peter N., *The Odyssey of the Abraham Lincoln Brigade: Americans in the Spanish Civil War*, Stanford, CA, 1994.

Castledine, Jacqueline, "'In a Solid Bond of Unity': Anticolonial Feminism in the Cold War Era," *Journal of Women's History* 20, 2008, 57–81.

———, "Wake Up America: Peekskill, Anti-Communism and the Cold War," unpublished BA thesis, Mount Holyoke College, 1999.

Caute, David, *The Dancer Defects: The Struggle for Cultural Supremacy During the Cold War*, Oxford, 2003.

———, *The Great Fear: The Anti-Communist Purge Under Truman and Eisenhower*, New York, 1978.

Cha-Jua, Sundiata Keita and Lang, Clarence, "The 'Long Movement' as Vampire: Temporal and Spatial Fallacies in Recent Black

Freedom Studies," *Journal of African American History* 92, 2007, 265–88.

Chambers, Colin, *The Story of Unity Theatre*, London, 1989.

Chateauvert, Melinda, *Marching Together: Women of the Brotherhood of Sleeping Car Porters*, Urbana, IL, 1998.

Cherny, Robert W., Issel, William, and Taylor, Kieran Walsh, eds., *American Labor and the Cold War: Grassroots Politics and Postwar Political Culture*, New Brunswick, NJ, 2004.

Claudín, Fernando, *The Communist Movement: From Comintern to Cominform*, Harmondsworth, 1975.

Cohen, Harvey G., *Duke Ellington's America*, Chicago, IL, 2010.

Cohen, Ronald D., *Rainbow Quest: The Folk Music Revival and American Society, 1940–1970*, Amherst, MA, 2002.

Committee on Un-American Activities, *Hearings Regarding Communist Infiltration of Minority Groups*, Eighty-First Congress, First Session, Washington, D.C., 1949.

————, *Report on the Communist "Peace" Offensive: A Campaign to Disarm and Defeat the United States*, Washington, D.C., 1951.

*Congrès mondial des intellectuels pour la paix Wrocław – Pologne 25 – 28 août 1948*, Warsaw, 1949.

*Congrès mondial des partisans de la paix Paris-Prague 20–25 avril 1949*, Paris, 1949.

Cook, Lisa D., "Converging to a National Lynching Database: Recent Developments," unpublished paper, 2011.

Copel, Melinda Susan, "The State Department Sponsored Tours of José Limón and His Modern Dance Company, 1954 and 1957: Modern Dance, Diplomacy, and the Cold War," unpublished PhD dissertation, Temple University, 2000.

Corbould, Clare, *Becoming African Americans: Black Public Life in Harlem, 1919–1939*, Cambridge, MA, 2009.

Creighton, Sean, "Paul Robeson's British Journey," in *Cross the Water Blues: African American Music in Europe*, Neil A. Wynn, ed., Jackson, MS, 2007, 125–44.

Croft, Clare Holloway, "Funding Footprints: US State Department

Sponsorship of International Dance Tours, 1962–2009," unpublished PhD dissertation, University of Texas, 2010.

Cull, Nicholas J., *The Cold War and the United States Information Agency: American Propaganda and Public Diplomacy, 1945–1989*, Cambridge, 2008.

———, "Film as Public Diplomacy: The USIA's Cold War at Twenty-Four Frames per Second," in *The United States and Public Diplomacy: New Directions in Cultural and International History*, Kenneth A. Osgood and Brian C. Etheridge, eds., Leiden, 2010, 257–84.

Curran, John J., *Peekskill's African American History*, Charleston, SC, 2008.

Curthoys, Ann, "Paul Robeson's Visit to Australia and Aboriginal Activism, 1960," in *Passionate Histories: Myth, Memory and Indigenous Australia*, Frances Peters-Little, Ann Curthoys and John Docker, eds., Canberra, 2010, 163–84.

———, "'You Got Rave Notices Too': Eslanda Goode Robeson's Visit to Australia, 1960," unpublished paper (scheduled to appear in a special issue of *Journal of Social History*).

Dalfiume, Richard, M., *Desegregation of the U.S. Armed Forces: Fighting on Two Fronts 1939–1953*, Columbia, MO, 1969.

Davenport, Lisa E., *Jazz Diplomacy: Promoting America in the Cold War Era*, Jackson, MS, 2009.

David-Fox, Michael, "The Fellow Travelers Revisited: The 'Cultured West' Through Soviet Eyes," *The Journal of Modern History* 75, 2003, 300–35.

Davies, Carole Boyce, "Deportable Subjects: U.S. Immigration Laws and the Criminalizing of Communism," *The South Atlantic Quarterly* 100, 2002, 949–66.

———, *Left of Karl Marx: The Political Life of a Black Communist*, Durham, NC, 2007.

Davis, Lenwood J., *A Paul Robeson Research Guide: A Selected, Annotated Bibliography*, Westport, CN, 1982.

Dawson, Ashley, "The Rise of the Black Internationale: Anti-imperialist Activism and Aesthetics in Britain During the 1930s," *Atlantic Studies* 6, 2009, 159–74.

Decker, Todd R., "Black/White Encounters on the American Musical Stage and Screen (1924–2005)," unpublished PhD dissertation, University of Michigan, 2007.

———, "'Do You Want to Hear a Mammy Song?': A Historiography of *Show Boat*," *Contemporary Theatre Review* 19, 2009, 8–21.

———, *Show Boat: Performing Race in an American Musical*, New York, 2013.

———, "Who Should Sing 'Ol' Man River'?: Tales of American Singers Transforming a Classic Song," unpublished paper, 2013.

Deery, Phillip, "'A Blot Upon Liberty': McCarthyism, Dr. Barsky and the Joint Anti-Fascist Committee," *American Communist History* 8, 2009, 167–96.

———, "'A Divided Soul'? The Cold War Odyssey of O. John Rogge," *Cold War History* 6, 2006, 177–204.

———, "The Dove Flies East: Whitehall, Warsaw and the 1950 World Peace Congress," *Australian Journal of Politics and History* 48, 2002, 449–68.

———, "'Running With the Hounds': Academic McCarthyism and New York University, 1952–1953," *Cold War History* 10, 2010, 469–92.

Deery, Phillip and Calkin, Rachel, "'We All Make Mistakes': The Communist Party of Australia and Khrushchev's Secret Speech, 1956," *Australian Journal of Politics and History* 54, 2008, 69–84.

*Deuxième congrès mondial des partisans de la paix, Varsovie 16–22 Novembre 1950*, Paris, 1951.

Defty, Andrew, *Britain, America, and Anti-Communist Propaganda, 1945–1953: The Information Research Department*, London, 2004.

De Rosa, Peter L. "American Legion Firing Line 1952–," in *The Conservative Press in Twentieth-Century America*, Ronald Lora and William Henry Longton, eds., Westport, CN, 1999, 479–88.

Devinatz, Victor G., "Filling In the Interstices of US Communist Trade Union Historiography During the Ages of Labour Radicalism and McCarthyism," *American Communist History* 9, 2010, 211–24.

Dewey, Thomas E., *Public Papers of Thomas E. Dewey Fifty-First Governor of the State of New York, 1949*, Albany, NY, 1949.

Di Biagio, Anna, "The Cominform as the Soviet Response to the Marshall Plan," in *The Failure of Peace in Europe, 1943–48*, Antonio Varsori and Elena Calandri, eds., Basingstoke, 2002, 297–305.

Dougherty, Thomas, *Cold War, Cool Medium: Television, McCarthyism, and American Culture*, New York, 2003.

Dorinson, Joseph and Warmund, Joram, eds., *Jackie Robinson: Race, Sports, and the American Dream*, Armonk, NY, 1998.

Duberman, Martin, *Paul Robeson*, New York, 1989.

Dudziak, Mary L., *Cold War Civil Rights: Race and the Image of American Democracy*, Princeton, NJ, 2000.

Dunaway, David King, *How Can I Keep From Singing: Pete Seeger*, London, 1985.

Early, Gerald L., *A Level Playing Field: African American Athletes and the Republic of Sports*, Cambridge, MA, 2011.

Eburne, Jonathan and Braddock, Jeremy, "Introduction: Paris, Capital of the Black Atlantic," *MFS Modern Fiction Studies* 51, 2005, 731–40.

Eckberg, Douglas, "Reported Victims of Lynching, By Race: 1882–1964," in *Historical Statistics of the United States, Earliest Times to the Present: Millennial Edition*, Susan B. Carter, et al., Cambridge, UK, 2006, Table Ec251–253.

Edwards, Brent Hayes, *The Practice of Diaspora: Literature, Translation, and the Rise of Black Internationalism*, Cambridge, MA, 2003.

Elias, Robert, *The Empire Strikes Out: How Baseball Sold U.S. Foreign Policy and Promoted the American Way Abroad*, New York, 2010.

Esedebe, P. Olisanwuche, *Pan-Africanism: The Idea and Movement, 1776–1991*, Washington, D.C., 1994.

Everitt, David, *A Shadow of Red: Communism and the Blacklist in Radio and Television*, Chicago, 2007.

Exton, Mark A., "Paul Robeson and South Wales: A Partial Guide to a Man's Belief," unpublished MA thesis, University of Exeter, 1984.

Fabre, Michel, "The Ring and the Stage: African Americans in Parisian Public and Imaginary Space before World War I," in *Space in America: Theory, History, Culture*, Klaus Benesch and Kerstin Schmidt, eds., Amsterdam, 2005, 521–8.

Falkner, David, *Great Time Coming: The Life of Jackie Robinson from Baseball to Birmingham*, New York, 1995.

Fast, Howard, *Peekskill USA: Inside the infamous 1949 Riots*, Mineola, NY, 2006.

Fetter, Henry D., "The Party Line and the Color Line: The American Communist Party, the *Daily Worker*, and Jackie Robinson," *Journal of Sport History* 28, 2001, 375–402.

Fisher, David James, *Romain Rolland and the Politics of Intellectual Engagement*, Berkeley, CA, 1988.

Fishman, Nina, *Arthur Horner: A Political Biography*, London, 2010.

Fosler-Lussier, Danielle, "Music Pushed, Music Pulled: Cultural Diplomacy, Globalization, and Imperialism," *Diplomatic History* 36, 2012, 53–64.

Francis, Megan Ming, "The Battle for the Hearts and Minds of America," *Souls* 13, 2011, 46–71.

Foner, Philip S., ed., *Paul Robeson Speaks: Writings, Speeches, Interviews, 1918–1974*, New York, 2002.

Franklin, John Hope, "A Half-Century of Presidential Initiatives: Some Reflections," *Journal of Supreme Court History* 24, 1999, 226–237.

Frazier, Robert, "Kennan, 'Universalism,' and the Truman Doctrine," *Journal of Cold War Studies* 11, 2009, 3–34.

Friedman, Andrea, "The Strange Career of Annie Lee Moss: Rethinking Race, Gender, and McCarthyism," *Journal of American History* 94, 2007, 445–68.

Fryer, Peter, *Staying Power: The History of Black People in Britain*, London, 1984.

Gallagher, Julie A., "The National Council of Negro Women, Human Rights, and the Cold War," in *Breaking the Wave: Women, Their Organizations, and Feminism, 1945–1985*, Kathleen A. Laughlin and Jacqueline L. Castledine, eds., New York, 2010, 80–98.

Gardner, Michael R., *Harry Truman and Civil Rights: Moral Courage and Political Risks*, Carbondale, IL, 2002.

Geduld, Victoria Phillips, "Performing Communism in the American Dance: Culture, Politics and the New Dance Group," *American Communist History* 7, 2008, 39–65.

Gellman, Erik S., *Death Blow to Jim Crow: The National Negro Congress and the Rise of Militant Civil Rights*, Chapel Hill, NC, 2012.

Gienow-Hecht, Jessica C. E., "*The World Is Ready To Listen*: Symphony Orchestras and the Global Performance of America," *Diplomatic History* 36, 2012, 17–28.

Gillett, Rachel Anne, "Crossing the Pond: Jazz, Race, and Gender in Interwar Paris," unpublished PhD dissertation, Northeastern University, 2010.

Gladchuk, John Joseph, *Hollywood and Anticommunism: HUAC and the Evolution of the Red Menace, 1935–1950*, New York, 2007.

Goldstein, Robert Justin, *American Blacklist: The Attorney General's List of Subversive Organizations*, Lawrence, KS, 2008.

———, "Prelude to McCarthyism: The Making of a Blacklist," *Prologue* 38, 2006, 22–33.

Goodman, Giora, "The British Government and the Challenge of McCarthyism in the Early Cold War," *Journal of Cold War Studies* 12, 2010, 62–97.

Goodman, Walter, *The Committee: The Extraordinary Career of the House Committee on Un-American Activities*, London, 1969.

Gore, Dayo F., "From Communist Politics to Black Power: The Visionary Politics and Transnational Solidarities of Victoria "Vicki" Ama Garvin," in *Want To Start a Revolution? Radical Women in the Black Freedom Struggle*, Dayo F. Gore, Jeanne Theoharis and Komozi Woodard, eds., New York, 2009, 72–94.

———, "'The Law Again. The Precious Law': Black Women Radicals and the Fight To End Legal Lynching," in *Crime and Punishment: Perspectives from the Humanities*, Austin Sarat, ed., Amsterdam, 2005, 53–83.

———, *Radicalism at the Crossroads: African American Women Activists in the Cold War*, New York, 2011.

Gore, Dayo F., Theoharis, Jeanne and Woodard, Komozi, eds., *Want To Start a Revolution? Radical Women in the Black Freedom Struggle*, New York, 2009.

Green, Jeffrey, *Black Edwardians: Black People in Britain 1901–1914*, London, 1998.

————, "Boxing and the 'Colour Question' in Edwardian Britain: The 'White Problem' of 1911," *International Journal of the History of Sport* 5, 1988, 115–19.

Green, Jeffrey P., "The Negro Renaissance and England," in *Black Music in the Harlem Renaissance: A Collection of Essays*, Samuel A. Floyd, ed., New York, 1990, 151–71.

————, "Roland Hayes in London, 1921," *The Black Perspective in Music* 10, 1982, 29–42.

Greene, Kate, "Burnita Shelton Matthews (1894–1988)," *Mississippi Women: Their Histories, Their Lives*, in Martha H. Swain, Elizabeth Anne Payne and Marjorie Julian Spruill, eds., Athens, GA, 2003, 144–59.

Greene, L.A., "A History of Afro-Americans in New Jersey," *Journal of the Rutgers University Libraries* 56, 1994, 4–71.

Guttenplan, D. D., *American Radical: The Life and Times of I. F. Stone*, New York, 2009.

Hall, Jacquelyn Dowd, "The Long Civil Rights Movement and the Political Uses of the Past," *Journal of American History* 91, 2005, 1233–1263.

Harris, Joseph E., *African-American Reactions to War in Ethiopia 1936–1941*, Baton Rouge, LA, 1994.

Haynes, John Earl and Klehr, Harvey, *Venona: Decoding Soviet Espionage in America*, New Haven, CN, 1999.

Hazlett, Katharine B., "The Nineteenth Century Origins of the Fifth Amendment: Privilege Against Self-Incrimination," *American Journal of Legal History* 42, 1998, 235–60.

*Hearing Before the Committee On Un-American Activities, House of Representatives, Eighty-Fourth Congress, Second Session, Investigation of the Unauthorized Use of United States Passports – Part 1*, Washington, D.C., 1956.

*Hearings Before the Committee On Un-American Activities, House of Representatives, Eighty-Fourth Congress, Second Session, Investigation of the Unauthorized Use of United States Passports – Part 3*, Washington, D.C., 1956.

Henderson, Carol E., "Policing the Racial Divide: The Body, The Nation, and the Emmett Till Murder," in *America and the Black*

*Body: Identity Politics in Print and Visual Culture*, Carole E. Henderson, ed., Madison, NJ, 2009, 224–236.

Herbert, Michael, *Never Counted Out: The Story of Len Johnson, Manchester's Black Boxing Hero and Communist*, Manchester, 1992.

Higadisha, Cheryl, "To Be(come) Young, Gay, and Black: Lorraine Hansberry's Existentialist Routes to Anticolonialism," *American Quarterly* 60, 2008, 899–924.

Hildebrand, Jennifer, "'Two Souls, Two Thoughts, Two Unreconciled Strivings': The Sound of Double Consciousness in Roland Hayes's Early Career," *Black Music Research Journal* 30, 2010, 273–302.

Hill, Rebecca N., *Men, Mobs, and Law: Anti-Lynching and Labor Defense in U.S. Radical History*, Durham, NC, 2008.

Hixson, Walter L., *Parting the Curtain: Propaganda, Culture, and the Cold War, 1945–1961*, London, 1997.

Høgsbjerg, Christian, "C.L.R. James in Imperial Britain, 1932–38," unpublished PhD dissertation, University of York, 2009.

———, ed., *Toussaint Louverture: The Story of the Only Successful Slave Revolt in History: A Play in Three Acts*, Durham, NC, 2013.

Horne, Gerald, *Communist Front? The Civil Rights Congress, 1946–1956*, Rutherford, NJ, 1988.

———, *The Final Victim of the Blacklist: John Howard Lawson, Dean of the Hollywood Ten*, Berkeley, CA, 2006.

———, "William Patterson," in *Research Guide to American Historical Biography*, Robert Muccigrosso, ed., Washington, D.C., 1991, 2675–79.

Howard, Ron, *Len Johnson and the Colour Bar: The Life and Times of Len Johnson: Boxing's Uncrowned Champion*, Stockport, UK, 2009.

Hughes, C. Alvin, "We Demand Our Rights: The Southern Negro Youth Congress, 1937–1949," *Phylon* 48, 1987, 38–50.

*Internal Security Manual*, Senate Document No. 47, 83rd Congress, 1st Session, Washington, D.C., 1953.

Isitt, Benjamin, *Militant Minority: British Columbia Workers and the Rise of a New Left, 1948–1972*, Toronto, ON, 2011.

Jackson, Esther Cooper, ed., *Freedomways Reader*, Boulder, CO, 2000.

Jackson, Jeffrey H., *Making Jazz French: Music and Modern Life in Interwar Paris*, Durham, NC, 2003.

James, Leslie Elaine, "'What We Put in Black and White': George Padmore and the Practice of Anti-Imperial Politics," unpublished PhD dissertation, London School of Economics, 2012.

Janken, Kenneth R., "From Colonial Liberation to Cold War Liberalism: Walter White, the NAACP, and Foreign Affairs, 1941–1955," *Ethnic and Racial Studies* 21, 1998, 1074–1095.

———, *White: The Biography of Walter White, Mr. NAACP*, New York, 2003.

Jenks, John, "Fight Against Peace? Britain and the Partisans of Peace, 1948–1951," in *Cold War Britain, 1945–1964: New Perspectives*, Michael F. Hopkins, Michael D. Kandiah and Gillian Staerck, eds., Basingstoke, 2003, 55–66.

Jerome, Fred, "Einstein, Race, and the Myth of the Cultural Icon," *Isis* 95, 2004, 627–39.

———, *The Einstein File: J. Edgar Hoover's Secret War Against the World's Most Famous Scientist*, New York, 2002.

Jerome, Fred and Taylor, Rodger, *Einstein on Race and Racism*, New Brunswick, NJ, 2005.

Johnson, A. Ross, *Radio Free Europe and Radio Liberty: The CIA Years and Beyond*, Palo Alto, CA, 2010.

Johnson, Timothy V., "'We Are Illegal Here': The Communist Party, Self-Determination and the Alabama Share Croppers Union," *Science & Society* 75, 2011, 454–79.

Johnston, Timothy, "Peace or Pacifism? The Soviet 'Struggle for Peace in All the World,' 1948–54," *Slavonic and East European Review* 86, 2008, 259–82.

Judt, Tony, *Postwar: A History of Europe since 1945*, London, 2005.

Kahn, Jeffrey, "The Extraordinary Mrs. Shipley: How the United States Controlled International Travel Before the Age of Terrorism," *Connecticut Law Review* 43, 2011, 819–88.

Kahn, Roger, *The Era 1947–1957: When the Yankees, the Giants, and the Dodgers Ruled the World*, New York, 1993.

Kanstroom, Daniel, *Deportation Nation: Outsiders in American History*, Cambridge, MA, 2007.

Keith, Joseph, "AT THE FORMAL LIMITS: C.L.R. James, *Moby Dick* and the Politics of the Realist Novel," *Interventions: International Journal of Postcolonial Studies* 11, 2009, 352–66.

Kelley, Robin D.G., *Hammer and Hoe: Alabama Communists During the Great Depression*, Chapel Hill, NC, 1990.

———, *Race Rebels: Culture, Politics, and the Black Working Class*, New York, 1994.

Kendhammer, Brandon, "Du Bois the Pan-Africanist and the Development of African Nationalism," *Ethnic and Racial Studies* 30, 2007, 51–71.

King, Al (with Kate Braid), *Red Bait! Struggles of a Mine Mill Local*, Vancouver, BC, 1998.

Klein, Christina, *Cold War Orientalism: Asia in the Middlebrow Imagination, 1945–1961*, Berkeley, CA, 2003.

Knepper, Cathy D., *Jersey Justice: The Story of the Trenton Six*, New Brunswick, NJ, 2011.

Kofas, Jon V., "U.S. Foreign Policy and the World Federation of Trade Unions, 1944–1948," *Diplomatic History* 26, 2002, 21–60.

Kornweibel, Theodore, Jr., *No Crystal Stair: Black Life and the Messenger, 1917–1928*, Westport, CN, 1975.

Korstad, Robert and Lichtenstein, Nelson, "Opportunities Found and Lost: Labor, Radicals, and the Early Civil Rights Movement," *The Journal of American History* 75, 1988, 786–811.

Kristmanson, Mark, *Plateaus of Freedom: Nationality, Culture, and State Security in Canada, 1940–1960*, Don Mills, ON, 2003.

Krugler, David F., *The Voice of America and the Domestic Propaganda Battles, 1945–1953*, Columbia, MO, 2000.

Kynaston, David, *Austerity Britain 1945–51*, London, 2007.

Lamphere, Lawrence, "Paul Robeson, *Freedom* Newspaper, and the Black Press," unpublished PhD dissertation, Boston College, 2003.

———, "Paul Robeson, *Freedom* Newspaper, and the Korean War," in *Paul Robeson: Essays on His Life and Legacy*, Joseph Dorinson, Joseph and William Pencak, eds., Jefferson, NC, 2002, 133–42.

Laursen, Thomas, E., "Constitutional Protection of Foreign Travel," *Columbia Law Review* 81, 1981, 902–31.

Laville, Helen and Lucas, Scott, "The American Way: Edith Sampson, the NAACP, and African American Identity in the Cold War," *Diplomatic History* 20, 1996, 565–90.

Lawless, Ken, "'Continental Imprisonment': Rockwell Kent and the Passport Controversy," *The Antioch Review* 38, 1980, 304–12.

Lawson, Autumn Anne, "Kwame Nkrumah's Quest for Pan Africanism: From Independence Leader to Deposed Despot," unpublished MA thesis, Wichita State University, KS, 2010.

Le Cour Grandmaison, Olivier, "Le mouvement de la paix pendant la guerre froide: le cas français, 1948–1952," *Communisme* 18/19, 1988, 120–38.

Lemelle, Sidney J. and Kelley, Robin D.G., "Introduction Imagining Home: Pan-Africanism Revisited," in *Imagining Home: Class, Culture and Nationalism in the African Diaspora*, Sidney J. Lemelle, and Robin D. G. Kelley, eds., London, 1994, 1–16.

Lewis, David Levering, "Paul Robeson and the U.S.S.R.," *Paul Robeson: Artist and Citizen*, in Jeffrey C. Stewart, ed., New Brunswick, NJ, 1998, 217–33.

———, *When Harlem Was in Vogue*, New York, 1989.

Lewis, David Levering, Nash, Michael H., and Leab, Daniel J., eds., *Red Activists and Black Freedom: James and Esther Jackson and the Long Civil Rights Revolution*, London, 2010.

Lieberman, Robbie, "The Culture of Politics: Communism, Americanism, and the People's Songs Hootenanny," *The South Atlantic Quarterly* 85, 1986, 78–88.

Lieberman, Robbie, "'Measure Them Right': Lorraine Hansberry and the Struggle for Peace," *Science & Society* 75, 2011, 206–35.

———, *"My Song Is My Weapon": People's Songs, American Communism, and the Politics of Culture, 1930–50*, Urbana, IL, 1989.

———, "People's Songs: American Communism and the Politics of Culture," *Radical History Review* 36, 1986, 63–78.

———, *The Strangest Dream: Communism, Anticommunism, and the U.S. Peace Movement, 1945–1963*, Syracuse, NY, 2000.

Lieberman, Robbie and Lang, Clarence, eds., *Anticommunism and the African American Freedom Movement*, Basingstoke, 2009.

Little, Sharoni Denise, "'Death at the Hands of Persons *Known*': Victimage Rhetoric and the 1922 Dyer Anti–Lynching Bill," unpublished PhD dissertation, Indiana University, 2005.

Litvak, Joseph, *The Un-Americans: Jews, the Blacklist, and Stoolpigeon Culture*, Durham, NC, 2009.

Lloyd, Craig, *Eugene Bullard: Black Expatriate in Jazz-Age Paris*, Athens, GA, 2006.

Loeser, Franz, *Sag Nie, Du Gehst Den Letzten Weg: Ein Deutsches Leben*, Cologne, 1986.

Lomax, Michael E., "Baseball's Great Experiment Revisited," *Journal of Sport History* 37, 2010, 199–205.

———, "'I Never Had It Made' Revisited: The Political, Economic, and Social Ideology of Jackie Robinson," *Afro-Americans in New York Life and History* 23, 1999, 39–60.

———, "Introduction: The African American and Latino Athlete in Post-World War II American: A Historical Review," in *Sports and the Racial Divide: African American and Latino Experience in an Era of Change*, Michael E. Lomax, ed., Jackson, MS, 2008, xiii–xxxix.

Long, Michael G., *First Class Citizenship: The Civil Rights Letters of Jackie Robinson*, New York, 2007.

Lorence, James J., *The Suppression of Salt of the Earth: How Hollywood, Big Labor, and Politicians Blacklisted a Movie in Cold War America*, Albuquerque, NM, 1999.

Lotz, Rainer E., *Black People: Entertainers of African Descent in Europe, and Germany*, Bonn, 1997.

Lynch, Hollis R., *Black American Radicals and the Liberation of Africa: The Council on African Affairs 1937–1955*, Ithaca, NY, 1978.

Lynskey, Dorian, *33 Revolutions Per Minute: A History of Protest Songs*, London, 2010.

McConnell, Lauren, "Understanding Paul Robeson's Soviet Experience," *Theatre History Studies* 30, 2010, 138–54.

MacDonald, J. Fred, *Blacks and White TV: African Americans in Television Since 1948 (Second Edition)*, Chicago, 1992.

Macdonald, Roderick J., "'The Wisers Who Are Far Away': The Role of London's Black Press in the 1930s and 1940s," in *Essays in the History of Blacks in Britain: From Roman Times to the Mid-Twentieth Century*, Jagdish S. Gundara and Ian Duffield, eds., Aldershot, 1992, 150–72.

MacDowall, Laurel Sefton, "Paul Robeson in Canada: A Border Story," *Labour/Le Travail* 51, 2003, 177–221.

McDonald, Kathlene, *Feminism, the Left, and Postwar Literary Culture*, Jackson, MS, 2012.

McDuffie, Erik, "A 'New Freedom Movement of Negro Women': Sojourning for Truth, Justice, and Human Rights during the Early Cold War," *Radical History Review* 101, 2008, 81–106.

———, *Sojourning For Freedom: Black Women, American Communism, and the Making of Black Left Feminism*, Durham, NC, 2011.

McGilligan, Patrick, *Oscar Micheaux: The Great and Only*, New York, 2007.

McKeon, Michael K., "The Robeson Riots: Two Incidents Which Foreshadowed the Rise of McCarthyism," unpublished MA thesis, Adelphi and Hofstra Universities, 1985.

McLeod, John, "'A Night at the Cosmopolitan': Axes of Transnational Encounter in the 1930s and 1940s," *Interventions* 4, 2002, 53–67.

McMillin, Scott, "Paul Robeson, Will Vodery's 'Jubilee Singers,' and the Earliest Script of the Kern-Hammerstein *Show Boat*," *Theatre Survey* 41, 2000, 51–70.

Makalani, Minkah, *In the Cause of Freedom: Radical Black Internationalism from Harlem to London, 1917–1939*, Chapel Hill, NC, 2011.

Makonnen, Ras, *Pan-Africanism From Within*, Nairobi, 1973.

Martelle, Scott, *The Fear Within: Spies, Commies, and American Democracy on Trial*, New Brunswick, NJ, 2011.

Martin, Charles H., "The Civil Rights Congress and Southern Black Defendants," *The Georgia Historical Quarterly* 71, 1987, 25–52.

———, "Internationalizing 'The American Dilemma': The Civil Rights Congress and the 1951 Genocide Petition to the United Nations," *Journal of American Ethnic History* 16, 1997, 35–61.

————, "The International Labor Defense and Black America', *Labor History* 26, 1985, 165–94.

Martin, Ruth, "Securing the Borders? Defending the Right to Travel, 1947–1958," unpublished paper, 2011.

Matera, Marc,, "Black Internationalism and African and Caribbean Intellectuals in London, 1919–1950," unpublished PhD dissertation, Rutgers University, 2008.

————, "Black Intellectuals in the Imperial Metropolis and the Debate Over Race and Empire in *Sanders of the River*," in *Brave New World: Imperial and Democratic Nation Building in Britain Between the Wars*, Laura Beers and Thomas Geraint, eds., London, 2011, 227–48.

Matthews, Lopez Denoble Jr., "The Southern Negro Youth Congress: Its Legacy and Impact," unpublished PhD dissertation, Howard University, 2009.

Matusevich, Maxim, "An Exotic Subversive: Africa, Africans and the Soviet Everyday," *Race & Class* 49, 2008, 57–81.

————, "Black in the U.S.S.R.: Africans, African Americans, and the Soviet Society," *Transition* 100, 2008, 56–75.

Meriwether, James H., *Proudly We Can Be Africans: Black Americans and Africa, 1935–1961*, Chapel Hill, NC, 2002.

Merrill, Dennis, "The Truman Doctrine: Containing Communism and Modernity," *Presidential Studies Quarterly* 36, 2006, 27–37.

Metress, Christopher, ed., *The Lynching of Emmett Till: A Documentary History*, Charlottesville, VA, 2002.

Mishler, Paul C., *Raising Reds: The Young Pioneers, Radical Summer Camps, and Communist Political Culture in the United States*, New York, 1999.

Monod, David, "Disguise, Containment and the *Porgy and Bess* Revival of 1952–1956," *Journal of American Studies* 35, 2001, 275–312.

Monod, David, "'He is a Cripple an' Needs my Love': *Porgy and Bess* as Cold War Propaganda," *Intelligence and National Security* 18, 2003, 300–12.

Monson, Ingrid, *Freedom Sounds: Civil Rights Call Out to Jazz and Africa*, New York, 2007.

Morgan, Kevin, "The Communist Party and the Daily Worker 1930–1956," in *Opening the Books: Essays on the Social and Cultural History of the British Communist Party*, Geoff Andrews, Nina Fishman and Kevin Morgan, eds., London, 1995, 142–59.

Morris, Jeffrey Brandon, *Calmly to Poise the Scales of Justice: A History of the Courts of the District of Columbia Circuit*, Durham, NC, 2001.

Morrison, Michael A., "Paul Robeson's Othello at the Savoy Theatre, 1930," *NTQ* 27, 2011, 114–40.

Mukherji, Ani, "The Anticolonial Imagination: The Exilic Productions of American Radicalism in Interwar Moscow," unpublished PhD dissertation, Brown University, 2011.

Müller-Enbergs, Helmut, et al., eds., *Wer War Wer in der DDR: Ein Lexikon Ostdeutscher Biographien*, Berlin, 2010.

Munro, John J., "The Anticolonial Front: Cold War Imperialism and the Struggle Against Global White Supremacy," unpublished PhD dissertation, University of California at Santa Barbara, 2009.

Murphy, Andrea, *From the Empire to the Rialto: Racism and Reaction in Liverpool, 1918–1948*, Birkenhead, 1995.

Murphy, Brenda, *Congressional Theatre: Dramatizing McCarthyism on Stage, Film, and Television*, Cambridge, UK, 1999.

Musser, Charles, "Paul Robeson and the Cinema of Empire," in *Empire and Film*, Lee Grieveson and Colin McCabe, eds., London, 2011, 261–80.

———, "To Redeem the Dreams of White Playwrights: Reappropriation and Resistance in Oscar Micheaux's *Body and Soul*," *Oscar Micheaux and His Circle*, in Pearl Bowser, Jane Gaines and Charles Musser, eds., Bloomington, IN, 2001, 97–131.

Narinskii, Mikhail M., "The Soviet Union and the Marshall Plan," in *The Failure of Peace in Europe, 1943–48*, Antonio Varsori and Elena Calandri, eds., Basingstoke, 2002, pp. 275–87.

Nash, Michael and Leab, Daniel J., "*Freedomways*," *American Communist History* 7, 2008, 227–37.

Navasky, Victor S., *Naming Names*, London, 1982.

Nehring, Holger, "Resisting the Imaginary War: Reconceptualising the Role of Peace Movements in the Cold War," unpublished paper,

Peace Movements in the Cold War and Beyond: An International Conference, London School of Economics, 2008.

Newman, Robert P., *Owen Lattimore and the "Loss" of China*, Berkeley, CA, 1992.

Nollen, Scott Allen, *Paul Robeson: Film Pioneer*, Jefferson, NC, 2010.

Ogbar, Jeffrey O. G., ed., *The Harlem Renaissance Revisited*, Baltimore, MD, 2010.

Osgood, Kenneth, *Total Cold War: Eisenhower's Secret Propaganda Battle at Home and Abroad*, Lawrence, KS, 2006.

Parsonage, Catherine, *The Evolution of Jazz in Britain, 1880–1935*, Aldershot, 2005.

Patterson, William L., *The Man Who Cried Genocide: An Autobiography*, New York, 1971.

Pennybacker, Susan D., *From Scottsboro to Munich: Race and Political Culture in 1930s Britain*, Princeton, NJ, 2009.

Perucci, Tony, *Paul Robeson and the Cold War Performance Complex*, Ann Arbor, MI, 2012.

Perucci, Tony, "The Red Mask of Sanity: Paul Robeson, HUAC, and the Sound of Cold War Performance," *TDR: The Drama Review* 53, 2009, 18–48.

Petitjean, Patrick, "The Joint Establishment of the World Federation of Scientific Workers and of UNESCO after World War II," *Minerva* 46, 2008, 247–70.

Petty, Miriam J., "'Doubtful Glory': 1930s Hollywood and the African American Actor as Star," unpublished PhD dissertation, Emory University, 2004.

Pfeffer, Paula F., *A. Philip Randolph, Pioneer of the Civil Rights Movement*, Baton Rouge, LA, 1990.

Pinault, Michel, "Le Conseil mondial de la paix dans la guerre froide," in *Cultures communistes au XXe siècle: entre guerre et modernité*, Jean Vigreux and Serge Wolikow, eds., Paris, 2003.

——, *Frédéric Joliot-Curie*, Paris, 2000.

——, "The Joliot-Curies: Science, Politics, Networks," *History and Technology* 13, 1997, 307–24.

Pollack, Harriet and Metress, Christopher, eds., *Emmett Till in Literary Memory and Imagination*, Baton Rouge, LA, 2008.

Powers, Joe and Rogovin, Mark, *Paul Robeson Rediscovered: An Annotated Listing of His Chicago History From 1921 to 1958*, Chicago, IL, 2000.

Prais, Jinny Kathleen, "Imperial Travelers: The Formation of West African Urban Culture, Identity, and Citizenship in London and Accra, 1925–1935," unpublished PhD dissertation, University of Michigan, 2008.

Prevots, Naima, *Dance for Export: Cultural Diplomacy and the Cold War*, Hanover, NH, 1998.

Prial, Dunston, *The Producer: John Hammond and the Soul of American Music*, New York, 2006.

Pries, Anne, "Khrushchev's 'Secret Speech': Confusion of Tongues," *Journal of Communist Studies* 6, 1990, 81–5.

Procacci, Giuliano, ed., *The Cominform: Minutes of the Three Conferences, 1947/1948/1949*, Milan, 1994.

Putnam, Aric, "Ethiopia is Now: J. A. Rogers and the Rhetoric of Black Anticolonialism During the Great Depression," *Rhetoric & Public Affairs* 10, 2007, 419–44.

Rader, Melvin, *False Witness*, Seattle, 1969.

Raman, Parvathi, "Yusuf Dadoo: Transnational Politics, South African Belonging," *South African Historical Journal* 50, 2004, 27–48.

Rampersad, Arnold, *Jackie Robinson: A Biography*, New York, 1997.

Ransby, Barbara, *Eslanda: The Large and Unconventional Life of Mrs. Paul Robeson*, New Haven, CT, 2013.

Reid, Mark A., "Race, Working-Class Consciousness, and Dreaming in Africa: *Song of Freedom* and *Jericho*," in *Paul Robeson: Artist and Citizen*, Jeffrey C. Stewart, ed., New Brunswick, NJ, 1998, 165–76.

Relyea, Harold C., "National Emergency Powers," *CRS Report for Congress*, 2006, www.au.af.mil/au/awc/awcgate/crs/98-505.pdf.

Rettie, John, "How Khrushchev Leaked His Secret Speech to the World," *History Workshop Journal* 62, 2006, 187–93.

Reuss, Richard A. and Reuss, JoAnne C., *American Folk Music and Left-Wing Politics, 1927–1957*, Lanham, MD, 2000.

Richards, Johnetta, "The Southern Negro Youth Congress: A History," unpublished PhD dissertation, University of Cincinnati, 1987.

Rise, Eric W., *The Martinsville Seven: Race, Rape and Capital Punishment*, Charlottesville, VA, 1995.

Roberts, Geoffrey, "Moscow and the Marshall Plan: Politics, Ideology and the Onset of the Cold War, 1947," *Europe-Asia Studies* 46, 1994, 1371–86.

Robeson, Paul, *Here I Stand*, Boston, MA, 1988.

Robeson, Paul Jr., *The Undiscovered Paul Robeson: An Artist's Journey, 1898–1939*, New York, 2001.

————, *The Undiscovered Paul Robeson: Quest for Freedom, 1939–1976*, Hoboken, NJ, 2010.

Robeson, Susan, *The Whole World In His Hands: A Pictorial Biography of Paul Robeson*, Secaucus, NJ, 1981.

Robinson, Cedric J., "Black Intellectuals at the British Core: 1920s – 1940s," in *Essays in the History of Blacks in Britain: From Roman Times to the Mid-Twentieth Century*, Jagdish S. Gundara and Ian Duffield, eds., Aldershot, 1992, 173–201.

Robinson, Greg, "Internationalism and Justice: Paul Robeson, Asia, and Asian Americans," in *AfroAsian Encounters: Culture, History, Politics*, Heike Raphael-Hernandez, and Shannon Steen, eds., New York, 2006, 260–76.

Robinson, Jackie, *I Never Had It Made, By Jackie Robinson As Told To Alfred Duckett*, New York, 1972.

Rocksborough-Smith, Ian, "Bearing the Seeds of Struggle: *Freedomways* Magazine, Black Leftists, and Continuities in the Freedom Movement," unpublished MA thesis, Simon Fraser University, 2005.

Rocksborough-Smith, Ian, "'Filling the Gap': Intergenerational Black Radicalism and the Popular Front Ideals of *Freedomways* Magazine's Early Years, (1961–1965)," *Afro-Americans in New York Life and History* 31, 2007, 7–42.

Rogers, Alan, "Passports and Politics: The Courts and the Cold War," *Historian* 47, 1985, 497–511.

Rosenberg, Jonathan, "America on the World Stage: Music and Twentieth-Century U.S. Foreign Relations," *Diplomatic History* 36, 2012, 65–9.

———, "Fighting the Cold War with Violins and Trumpets: American Symphony Orchestras Abroad in the 1950's," in *Winter Kept Us Warm: Cold War Interactions Reconsidered*, Sari Autio-Sarasmo and Brendan Humphreys, eds., Helsinki, 2010, 23–43.

Rousseau, Sabine, "Les Mouvements de Paix en France depuis 1945. Un Objet de Recherche en Construction," in "Peace Movements in Western Europe, Japan and the USA since 1945: Historiographical Reviews and Theoretical Perspectives," Benjamin Ziemann, ed., in *Mitteilungsblatt des Instituts für soziale Bewegungen, Forschungen und Forschungsberichte* 32, 2004, 49–66.

Rowan, Carl T., *Breaking Barriers: A Memoir*, Boston, MA, 1991.

Rush, Anne, "Reshaping British History: The Historiography of West Indians in Britain in the Twentieth Century," *History Compass* 5, 2007, 463–84.

Rush, Barbara, *Imperialism, Race and Resistance: Africa and Britain, 1919–1945*, London, 1999.

Rusinack, Kelly E., "Baseball on the Radical Agenda: The *Daily Worker* and *Sunday Worker* Journalistic Campaign to Desegregate Major League Baseball, 1933–1947," in *Jackie Robinson: Race, Sports, and the American Dream*, Joseph Dorinson and Joram Warmund, eds., Armonk, NY, 1998, pp. 75–85.

Rye, Howard, "Southern Syncopated Orchestra: The Roster," *Black Music Research Journal* 30, 2010, 19–70.

———, "The Southern Syncopated Orchestra', *Black Music Research Journal* 29, 2009, 153–228.

Sabin, Arthur J., *Red Scare In Court: New York Versus the International Workers Order*, Philadelphia, 1993.

Sandage, Scott A., "A Marble House Divided: The Lincoln Memorial, the Civil Rights Movement, and the Politics of Memory, 1939–1963," in *Time Longer Than Rope: A Century of African American*

*Activism, 1850–1950*, Charles M. Payne and Adam Green, eds., New York, 2003, 492–535.

Sandeen, Eric J., *Picturing an Exhibition: The Family of Man and 1950s America*, Albuquerque, NM, 1995.

Santamaria, Yves, *Le Parti de l'ennemi: le parti communiste français dans la lutte pour la paix, 1947–1958*, Paris, 2006.

————, "Un prototype toutes missions: le Comité de lutte contre la guerre, dit 'Amsterdam-Pleyel,' 1932–1936," *Communisme* 18/19, 1988, 71–97.

Saunders, Frances Stonor, *Who Paid the Piper?: The CIA and the Cultural Cold War*, London, 1999.

Schaffer, Gordon, *Baby in the Bathwater: Memories of a Political Journalist*, Lewes, 1996.

Schlosser, Anatol I., "Paul Robeson: His Career in the Theatre, in Motion Pictures, and on the Concert Stage," unpublished PhD dissertation, New York University, 1970.

Schrecker, Ellen, "Immigration and Internal Security: Political Deportations During the McCarthy Era," *Science & Society* 60, 1996–1997, 393–426.

————, "Introduction," in *Records of the Subversive Activities Control Board, 1950–1972*, Mark Naison and Maurice Isserman, eds., microfilm edition, Frederick, MD, 1988, v–xvi.

————, *Many are the Crimes: McCarthyism in America*, Boston, MA, 1998.

————, *No Ivory Tower: McCarthyism and the Universities*, New York, 1986.

Schwarz, Bill, "Black Metropolis, White England," in *Modern Times: Reflections on a Century of English Modernity*, Mica Nava and Alan O'Shea, eds., London, 1995, 176–207.

————, ed., *West Indian Intellectuals in Britain*, Manchester, 2003.

Scobie, Ingrid Winther, "Jack B. Tenney and the 'Parasitic Menace': Anti-Communist Legislation in California 1940–1949," *Pacific Historical Review* 43, 1974, 188–211.

Scott-Smith, Giles, "The 'Masterpieces of the Twentieth Century' Festival and the Congress for Cultural Freedom: Origins and

Consolidation 1947–52," *Intelligence and National Security* 15, 2000, 121–43.

——, *The Politics of Apolitical Culture: The Congress for Cultural Freedom and the Political Economy of American Hegemony, 1945– 1955*, London, 2001.

*Second Women's International Congress: Account of the Work of the Congress Which Took Place in Budapest (Hungary) from the 1st to the 6th of December, 1948*, Paris, 1949.

Seniors, Paula Marie, "Jack Johnson, Paul Robeson, and the Hypermasculine African American *Übermensch*," in *The Harlem Renaissance Revisited*, Jeffrey O. G. Ogbar, ed., Baltimore, 2010, 155–76.

Seroff, Doug, "The Fisk Jubilee Singers in Britain," in *Under the Imperial Carpet: Essays in Black History 1780–1950*, Rainer Lotz and Ian Pegg, eds., Crawley, 1986, 42–54.

Seton, Marie, *Paul Robeson*, London, 1958.

Shapiro, Herbert, *White Violence and Black Response: From Reconstruction to Montgomery*, Amherst, MA, 1988.

Shargel, Baila Round, "Leftist Summer Colonies of Northern Westchester County, New York," *American Jewish History* 83, 1995, 337–58.

Sherwood, Marika, "The Comintern, the CPGB, Colonies and Black Britons, 1920–1938," *Science & Society* 60, 1996, 137–63.

——, "Kwame Nkrumah: The London Years, 1945–47," *Immigrants & Minorities* 12, 1993, 164–94.

——, *Manchester and the 1945 Pan-African Congress*, London, 1995.

——, "Peter Blackman, 1909–1993," *History Workshop Journal* 37, 1994, 266–7.

Sherwood, Marika and Adi, Hakim, *Pan-African History: Political Figures from Africa and the Diaspora Since 1787*, London, 2003.

Sivanandan, A., *A Different Hunger: Writings on Black Resistance*, London, 1982.

Silber, Irwin, *Press Box Red: The Story of Lester Rodney, the Communist Who Helped Break The Color Line in American Sports*, Philadelphia, 2003.

Singh, Nikhil Pal, *Climbin' Jacob's Ladder: The Black Freedom Movement Writings of Jack O'Dell*, Berkeley, CA, 2010.

Slagle, Mark, "Mightier than the Sword? The Black Press and the End of Racial Segregation in the U.S. Military, 1948–1954," unpublished PhD dissertation, University of North Carolina, 2010.

Semthurst, James, "SNYC, *Freedomways*, and the Influence of the Popular Front in the South on the Black Arts Movement," *reconstruction* 8.1, 2008, np.

Smith, Evan, "'Class Before Race': British Communism and the Place of Empire in Postwar Race Relations," *Science & Society* 72, 2008, 455–81.

Smith, O. Joyce, "Channing H. Tobias: An Educational Change Agent in Race Relations, 1940–1960," unpublished PhD. dissertation, Loyola University, 1993.

Smith, Richard Norton, *Thomas E. Dewey and His Times*, New York, 1982.

Smith, Ronald A., "The Paul Robeson–Jackie Robinson Saga and a Political Collision," *Journal of Sport History* 6, 1979, 5–27.

Solski, Mike and Smaller, John, *Mine Mill: The History of the International Mine, Mill, and Smelter Workers in Canada Since 1895*, Ottawa, ON, 1985.

Spina, Raphaël, "Yves Farge (1899–1953) and the First Years of the French Peace Movement. From the Committed Citizen to the Fellow Traveller, a Biographical Approach," unpublished paper, Peace Movements in the Cold War and Beyond: An International Conference, London School of Economics, 2008.

Spohrer, Erika, "Becoming Extra-Textual: Celebrity Discourse and Paul Robeson's Political Transformation," *Critical Studies in Media Communication* 24, 2007, 151–68.

Stephens, Michelle A., "'I'm the Everybody Who's Nobody': Genealogies of the New World Slave in Paul Robeson's Performances of the 1930s," in *Hemispheric American Studies*, Caroline F. Lavender and Robert S. Levine, eds., New Brunswick, NJ, 2008, 166–86.

Stern, Ludmila, *Western Intellectuals and the Soviet Union, 1920–40: From Red Square to the Left Bank*, London, 2006.

Stewart, Jeffrey C., "The Black Body: Paul Robeson as a Work of Art and Politics," in *Paul Robeson: Artist and Citizen*, Jeffrey C. Stewart, ed., New Brunswick, NJ, 1998, 135–63.

———, "I Sing the Black Body Electric: Transnationalism and the Black Body in Walt Whitman, Alain Locke, and Paul Robeson," in *Recharting the Black Atlantic: Modern Cultures, Local Communities, Global Connections*, Annalisa Oboe and Anna Scacchi, eds., London, 2008, 259–81.

———, "Paul Robeson and the Problem of Modernism," in *Rhapsodies in Black: Art of the Harlem Renaissance*, Joanna Skipwith, ed., London, 2007, 90–101.

Stockwell, A. J., "Leaders, Dissidents and the Disappointed: Colonial Students in Britain as Empire Ended," *Journal of Imperial and Commonwealth History* 36, 2008, 487–507.

Stovall, Tyler, *Paris Noir: African Americans in the City of Light*, New York, 1996.

Stromquist, Shelton, ed., *Labor's Cold War: Local Politics in a Global Context*, Urbana, IL, 2008.

Swain, Geoffrey, "The Cominform: Tito's International?," *The Historical Journal* 35, 1992, 641–63.

Swann, Brenda and Aprahamian, Francis, eds., *J.D. Bernal: A Life in Science and Politics*, London, 1999.

Swindall, Lindsey R., *Paul Robeson: A Life of Activism and Art*, Lanham, MD, 2013.

———, *The Politics of Paul Robeson's Othello*, Jackson, MS, 2011.

Taylor, John Harper, "Ambassadors of the Arts: An Analysis of the Eisenhower Administration's Incorporation of 'Porgy and Bess' into its Cold War Foreign Policy," unpublished PhD dissertation, Ohio State University, 1994.

Theoharis, Athan, *Chasing Spies: How the FBI Failed in Counterintelligence But Promoted the Politics of McCarthyism in the Cold War Years*, Chicago, 2002.

Thomas, Damion, *Globetrotting: African American Athletes and Cold War Politics*, Urbana, IL, 2012.

———, "Let the Games Begin: Sport, U.S. Race Relations and Cold

War Politics," *The International Journal of the History of Sport* 24, 2007, 151–71.

——, "Playing the 'Race Card': US Foreign Policy and the Integration of Sports," in *East Plays West: Sport and the Cold War*, Stephen Wagg and David L. Andrews, eds., London, 2007, 207–21.

Thomas, Martin, Moore, Bob and Butler, L.J., *Crises of Empire: Decolonization and Europe's Imperial States, 1918–1975*, London, 2008.

Thornton, Brian, "The Murder of Emmett Till: Myth, Memory, and National Magazine Response," *Journalism History* 36, 2010, 96–104.

Till-Mobley, Mamie and Benson, Christopher, *Death of Innocence: The Story of the Hate Crime That Changed America*, New York, 2003.

Tygiel, Jules, *Baseball's Great Experiment: Jackie Robinson and His Legacy*, New York, 1997.

Ullrich, Weston, "Preventing 'Peace': The British Government and the Second World Peace Congress," *Cold War History* 11, 2011, 341–62.

Vaïsse, Maurice, ed., *Le Pacifisme en Europe des années 1920 aux années 1950*, Brussels, 1993.

Verzuh, Ron, "Mine Mill's Peace Arch Concerts: How a 'Red' Union and a Famous Singer-Activist Fought for Peace and Social Justice During the Cold War," *BC Studies* 174, 2012, 61–99.

Von Eschen, Penny M., *Race Against Empire: Black Americans and Anticolonialism*, Ithaca, NY, 1997.

——, *Satchmo Blows Up the World: Jazz Ambassadors Play the Cold War*, Cambridge, MA, 2004.

Wade, Wyn Craig, *The Fiery Cross: The Ku Klux Klan in America*, London, 1987.

Walwik, Joseph, *The Peekskill, New York, Anti-Communist Riots of 1949*, Lewiston, NY, 2002.

Warren, Wallace H., "'The Best People in Town Won't Talk': The Moore's Ford Lynching of 1946 and Its Cover-Up" in *Georgia in Black and White: Explorations in the Race Relations of a Southern State, 1865–1950*, John C. Inscoe, ed., Athens, GA, 1994, 266–88.

Washburn, Patrick S., *The African American Newspaper: Voice of Freedom*, Evanston, IL, 2006.

———, *A Question of Sedition: The Federal Government's Investigation of the Black Press During World War II*, New York, 1986.

Washington, Jack, *The Long Journey Home: A Bicentennial History of the Black Community of Princeton, New Jersey 1776–1976*, Trenton, NJ, 2005.

Washington, Mary Helen, "Alice Childress, Lorraine Hansberry, and Claudia Jones: Black Women Write the Popular Front," in *Left of the Color Line: Race, Radicalism, and Twentieth-Century Literature of the United States*, Bill V. Mullen and James Smethurst, eds., Chapel Hill, NC, 2003, 183–204.

Weaver, Bill L., "The Black Press and the Assault on Baseball's 'Color Line': October 1945–April 1947," *Phylon* 40, 1979, 303–17.

Weigand, Kate, *Red Feminism: American Communism and the Making of Women's Liberation*, Baltimore, MD, 2001.

Weinberg, Carl R., "*Salt of the Earth*: Labor, Film, and the Cold War," *OAH Magazine of History* 24, 2010, 41–5.

Welch, Rebeccah E., "Black Art and Activism in Postwar New York, 1950–1965," unpublished PhD dissertation, New York University, 2002.

———, "Spokesman of the Oppressed? Lorraine Hansberry at Work: The Challenge of Radical Politics in the Postwar Era," *Souls* 9, 2007, 302–19.

Wexler, Laura, *Fire in a Canebreak: The Last Mass Lynching in America*, New York, 2003.

White, Walter, *A Man Called White: The Autobiography*, London, 1949.

Wilkins, Fanon Che, "Beyond Bandung: The Critical Nationalism of Lorraine Hansberry, 1950–1965," *Radical History Review* 95, 2006, 191–210.

Williams, Daniel G., *Aneurin Bevan and Paul Robeson: Socialism, Class and Identity*, Cardiff, 2010.

Williams, Ronald II, "From Anticolonialism to Anti-Apartheid: African American Political Organizations and African Liberation,

1957–93," in *African Americans in Global Affairs: Contemporary Perspectives*, Michael L. Clemons, ed., Boston, 2010, 65–89.

Williamson, John, *Dangerous Scot: The Life and Work of an American "Undesirable*," New York, 1969.

Whittall, Daniel James, "Creolising London: Black West Indian Activism and the Politics of Race and Empire in Britain, 1931–1948," unpublished PhD dissertation, Royal Holloway, University of London, 2012.

Wittner, Lawrence S., *One World or None: A History of the World Nuclear Disarmament Movement Through 1953*, Stanford, CA, 1993.

Woods, Jeff, *Black Struggle, Red Scare: Segregation and Anti-Communism in the South, 1948–1968*, Baton Rouge, LA, 2004.

*World Congress for Peace Paris–Prague April 20–25, 1949*, supplement to *New Times*, no. 19, May 4, 1949.

Wright, Charles, H., *Robeson: Labor's Forgotten Champion*, Detroit, MI, 1975.

Yarrow, Andrew L., "Selling a Vision of America to the World: Changing Messages in Early U.S. Cold War Print Propaganda," *Journal of Cold War Studies* 11, 2009, 3–45.

Ybarra, Michael, J., *Washington Gone Crazy: Senator Pat McCarran and the Great American Communist Hunt*, Hanover, NH, 2004.

Ziemann, Benjamin, ed., "Peace Movements in Western Europe, Japan and the USA since 1945: Historiographical Reviews and Theoretical Perspectives," *Mitteilungsblatt des Instituts für soziale Bewegungen Forschungen und Forschungsberichte* 32, 2004.

# Index